780.9 B875w
Broughton, Simon.
World

100 ESSENTIA

There are more than one hundred and fifty Rough Guide travel, phrasebook, and music titles, covering destinations from Amsterdam to Zimbabwe, languages from Czech to Vietnamese, and musics from World to Opera and Jazz

Other 100 Essential CD titles

Blues • Classical • Country • Opera
Reggae • Rock • Soul

Rough Guides on the Internet

www.roughguides.com

Rough Guide Credits

Text editor: Joe Staines
Series editor: Mark Ellingham
Scanning and layout: Link Hall

Publishing Information

This first edition published October 2000 by
Rough Guides Ltd, 62–70 Shorts Gardens, London WC2H 9AH

Distributed by the Penguin Group

Penguin Books Ltd, 27 Wrights Lane, London W8 5TZ
Penguin Putnam, Inc., 375 Hudson Street, New York 10014, USA
Penguin Books Australia Ltd, 487 Maroondah Highway,
PO Box 257, Ringwood, Victoria 3134, Australia
Penguin Books Canada Ltd, 10 Alcorn Avenue,
Toronto, Ontario, Canada M4V 1E4
Penguin Books (NZ) Ltd, 182–190 Wairau Road,
Auckland 10, New Zealand

Typeset in Bembo and Helvetica to an original design by Henry Iles.
Printed in Spain by Graphy Cems.

No part of this book may be reproduced in any form
without permission from the publisher except for the
quotation of brief passages in reviews.

© Simon Broughton
208pp

A catalogue record for this book is available from the British Library.
ISBN 1-85828-598-4

World

| 100 ESSENTIAL CDs | THE ROUGH GUIDE |

by Simon Broughton

Contents

1. King Sunny Ade / Juju Music 1
2. Afro Celt Sound System / Vol.1: Sound Magic.....................3
3. Mahmoud Ahmed / Almaz 5
4. Amina Alaoui / Gharnati – Arabo-Andalusian Music of Morocco 7
5. Altan / Island Angel...9
6. Ankala / Rhythms of the Outer Core 11
7. Joe Arroyo / La Noche 13
8. Eleftheria Arvanitaki / Meno Ektos 15
9. Ashkabad / City of Love 17
10. Susana Baca / Eco de Sombras 19
11. Baka Beyond / Spirit of the Forest 21
12. The Balfa Brothers / Play Traditional Cajun Music Vols. 1 & 2 23
13. Asha Bhosle and Ali Akbar Khan / Legacy 25
14. Věra Bílá / Queen of Romany 27
15. João Bosco / João Bosco 29
16. La Bottine Souriante / En Spectacle 31
17. Boukman Eksperyans / Libète (Pran Pou Pran'l) 33
18. Budowitz / Mother Tongue 35
19. Buena Vista Social Club / Buena Vista Social Club 37
20. Camarón / Calle Real 39
21. Manu Chao / Clandestino 41
22. Hariprasad Chaurasia and Shirkumar Sharma / Call of the Valley 43
23. Clifton Chenier / Bogalusa Boogie 45
24. The Chieftains / Santiago 47
25. Willie Colon and Ruben Blades / Siembra 49
26. Toumani Diabate / Djelika 51
27. Manu Dibango and Cuarteto Patria / CubAfrica..............53
28. Donnisulana / Per Agata 55
29. Cesaria Evora / Cesaria 57
30. Mahmoud Fadl / Love Letters from King Tut-Ank-Amen 59
31. Fania All Stars / Live at Yankee Stadium 61
32. Franco / 20ème Anniversaire 63
33. Ghazal / Moon Rise Over the Silk Road 65

34	Gipsy Kings / Gipsy Kings	67
35	Juan Luís Guerra and 4.40 / Bachata Rosa	69
36	Hassan Hakmoun / The Fire Within: Gnawa Music of Morocco	71
37	Ofra Haza / Yemenite Songs	73
38	Huun-Huur-Tu / The Orphan's Lament	75
39	Istanbul Oriental Ensemble / Gypsy Rum	77
40	Jali Musa Jawara / Yasimika	79
41	Carlo Jones & the Surmam Kaseko Troubadours / Carlo Jones & the Surinam Kaseko Troubadours	81
42	Kepa Junkera / Bilbao 00:00h	83
43	Salif Keita / Soro	85
44	Khaled / Khaled	87
45	Nusrat Fateh Ali Khan / Musst Musst	89
46	The Klezmatics / Rhythm + Jews	91
47	Euis Komariah & Yus Wiradiredja / The Sound of Sunda	93
48	Kronos Quartet / Pieces of Africa	95
49	Fela Kuti / The Best Best of Fela Kuti: The Black President	97
50	Ladysmith Black Mambazo / The Star and the Wiseman	99
51	Famille Lela de Permet / Polyphonies vocales et instrumentales d'Albanie	103
52	Oscar D'Leon / Los Oscares de Oscar	101
53	Cheikh Lô / Né La Thiass	105
54	Paco de Lucía / Siroco	107
55	Baaba Maal / Nomad Soul	109
56	Miriam Makeba and the Skylarks / The Best of Miriam Makeba and the Skylarks	111
57	Samba Mapangala and Orchestre Virunga / Virunga Volcano	113
58	Thomas Mapfumo / The Best of Thomas Mapfumo	115
59	Maurice El Médioni / Café Oran	117
60	Mighty Sparrow / 25th Anniversary	119
61	Mila Na Utamaduni / Spices of Zanzibar	121
62	Beny Moré / Cuban Originals – Beny Moré	123
63	Muzsikás and Márta Sebestyén / Morning Star	125
64	Le Mystère des Voix Bulgares / Le Mystère des Voix Bulgares	127
65	Najma / Qareeb	129
66	Milton Nascimento / Clube da Esquina	131

67 Youssou N'Dour / The Guide (Wommat)..................................133
68 NG La Banda / The Best OF NG La Banda 135
69 Orchestra Baobab / Pirates Choice 137
70 Geoffrey Oreyma / Exile 139
71 Orquesta Aragon / Cuban Originals – Orquesta Aragon 141
72 The Gabby Pahinui Hawaiian Band / The Gabby Pahinui Hawaiian Band 143
73 Ivo Papasov / Orpheus Ascending 145
74 Astor Piazzola / Tango: Zero Hour 147
75 Tito Puente / 50 Years of Swing 149
76 Purna Das Baul / Bauls of Bengal 151
77 Ismael Rivera / El Sonero Mayor 153
78 Abdel Gadir Salim All-Stars / The Merdoum Kings Play Songs of Love...155
79 Nitin Sawhney / Beyond Skin 157
80 Shakti / The Best of Shakti 159
81 Ravi Shankar / Live at the Monterey International Pop Festival....161
82 Shooglenifty / Venus in Tweeds 163
83 Paul Simon / Graceland 165
84 Songhai / Songhai 167
85 Mercedes Sosa / 30 Años 169
86 Rashid Taha / Diwân 171
87 Taraf de Haidouks / Honourable Brigands, Magic Horses and Evil Eye 173
88 Tarika / Son Egal 175
89 3 Mustaphas 3 / Shopping 177
90 Totó la Momposina / Pacantó 179
91 Ali Farka Toure with Ry Cooder / Talking Timbuktu 181
92 Transglobal Underground / Dream of 100 Nations 183
93 Rokia Traoré / Mouneïssa..185
94 Värttinä / Vihma 187
95 Caetano Veloso / Circuladô Vivo 189
96 Waterson:Carthy / Waterson:Carthy......................................191
97 Papa Wemba / Le Voyageur 193
98 Zap Mama / Zap Mama 195
99 Various Artists / The Indestructible Beat of Soweto: Vol.1 197
100 Various Artists / Road of the Gypsies...................................199

Introduction

Over the past ten years World Music has been the fastest-growing area of the record industry. From an admittedly small base the scene has mushroomed and there are now literally thousands of CDs in the megastores featuring artists from all over the globe. Because many of the names and much of the music is unfamiliar, the choice can be bewildering, but that's no reason to miss out on the wonderful music out there. The **Rough Guide to 100 Essential World Music CDs**, a hand-picked selection of some of the all-time great albums, shows you the best places to start.

While the term "World Music" has gained common currency and served to win the genre its place in record stores, it still hasn't got a universally agreed definition. For some, World Music is simply the fashionable fusing of different global sounds, while for others the name is so all-embracing that it's virtually meaningless. This book takes its cue from the *Rough Guide to World Music*, the leading handbook on the subject, which includes popular, folk and (excluding the Western canon) classical traditions from around the globe. As a result you'll find an Albanian village band rubbing shoulders with Zimbabwean superstar Thomas Mapfumo, and classical sitar maestro Ravi Shankar alongside such dance-led fusionists as Afro Celt Sound System.

This book doesn't list the hundred best World Music CDs, but attempts to give a wide geographical spread and a varied selection of global styles. Inevitably, though, the choice reflects the popularity of African and Latin music and the relatively small impact of music from the Far East. So, while the Chinese make up a quarter of the world's population, there is no Chinese disc in this book, whereas there are three from Cuba and three from Senegal. In fact, certain countries had so many hot contenders that we decided to limit the choice to three discs from any one country. Each entry finishes with a Further listening section, which might recommend another album by the same artist or push you in a slightly different direction towards new but related material.

As this book is primarily intended for people coming to the music for the first time, the selected albums are generally the most commercial in an artist's catalogue – thus we have Youssou N'Dour's *The Guide (Wommat)*, rather than one of his earlier rootsy recordings. Of the many compilation discs arranged by country (or ethnically), we have selected two, although other country compilations have been included in the Further Listening section, for instance the excellent *Soul of Cape Verde*, which gives a broad picture of the islands' music, is mentioned in the "Further listening" to Cesaria Evora.

While a lot of recordings have become universally accepted as classics – like the *Buena Vista Social Club*, Salif Keita's *Soro* and Ali Farka Toure and Ry Cooder's *Talking Timbuktu* – part of the joy of the World Music phenomenon is the way in which barely known, but wonderful, music regularly emerges from relative obscurity. Alongside the classics, this selection is liberally sprinkled with gems, such as Euis Komariah and Yus Wiradiredja's *The Sound of Sunda* from Indonesia, which deserve to be better known.

Acknowledgements

After I'd drawn up around 130 possibilities for this book I had a meeting with some of the key observers and players on the World Music scene to expand, refine and discuss the list. Virtually everything that was agreed and disagreed on at that meeting has filtered through to this selection, so I offer my thanks to Ben Mandelson, Ian Anderson, Kim Burton and fellow editors of the *Rough Guide to World Music*, Mark Ellingham and Richard Trillo.

Thanks also to those who helped write some of the entries and fill in where I hadn't got the expertise: Nigel Williamson, Sue Steward, Jan Fairley, Andy King-Dabbs, Sue Wilson, Dave Abram, David Flower, Ronnie Graham, Julian May, Robert Maycock, Andy Morgan, Doug Paterson, Mike Cooper and Alex Robinson. At Rough Guides, thanks to Joe Staines for editing and Link Hall for typesetting, and at home, to Kate for huge support through difficult times.

Simon Broughton

King Sunny Ade

Juju Music

Island, 1982

Sunny Ade (guitar and vocals) and the African Beats, featuring Bob Ohiri (guitar), Demola Adepoju (Steel guitar) and Timmy Olaitan (lead talking drum).

In the summer of 1982, amidst the jaded aftermath of glam rock and punk, Nigerian juju music single handedly, and irreversibly, started to expand western musical parameters. Within a couple of years, all the top African stars were playing in London, specialist labels were up and running, African music stores had been opened, and African music had established a solid foothold in the world's most influential pop market.

The pioneering exponent of this new African ambience was Sunny Ade, the son of a Nigerian pastor, aka Alujonu Onigita ("Wizard of the Guitar"), and, ultimately, "The King of World Beat". The vehicle for this trans-continental shift was Island Records – hero and villain in the first world music set-piece of market fickleness and musical frustration.

Juju Music is a vitally important recording, both as a pinnacle of achievement in one of Africa's most potent dance styles, and as the single album which opened western ears to the cultural riches of Africa. After *Juju Music*, for hundreds of thousands of music lovers, there was no going back.

Yet the rise of Sunny Ade, from Nigerian superstardom to global fame, was no flash in the pan. By the time *Juju Music* appeared, Sunny Ade had already served his apprenticeship in Lagos with Moses Olaiya, formed his first band the Green Spots in 1966 and recorded over forty best selling LPs. Slim, handsome, worldly, and in absolute control of the 25 strong African Beats, the 42-year-old Sunny Ade was a virtuoso guitarist and arranger at the very peak of his powers. If ever an African musician was ready for international exposure, then it was Sunny Ade in 1982.

Meanwhile, over in the UK, Island records was looking for a star to open up a new mother lode of music. With its hypnotic, compelling beat, tight, breathless, vocal harmonies, scintillating steel guitar work and time-bending talking drums, *Juju Music* fitted the bill perfectly and, amidst unprecedented media frenzy for music from south of the Sahara, the marriage of music and marketing was consummated.

Recorded in Togo, the album opens with the initially sombre but ultimately exhuberant Ja Funmi, before hurtling through a tightly synchronised series of classic juju riffs in Eje Nio Gba Ara Mi. Underpinned by a gallery of pounding talking drums and with the precise discipline of a finely tuned express train, the track then opens out into the finest exposition of driving percussion and guitar work since the Allman Brothers travelled south. The fourth track, Sunny Ti De Ariya, introduces a more festive, party air with enough call and response to satisfy the most ardent purists of the style.

Ma Jaiye Oni is a mid-tempo outing for steel guitarist Demola Adepoju with a rhythmic feel that owes as much to Steely Dan as to Lagos street-life. King Sunny then takes centre stage with his signature song, 365 Is My Number, taken at twice the usual speed. Subtitled "The Message", "365" remains one of the finest statements of modern juju, an experimental, post-modern foray into traditional Nigerian music. E Falabe Lewe closes off the album, following an all too brief samba intro to a final and potent reminder of roots juju.

Historic, majestic, nostalgic, *Juju Music* is much more than a footnote in the evolution of world music. It is the culmination of an astonishing, century-old Yoruba musical tradition which – almost 20 years on – remains a living masterpiece.

Further listening: Get Yer Jujus Out (Rykodisc) is a great live album from King Sunny's main rival, Chief Commander Ebenezer Obey. **Juju Roots 1930s-1950s** (Rounder) is an excellent introduction to juju's early years.

Afro Celt Sound System

Vol.1: Sound Magic

Real World, 1996

Simon Emmerson (guitars, programming), Ronan Browne (uilleann pipes), Iarla O'Lionaird (vocals), James McNally (bodhrán, whistle), Davy Spillane (pipes, whistle), Myrdhin (harp), Kauwding Cissokho (kora), Masamba Diop (tama), Jo Bruce (keyboards), Martin Russell (keyboards).

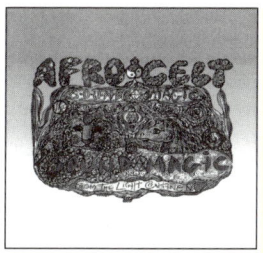

The brain-child of Grammy-nominated producer Simon Emmerson, the Afro Celt Sound System's astonishing debut album, **Sound Magic**, creates an ambitious and innovative soundscape of swirling cross-cultural musical patterns. Elements of modern dance, techno and trance styles are fused with rhythms from West African and Celtic traditions to create one of the richest and least self-conscious "global fusion" projects ever assembled. Emmerson's musical vision was fired by the theory that the Celts had originated in Africa, moving across mainland Europe until they reached the west coast of Ireland. Whatever the truth of "the black Celts" theory, such inspired music-making requires no such cultural justification, although even the casual listener will find it hard not to be struck by the musical empathy between the African kora and the Celtic harp, or the talking tama drum and the Irish bodhrán.

Emmerson spent two years preparing for the project, which eventually took shape at the biennial recording week at Real World's bucolic studios at Box, Wiltshire, in July 1995. The intention of the week is to bring together musicians from around the globe working in different traditions and then to allow them the space to cross-fertilize. It created the perfect environment for Emmerson's visionary project and he collected together a diverse musical crew. He had already produced two Baaba Maal (see p.109) albums and from the Senegalese star's band he took the kora virtuoso Kauwding Cissokho and talking drum player Masamba Diop. From the Irish side came the pipers Ronan Browne and Davy Spillane, as well as the bodhrán and whistle of James McNally (the Pogues) and the bardic singing of Iarla O'Lionaird in the Gaelic style known as sean nós. The Breton harpist Myrdhin added a broader Euro-Celt perspective while Emmerson, Martin Russell and Jo Bruce worked on the programming. Edinburgh's "acid croft" purveyors Shooglenifty (see p.163) happened to be in the studio the same week and so were also pressed into service on two tracks.

Although Emmerson began with pre-prepared basic rhythms and beats, the week was spent improvising over the top of the backing tracks. He then spent three months working on the tapes, judiciously editing and refining but without losing the spontaneous feel or making the results sound self-conscious or overarranged. The album was released a year later with an eye-catching sleeve design by Jamie Reed (designer of the Sex Pistols' *Never Mind the Bollocks* album). Miraculously it works. The Celtic harps, the nyati and the kora form a perfect mesh, particularly on the hypnotic Sure-as-Not. Floating and ethereal pieces of extraordinary beauty can suddenly burst into explosive dance rhythms without warning, and on tracks such as Whirl-y-Reel the Celtic and African percussion find a perfect synergy. Emmerson's production sparkles throughout while the emotive singing of O'Lionaird is a revelation, heard to best effect on the stark House of the Ancestors.

The album made the Afro Celts huge festival favourites across the land but the follow-up was delayed by the death in 1997 of Bruce at the tragically early age of 28. *Volume 2: Release* eventually appeared in 1999, with O'Lionaird's vocals taking a more prominent role. Arguably, it was musically even stronger than *Sound Magic*, although, perhaps inevitably, could not quite match the ground-breaking impact of it's extraordinary predecessor.

Further listening: Although the elements he is fusing are markedly different, Talvin Singh's Mercury Music Prize-winning album **OK** (Island) shares a similarly eclectic spirit of musical adventure.

Mahmoud Ahmed

Almaz

Buda, 1999

Mahmoud Ahmed (vocals), Téwodros Meteku (sax), Fèqadu Amdè-Mèsqèl (sax, flute), Andrew Wilson (guitar), Mèssèlè Gèssèssè (keyboards), Giovanni Rico (bass), Tèsfayé Mèkonnen (drums), Ismael Djingo (percussion).

Mahmoud Ahmed, probably the most popular musical voice in Ethiopia, came to prominence in the "swinging Addis" music scene of the early 1970s as bars, cabarets and an independent record label sprung up in the capital in the closing years of Emperor Haile Selassie's reign. After his overthrow in 1974, Ethiopia was subjected to eighteen years of Marxist dictatorship, which brought an end to the nightlife and halted record production in 1978. Since the collapse of the Mengistu regime in 1991, normality has returned to Addis Ababa but Ethiopian music remains pretty much unknown outside of the country. This is a great shame, as it has a sound and character which is very much its own. Fortunately Buda's "Éthiopiques" series, of which this disc is part, is making some of the vintage recordings of those extraordinary years internationally available.

For those in the know, there is one cult Mahmoud Ahmed record – 1975's *Erè Mèla Mèla*, the first recording of Ethiopian popular music to be released in the West. This is an album with all the brilliance of Orchestra Baobab's *Pirates Choice* (see p.137); but, whereas that disc communicates a particular time and place, Ahmed's has a magic that's eternal. So why isn't it included in this book? Because there's an even better one – his first album, **Almaz**, recorded in 1973, which has the same extraordinary intensity but a greater variety of mood. Until recently this album was virtually unknown.

Mahmoud Ahmed's story is the stuff of legend. Born in Addis in 1941, he started as a shoeshine boy and then found work as an odd-job man in the *Arizona Club*, one of the capital's best nightclubs of the 1960s. He was already a keen singer, but had been turned down when he auditioned because he couldn't read music. However, one night at the club, when the billed singers didn't show, Ahmed stepped in and, since then, he has never looked back. He went on to become one of the country's most popular singers, recording several hits in the 1970s and performing in the luxury hotels during the years of the dictatorship, the only place where musical life took place. Today's he's still one of the country's biggest stars and has a nightclub of his own.

The muddy sonic quality of these Ethiopian discs from the '70s somehow adds to their allure. The title track, **Almaz men eda nèw**, opens with a garage drum-kit groove, over which saxes enter with a distinctively Ethiopian recurring melody. Many of the melodies are in a slightly awkward-sounding five-note scale, with some uneasy intervals that help to give the music an unresolved, soulful feel. But it's when the pace slows down for **Feqer endègèna** that this album's real magic begins. Spiced by gentle backbeats, the saxes swing through a languorous melody that arches up and down while Ahmed's warm baritone sings of trying to rekindle love. The following track, **Ambassel** – the most beautiful on the album – has a strangely Indonesian-like flavour, with a gorgeously doodling flute, plus keyboards and bass. The pace ups for the melismatic **Kulun mankwalèsh** with an insistent bass pattern and rattling percussion, while **Mèla mèla** is a dead ringer for the title track from Ahmed's cult album – and is equally appealing. The 1973 release is supplemented by two additional singles, Ahmed's first vinyl recordings from 1971, which have a rough and ready appeal. Aside from being a marvellous CD, it comes with comprehensive sleeve notes and great photos.

Further listening: Swinging Addis (Buda), vol. 8 in the Éthiopiques series, gives a taste of the Ethiopian capital's groovy music at its height. For the best-available, all-round introduction to the country's traditional music, **Music from Ethiopia** (Caprice) is unbeatable.

Amina Alaoui

Gharnati – Arabo-Andalusian Music of Morocco

Auvidis Ethnic, 1995

Amina Alaoui (vocals), Ahmed Piro (banjo, vocals) and his orchestra.

The tradition of Arab-Andalucian music is a rich and distinguished one, but it can be daunting to the uninitiated, with extended suites of pieces often containing complex modal and rhythmic structures. There's a freshness and directness about Amina Alaoui's performances, however, that make such difficulties fall away. Here is a voice that is clear and gentle, employing just the right caressing tone where necessary. She is supported by one of Morocco's leading Arab-Andalucian orchestras led by Ahmed Piro.

The album opens with the strings of the orchestra playing a low unison C, over which Alaoui's alto voice enters with a warm, seductive melody. Although the end of each phrase heads for the key note, on the way there are some wonderful harmonic tensions with the delicate ornamentations and passing notes clashing with the underlying drone. You don't need to know any of this, of course, you just feel it in the music and Alaoui's performance works its magic. This opening lament, Li Ayyi Sabab, is all too brief, its delicacy and poise virtually unmatched by any music on earth. Most of the texts are laments expressing the sorrow of abandonment by a lover and devotion to God, combining the profane and sacred in a way that is typical of Sufi music, where love for God and an amorous partner are cunningly blurred.

The origins of Arab-Andalucian music are ascribed to Ziryab, who came from Baghdad to Andalucia in the ninth century and founded a musical style that flourished there until the Catholic reconquest of Spain, which culminated in the expulsion of the Moors from Granada in 1492. The musicians relocated to Morocco and the music has developed up to the present day in centres like Tangier, Fez, Tetouan and Rabat, where Ahmed Piro is based. The style is referred to as gharnati (the title of the album), which means "from Granada" – the last great cultural centre of Moorish Spain.

Normally the extended suites of gharnati music are each based in a single mode, but what Alaoui and Piro do here is break with convention by performing a sequence that runs through several rhythmic patterns and a range of different modes. The orchestra is an ensemble of banjo, lute, Moroccan percussion of derbouka (goblet drum) and taar (tambourine), plus violins and violas (played upright) and cello – a mixture of Arabic and Western instruments that has become standard in Arab-Andalucian orchestras.

The suite of sixteen pieces also includes vocals from Piro, an acknowledged veteran of the gharnati tradition, as well as duets between the master and his young protégé, who was just over 30 when this album was recorded. It's the slow numbers, like "Li Ayyi Sabab" and 'An Hwakoum, that are the most poetic, but there's plenty of variety on offer, including some catchy uptempo numbers like Ya Lailatan and Lachjar Barza, the first of which is surely a veiled celebration of consummated sex (the lyrics are translated). The voices soar and are spurred on to greater heights by brief instrumental breaks for the strings as the lyrics become more spiritual in mood and the world of the senses slips (only just) into second place. The strings have that slightly edgy quality typical of Arab orchestras. The disc concludes with Ida Yahij, an unaccompanied solo which returns to the mood of the opening track. Alaoui's voice is in all its glory here, expressing desire, resignation and faith all in one – a wonderful climax to the album.

Further listening: Encuentros (GlobeStyle) is a collaboration of flamenco singer and guitarist Juan Peña "El Lebrijano" and the Orquestra Andalusi de Tanger.

Altan

Island Angel

Green Linnet, 1993

Mairéad Ni Mhaonaigh (vocals, fiddle), Frankie Kennedy (flute, low whistle, backing vocals), Mark Kelly (guitars, backing vocals), Ciaran Curran (bouzouki, bouzouki-guitar), Ciaran Tourish (fiddle, whistle, backing vocals), Daithi Sproule (guitar, backing vocals) plus guests,

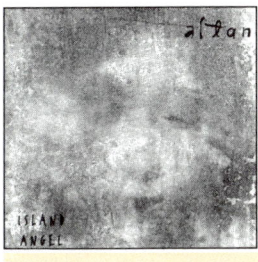

Since their inception in 1987, around Donegal singer and fiddler Mairéad Ni Mhaonaigh and Belfast flute/whistle player Frankie Kennedy, Altan have stood as a contemporary benchmark for Irish traditional music, earning a place among Ireland's leading cultural ambassadors, while never losing touch with the localized heart of the music they play.

That heart resides in Ni Mhaonaigh's native Gaeltacht (Gaelic-speaking) region of Gweedore, in northwest Donegal, an area rich in distinctive musical traditions thanks to the area's geographical isolation from the rest of Ireland and relative proximity to Scotland. Fiddle music is particularly strong, and Altan's exhilarating twin fiddle attack, driven by the region's forcefully accented bowing style, has long been a particular trademark. Their repertoire, too, centres on turbocharged sets of fiddle-led reels and the slower but still insistently jaunty "highlands" – Donegal variants on the Scottish strathspey – together with centuries-old Irish Gaelic songs. What has always set Altan apart, besides Ni Mhaonaigh's bewitching spun-glass vocals, is their collective ability to combine joyous abandon with rigorous technical control. Many a young band's sound possesses that avid, intoxicating energy, but Altan have retained their early edge to a remarkable degree.

For such a long-lived oufit, Altan's line-up has remained unusually stable over the years. By far the biggest mountain they've had to climb, in personal terms, was Frankie Kennedy's death from cancer in 1994. It was his fervent wish, however, that Altan keep going, and in due course they did, bringing in accordionist Dermot Byrne, a regular guest, as a permanent member. Their subsequent signing to Virgin has seen them enjoying the financial benefits of major-label backing, while refusing to compromise the music. **Island Angel** was the last album they made before Kennedy fell ill, and is generally regarded as one of their finest achievements.

The opening set of reels, **Tommy Peoples/The Windmill/Fintan McManus's**, is vintage Altan, diving headlong and without preamble into the rushing current of the tune. Fiddles and flute tumble and scurry through the melodies, backed by resonant, precision-honed rhythm work on bouzouki and guitar. The band's boldness and fluency in handling dynamic shifts and contrasts, together with their seemingly inexhaustible capacity to ring fresh changes on harmony, counterpoint and tonal texture, are gloriously exemplified here, as in several other instrumental sets, notably **Humours of Andytown/Kylebrack Rambler/The Gladstone** and **Glory Reel/The Heathery Cruach**. **Mazurka**, meanwhile, with its strutting, dotted metre and exotically tinged harmonies, is a striking instance of a triple-time dance tune originally from Poland but long incorporated into Donegal tradition.

Of the five songs on the album, three – **Brid Og Ni Mhaille**, **An Mhaighdean Mhara** and **An Cailin Gaelach** – are exactly the kind of gorgeously woebegone love-laments that Ni Mhaonaigh's crystal-pure soprano and exquisitely measured phrasing were made for, sparsely accompanied by plangent guitar figures, moody cello strokes and occasional, subtle layers of synth. These are deftly complemented by **Dulaman**, a luminously rendered, hypnotically swinging children's nonsense rhyme, and a winsomely sunny version of an English-language drinking song, **The Jug of Punch**.

> **Further listening:** Dervish display a comparable calibre on **At the End of the Day** (Whirling Discs), while the all-instrumental Lunasa combine virtuoso playing with innovative arrangements on **Otherworld** (Green Linnet).

Ankala

Rhythms of the Outer Core

Network, 1997

Mark Atkins (didgeridu), Janawirri Yiparrka (yidaki, clapsticks, vocals), Michael Atherton (bouzouki, dobro, marimba, darabuka, etc) plus guests.

When a group of scientists and geologists lowered a microphone as close as they could to the earth's core, they heard a deep, vibratory drone with an almost mystical effect. Was it the sound of man's primal roots? The essence of creation? When asked to describe it, all were unanimous. It was the sound, they said, of the didgeridu, the instrument of the Aboriginal cultures of Australia and the oldest instrument – apart from the human voice – ever invented. The title of this album was presumably suggested by that experiment.

Along with the boomerang, the didgeridu has become a totem for Aboriginal culture. Thanks to New Age fads and buskers on the underground, the instrument is very familiar, but in the hands of a real artist it has a musical power that is astonishing and, of course, a symbolic power for Aborigines that links them to the land and their history. Recently discovered cave and rock paintings in Western Australia including depictions of didgeridus have been dated to 200,000 years old, so the Aborigines can safely claim the oldest intact civilization on the planet. That, of course, is no thanks to white settlers who, over much of the past two hundred years, have been shamefully responsible for destroying Aboriginal society, culture and desecrating the land. Over the past decade there's been a strong Aboriginal rights movement and its musical representatives have all seized on the potency and power of the didgeridu.

Part of the instrument's appeal is that it's made from natural resources – it's basically a termite-hollowed log. Mark Atkins favours the didgeridus from "red dirt country" and finds them by putting his ear to the trees and knocking to find one that's hollow. Then it's a matter of emptying it out, peeling the bark and patching any holes with beeswax. This album includes some fantastic improvisations on the didgeridu, which create vivid sound pictures and various fusion tracks drawing on the traditions of some of Australia's more recent inhabitants.

In **Walya Ngaamadiki**, the brief introductory track of this CD, Atkins describes an evening in the red dirt country and then, over a background of natural bush sounds of frogs, insects and birds, the didgeridu enters to give a rich and resonant backing to **Kuwaritja**, a wistful love song sung by Janawirri Yiparrka. **Scrub Beat** is an improvised didgeridu duet that builds up into what sounds like the stalking and fighting of two wild animals in the bush, complete with the most incredible shrieks and screams. Other tracks that really highlight the elemental power of the instrument are **City Circle**, a spectacular rhythmic solo which sounds like a compendium of virtuoso techniques inspired by urban culture, and **Chitty Chitty**, named after an Australian bird, another example of the way the didgeridu is often used to imitate the natural bush sounds. By contrast, **Ngurili** is an acoustic didgeridu solo which takes its cue from techno music. Among the more eclectic tracks, **Road Train**, **Ghan** and **Café Izmir** bring in European, Pakistani and Turkish ingredients and evoke the Afghan and Pakistani camel trains that crossed the continent. **Dobro Matilda** is a version of "Waltzing Matilda", one of Australia's most popular songs, while **Wongi Wongi**, which closes the album, is a frenetic dash for two drummers, on djembe and darabuka (West African and Arabic goblet drums) and two digderidus. An inventive and inspired album.

Further listening: Yothu Yindi's 1991 **Tribal Voice** (Mushroom) was a landmark of contemporary Aboriginal music that confronted the question of land rights and other contentious issues. **The Rough Guide to Australian Aboriginal Music** (World Music Network) is a good overview of traditional and contemporary Aboriginal music.

Joe Arroyo

La Noche

World Music Network, 1999

Joe Arroyo (vocals) with Fruko (bass, piano, arrangements), Alberto Barros (trombone), Wilson Saoco (shared vocals).

Colombians have a very soft spot for singer Joe Arroyo. His popularity breaks down age and regional barriers and his longevity as a singer has made his music a national passion. A barrio boy made good, Arroyo's life includes the kind of dramatic incidents beloved of Latin American soaps: childhood in a convent and a brothel, a place in a church choir in the Caribbean resort of Cartagena, talent-spotted at 17 by Fruko, Colombia's leading salsa producer, and given a deal with the hit factory label, 3Discos Fuentes. With Fruko's bands, Los Tesos and The Latin Brothers, he accumulated a string of hits, until he formed his own outfit, La Verdad, in 1981 and went stratospheric. This compilation records the peak songs of those periods and reveals his unique salsa style – a fusion of local folk rhythms with other non-Latin Caribbean music grafted onto Cuban rhythms and classic New York salsa.

Arroyo's first recording (and hit) was a fast, brassy version of Celina Gonzalez's sedate anthem to Cubanism, **Yo Soy El Punto Cubano**. It reveals a sharp, ungroomed, edgy voice, and all the confidence of a star in the making. From the same era, trumpet-led, New York salsa influence is also evident in **El Caminante**, with its barroom piano solo and simple blocks of trumpets behind Arroyo's youthful tone. The Latin Brothers were a more sophisticated and distinctively Colombian adventure. By the time of **El Son de Caballo**, Fruko's team included trombonist Alberto Barros, whose lurching legato choruses and solos became a selling point. Electric piano adopts the melody role played by the tres guitar in Cuban son, and Fruko takes the rhythms on jerky son roller-coaster detours.

By the time of the album's opener, La Noche, Arroyo was leading La Verdad, and such upbeat songs (known as joeson) had become his trademark. The stop-start rhythms, outbursts of trumpet and trombone, tinkly bright electric piano melodies, and Arroyo's carefree, high singing and excited high-pitched interjections drove dancers wild. Pal'Bailador magically transforms a piano and trumpets son, while Suave Bruta has a rootsy cumbia rhythm spelled out on traditional Indian gourd shaker (guacharaca) with a solo clarinet, and choruses of "candela" recalling the candles that dancers originally carried in their hands. El Gavilan Pollero is rather easier to dance to; indeed its walking bass-line and see-sawing cumbia beat make it almost impossible not to. Other upbeat numbers – Fuego En Mi Mente and Te Quiero Mas, and the zouk-influenced, synthesizer-led Simula Timula, were favourites with UK audiences during Arroyo's frequent visits to London. In the wake of a near-fatal illness, Arroyo's songs included religious numbers like A Mi Dios Todo Le Debo and Somos Seres – both suggest that Arroyo's temple is more likely to be a nightclub than a church.

The album closes, appropriately, with Mis Zapatos Blancos – the story of a man from Cali desperately looking for his white shoes, an absolute requirement for dancing in that town. Arroyo brings back the trombones, a nod to Willie Colon's '70s hit song with Hector Lavoe, "La Murga", which was adapted from a Panamian folk dance. Many of these songs brought Arroyo and Colombian music to the wider non-Latin world; they still create a rush to the dance-floor years after their first successes.

Further listening: This CD includes a free sampler of Colombian salsa – including Fruko and some of his salsa protégés. Singer Carlos Vives' **Clasicos De La Provincia** (Philips) captures some more progressive developments in Colombian music.

Eleftheria Arvanitaki

Meno Ektos

Polygram Greece, 1991

Eleftheria Arvanitaki (vocals). G. Spathas (guitar), K. Papadoikas (pliktra), M. Klapakis (bauli, bass), N. Antipas (programming).

It's only quite recently that some of Greece's extraordinary female voices have started to become known internationally, but now Savina Yannatou, Melina Kana and Eleftheria Arvanitaki are significant names on the World Music circuit. Arvanitaki, in particular, has a light, focused voice with a silky freshness that is captivating to listen to – whether or not you understand a word of Greek. This isn't a disc for dancing on tables and breaking plates: there's a preponderance of slow music, and that's what Arvanitaki does best, singing with understated delicacy and poise.

Born in Athens, she grew up in the port district of Piraeus, the former heartland of rembetika – an urban blues form which developed with the return of Greek expatriates from Turkey following Greece's defeat in the Greco-Turkish war of 1919–1922. She first started to make a name for herself after becoming involved in the rembetika revival in the 1980s. What attracted her to the songs were the uncomplicated words and melodies, which were always simple but rich in meaning. Although it's not a rembetika album, the same could be said about the material on **Meno Ektos**, which consists of songs by a number of Greek composers, and by the Armenian/American musician and composer Ara Dinkjian. Arvanitaki wanted to record two of Dinkjian's songs after hearing the music of his group Night Ark, and it turned out that Dinkjian was a fan of Greek traditional music. The result was that both of them became interested in exploring the common connections between the sounds of the eastern Mediterranean – specifically Armenian, Turkish and Greek music. Dinkjian went on to write Arvanitaki's next album, *The Bodies and the Knives* (1994).

Those two Dinkjian songs which first appealed to Arvanitaki are included here. The title track, **Meno Ektos** (I Remain an Outcast), opens the album with a hushed delicacy. The tune is simple, but exquisitely beautiful and made instantly memorable by repeated falling phrases. An Armenian song of exile, it expresses a longing to return to a world that no longer exists. The transparent accompaniment on guitars is utterly magical. The other Dinkjian song, **Dinata** (Homecoming), is forceful and urgent, with a more hard-edged electronic accompaniment and Arvanitaki alternating with a chorus. It's a song of hope, about moving from darkness into light with music that is reminiscent of Mikis Theodorakis (famed composer of *Zorba the Greek*) in anthemic mode. It's followed by another of those magical slow numbers, **Omorfi Moi Agapi** (Guardian Angel), which has Eleftheria's voice singing as soft as possible, as if floating in space. Every track is beautiful in its way, but there are a couple of love songs that stand out: **Kima to Kima** (Wave After Wave), about dreaming of a loved one, and **Tis Kalinichtas Ta Filia** (The Goodnight Kisses) which shows off the ethereal quality of Arvanitaki's voice. The most robust song on the album is **Kathreftizo To Nou** (I Reflect the Mind), a Romany Gypsy song used in the film *Rom* by Manelaos Karamagiolis.

With its predominantly slow pace and elegiac, character, this is an album for the romantic at heart. Its strengths are the otherworldly quality of Arvanitaki's voice, the control with which she handles it and the lyrical writing throughout.

Further listening: The Greek rembetika music of the '20s and '30s gives an extraordinarily vivid picture of the era. **Greek-Oriental Rembetika** (Arhoolie) and **Historic Urban Folk Songs from Greece** (Rounder) are two excellent compilations of early recordings.

Ashkabad

City of Love

Real World, 1993

Atabai Tsharykuliev (vocals, dutar, tar), Gassan Mamedov (violin), Sabir Rizaev (clarinet, saxophone, etc), Kurban Kurbanov (accordion, piano), Khakberdy Allamuradov (percussion) plus guests.

Central Asia is a vast expanse of territory, ten times the size of Britain, full of fertile valleys, cotton fields and spectacular mountains ranges. It also has a rich and developed musical tradition almost unknown in the West. Well done to Real World for making some of it more widely available – although this is their only excursion, so far, into the territory. Ashkabad is the capital city of Turkmenistan, lying north of Iran and east of the Caspian Sea, and it's also the name of this Turkmen supergroup, who perform the "wild and romantic traditional wedding music" of their homeland. The name of the group, and the city, translates as the "city of love" and the album is a great set of catchy songs, swirling dance tunes and lyrical ballads tinged with melancholy.

This disc is a fine example of a distinctive Central Asian style in a contemporary context. All the musicians are recognized in their own right and familiar with Western music as well as their own traditional styles. Atabai Tsharykuliev, leader of the band, works in the national orchestra, but also grew up on the wedding circuit and was instrumental in keeping the tradition alive when it was discouraged by the Soviet authorities for being too Islamic. The instrumental ensemble is a combination of Western instruments – violin, clarinet and accordion – and Central Asian ones – the dutar (long-necked lute) and dep (frame drum), nagara (barrel drum) and serp (jingles) that tap out the rhythms. Some of the numbers are snakey, lyrical melodies (for example Bayaty) while others, are frenetic uptempo dances, for instance Shalakho with screaming violin and rattlingly good Central Asian-style drum solo.

Many of Ashkabad's song lyrics come from the celebrated eighteenth-century Turkmen poet Makhtumkuli, including the patriotic Ayrylsa (Separation) that opens the album: "I'm far from home, travelling the world. Every country has its own beauty, but my heart longs for the black stones and sweet people of Turkmenistan." The music, moving stepwise up and down in a melody that turns in on itself, is typically Central Asian in style. It's clean and taut in its instrumentation and intense in its emotional drive. Aglar Men (I'm Crying), which follows, is one of their slow, wistful ballads – also with words by Makhtumkuli. A song about the troubled fate of the country, it has some surprising and beautiful twists in the melody and harmony.

The same is true of the instrumental "Bayaty", which just occasionally verges on the schmaltzy. Aisha, another instrumental, with a soulful violin solo, also has a warm, meditative lyrical flavour. Yaman Ykbal (Sad Fate), composed by Atabai Tsharykuliev, is a beautiful slow ballad about ageing, with a languid melody and lyrical playing on the saxophone. Bibining is more typical wedding repertoire, with shrieks, vocal declamations and fiery instrumental interjections. Ketshpelek (Bitter Fate), which draws on the conservatoire background of several of the players, is a song and orchestral fantasy (with Western string players) about a musician unable to marry the girl he loves. After a strange bit of jiggery-pokery with a low-level vocal track, Gagagum Keshdeleri is a rousing percussion finale. The album is produced by John Leckie, who's brought his rock band skills to several excellent Real World albums.

> **Further listening:** Yulduz Usmanova is the best-known popular singer of Uzbekistan, but there is always a traditional feel to her music. **Yulduz: The Selection Album** (Blue Flame) is an excellent "greatest hits" collection.

Susana Baca

Eco de Sombras

Luaka Bop, 2000

Susana Baca (vocals), David Pinto (bass, vocals), Rafael Muñoz (acoustic guitar, vocals), Hugo Bravo (congas, quijada, checo, timpani, botijas, yembe, vocals), Juan Medrano Cotito (cajón, mesa, vocals) and guests.

Susana Baca's delicate, cool Afro-Peruvian styles has shown the world that there is more to Peruvian music than panpipes and quena flutes. Her songs come from the black-infused traditions which evolved out of the music brought by African slaves during the colonial period. Singing rhythmic festejos and landos, chants and dances, Susana's gentle voice glances against bass, guitar and percussion. Often elegantly dancing while singing, she is a performer who consistently entrances audiences.

Baca's music is rooted in Afro-Peruvian sounds, which were revived and became extremely popular in Latin America in the 1960s. Susana worked with the late, great Chabuca Grande, who she refers to as "the mother of my singing". Inspired by Chabuca's pioneering example, Susana founded the Instituto Negro Continuo in Lima – complete with its own archive, library and performance space – with the aim of preserving Black traditions and revitalizing them. The songs she sings are both old and new, and her own compositions have a contemporary, often jazz-like feel, her voice imbued with affection and tenderness.

Susana's work came to the attention of ex-Talking Head David Byrne, and his Luaka Bop label, who included one of her songs, "Maria Lando", on his *The Soul of Black Peru* compilation. Byrne was so charmed by Susana's music and quiet confidence, he joined her on her second album, **Eco de Sombras**. He also brought in a number of renowned US musicians who subtly embroider the rich timbres of Susana's own superb group.

The relaxed air of the album probably comes from the fact it was recorded in Susana's home in Chorrillos on the Lima coast. Susana was brought up there, in a world populated, as she describes it, by "cats and fisherman", where her father played guitar at neighbourhood parties and her mother danced and sang.

The album opens with clinking percussion, like children rapping on pots and boxes, which introduces De los Amores, a bitter-sweet love song beautifully combining plucked guitar with resonant bass. Reiña Mortal, another song by the same composer Javier Lozo, is equally subtle. Love songs with poetic lyrics have a special meaning for Susana, who calls them "small glimpses of emotion". One of the most exquisite examples on the album is Poema, with words by Carlos Oquendo de Amat, a surrealist poet from Puno. The fragility of the love described ("a smile printed on Japanese paper") is matched by the vulnerability of Susana's voice as it moves over cool guitar, bass and deft piano touches. A warmer more sensual take on the love experience can be found on Los Amantes, its final phrases infused with a deep and poignant melancholy. Valentín recalls the beatings and struggles of slavery, but the violence of its lyrics is belied by the mellow shades of percussion and guitar. El Mayoral, Golpe e' Tierra and Panalivio also come from the same slave root, but their message is largely nostalgic.

While producer Craig Street's mantra for this disc was clearly "the voice is the song", the album's arrangements are full of delicious instrumental touches, notably some richly varied guitar textures and David Byrne's charango. The finale Xanaharí, with its intoxicating theme, "Life shines through your radiant smile", is a wonderfully upbeat number – its percussive coda apparently played on Susana's table top while the band waited for their supper!

Further Listening: The pioneers of Peru Negro can be heard on **The Soul of Black Peru** (Luaka Bop). **The Best of Inti-Illimani** (Xenophile) showcases the radical politics of the finest exponents of modern Andean music.

Baka Beyond

Spirit of the Forest

Hannibal/Rykomusic, 1993

Martin Cradick (guitar, mandolin, bass, ndenge, percussion, samples), Su Hart (vocals and percussion), Paddy Le Mercier (violin, flutes), Sangowe (limbindi), Bounaka (ngombi), Nahwia (limbindi), Jerry Soffe (bass).

Ever since ethnographer Simha Arom's legendary field recordings first brought "Pygmy" music to the wider world's attention in 1978, Western musicians have experimented with the mesmerizing harmonies and complex syncopated rhythms of the central African rainforest. Jazz trumpeter Chet Baker, Brussels-based a cappella group Zap Mama (see p.195) and, most famously, Euro-synth supremos Deep Forest, have all drawn inspiration from Arom's archives over the years. But no recording artist actually played with living Pygmy musicians until former Outback guitarist, Martin Cradick, decided to do just that in 1992.

Cradick first came across the Pygmies' music through a television documentary about a group called the Baka, who live in the remote forest region lining the Cameroon–Congo border. Picking out chords on his guitar to fit with the soundtrack, he found he could play along with the Baka's tunes. Over time this seed of an idea grew into the insistent title track of Outback's last album, *Baka*, and an enduring desire to tap the source of those otherworldly sounds.

Three years later, he finally got his chance. Armed with a Sony-Pro Walkman, mandolin and a tent, Cradick and his wife, vocalist Su Hart, set off to Cameroon and spent six weeks in the forest, hunting, eating and jamming with their Baka hosts, whose irrepressible musicality was a constant source of wonder. The album that emerged ranked among the most original of the decade. Weaving together live field footage, tunes learned from the Baka, and improvised studio overdubs, **Spirit of the Forest** was an attempt to recreate the feel of those inspirational camp sessions.

A drone of nocturnal insect noise opens the trademark title track, broken by the lingering echoes of a yelli – haunting yodelled notes, descending in steps, with which the Baka traditionally entice animals to their hunt. Wood blocks, seedpod shakers and hand claps then set up an infectious fireside groove, over which Cradick lays the key notes of the yelli on his mandolin, with picked acoustic guitar chords filling out the melody. Short violin and flute breaks from French fiddler, Paddy Le Mercier, and periodic reversions to the Baka root rhythms, hold your interest for all five and a half minutes of the most lyrical, inspired fusion music you're ever likely to hear.

All eight tracks more or less follow this formula, but each strikes a distinctively different tone. While some – such as **The Man Who Danced Too Slowly** and **Eeya Bé** – are fuelled by bouncy soukous-style guitar riffs; others – notably **Ngombi** and **Nahwia** – cast trancier spells rooted in the looped licks of the Baka's forest-made instruments, the ngombi (harp zither) and limbindi (earth harp). Outshone only by the first track, the most memorable tune on the album is **Baka Play Baka**. This was the song inspired by the TV documentary soundtrack Cradick first jammed along to. The Baka themselves apparently loved it when he played them the Outback recording and immediately joined in with the wonderful layer of percussion that drives this later version, exploited to the full by funky bass-line and guitar riff.

Though less slickly produced than Baka Beyond's subsequent offerings, *Spirit of the Forest* has emerged as the band's most popular album. This is largely attributable to the more collaborative nature of its music, which possesses all the freshness and raw vitality you'd hope for from such a first encounter.

Further listening: Of Baka Beyond's later albums, **Meeting Pool** (Hannibal) retains the most "Pygmy" influence, blended with some spine-tingling Celtic ballads.

The Balfa Brothers

Play Traditional Cajun Music Vols. 1 & 2

Ace, 1990

Dewey Balfa (fiddle, vocals), Will Balfa (second fiddle, vocals), Hadley Fontenot (accordion), Rodney Balfa (guitar, vocals), Harry Balfa (guitar), Burke Balfa (triangle), plus guest Marc Savoy.

Cajun music is the distinctive sound of the French settlers of South Louisiana. Life there is hard and music has traditionally been an escape: a way of drowning sorrows or dancing them off at weekend parties. It's a tradition that continues at dancehalls and lounges to this day. Most songs are sung in French, although there's inevitably been a strong influence of Anglo-American culture, sometimes forcefully imposed.

The Balfa Brothers created, or more correctly recreated, what we think of as the quintessential sound of Cajun music with fiddles, accordion, guitar and triangle. Coming from a poor sharecropping family, they regularly played together for house parties from the 1940s, but were raised to celebrity status after Dewey Balfa appeared at the Newport Folk Festival in 1964. This heralded a revival in the rootsier sound of Cajun music after years of Americanization, with country-style steel guitars. The Balfas' acoustic sound was distinguished by the high, searing French vocals of Dewey and Rodney, the fiddle duets of Dewey and Will and the fine accordionists they worked with, including Nathan Abshire, Hadley Fontenot and the youthful (at that time) Marc Savoy. The other brothers provided the accompaniment on guitar and petit fer (triangle).

This CD combines two LPs the Balfas made for Swallow Records – one of the leading labels for Cajun music. The first was recorded in 1965 and the second, featuring Rodney's son Tony (triangle and drums) and Marc Savoy (accordion) in 1974. This is not concert music, but music for dancing – virtually all Cajun numbers are either waltzes or two-steps. The 24 tracks here have a genuine rawness and down-home quality and you can easily imagine the stomping feet on a wooden floor. The playing has such a natural quality that it's clear that this is a band that has played thousands of dances together for decades. The very first track, **Drunkard's Sorrow Waltz**, takes you straight into the distinctive world of intense, plaintive vocals and grinding fiddle playing with lots of double-stopping. There are informal cries of encouragement as the band lurches into the instrumental bridge passages between verses. The way the lyrics are set to the melody is strange and awkward, intensifying the grief (or maybe the drunkenness) of the song. This is followed by an upbeat two-step that's become a Cajun standard, **Lacassine Special**.

For a distinctive Balfa-style fiddle duet, try **La Valse de Grand Bois**, and for some really meaty accordion playing by Hadley Fontenot listen to **Family Waltz**. Other highlights from the first session include **Valse de Balfa**, **Parlez Nous à Boire** (which has become another standard) and the lonesome **Les Blues de Cajun** with vocal and soulful fiddle solo from Dewey. Classic numbers from the second set include the tight **'Tit Galop pour Mamou**, celebrating the town five miles from the Balfas' home in Bayou Grand Louie, and the suitably fiery **Les Flammes d'Enfer**.

Tragically Will and Rodney died in a car crash in 1979 (an alarming number of Cajun musicians have died on the roads), which brought the band's career to an end. Dewey Balfa continued recording with other musicians and was a respected teacher of Cajun music until his death in 1992.

> **Further listening:** One of Dewey's most successful students, fiddler, accordionist and vocalist Steve Riley, leads the best of Louisiana's contemporary Cajun bands. The title track of **'Tit Galop pour Mamou** (Rounder) is a homage to the Balfas and includes Dewey's daughter Christine "guesting" on triangle.

Asha Bhosle and Ali Akbar Khan

Legacy

AMMP/Triloka 1996

Asha Bhosle (vocal), Ali Akbar Khan (sarod), Swapan Chaudhuri (tabla, pakawaj), Ramesh Misra (sarangi), Dan Reiter (cello), James Pomerantz (sitar), Rajan Parrikar (harmonium), Kalpana Banerjee (tanpura), Alam Khan (tanpura).

For listeners in the West, the biggest names in Indian classical music are the instrumentalists, like sitarist Ravi Shankar (see p.161), or the veteran Ali Akbar Khan who, in 1955, gave the first major Indian music recital in America playing the sarod (a lute-like stringed instrument with a shiny fingerboard and a dark, teak-like tone). In India itself, however, it is the vocalists who reign supreme and Asha Bhosle is one of the most revered figures. One of the most recorded artists in the world, Bhosle's name isn't usually connected with the refined repertoire of Hindustani classical music, but with the razzmatazz of Bollywood, India's vast and fertile film industry.

The seeds of this album seem to go back as far as 1952, when Ali Akbar Khan was supplementing his earnings as a classical master with a bit of film work and found himself working with Bollywood's ubiquitous playback singers, Lata Mangeshkar and her younger sister Asha Bhosle. As Bhosle and Khan rose to the summit of two completely different careers, Khan cherished the idea of making a recording with her.

All the songs on this disc were learned by Ali Akbar Khan from his father Allaudin Khan, who had, in turn, received them from his father and so on for several generations. In theory it's an oral tradition stretching back to Tansen, principal court musician to the Mughal emperor Akbar in the sixteenth century and one of the legendary figures of Indian music. Ali Akbar Khan can, therefore, trace his lineage back to Tansen (there's a family tree to prove it), so it's remarkable that he decided to entrust such unique material to a playback artist who'd already dashed off around eight thousand songs. Bhosle, however, underwent an exacting training process in order to record the classical material, and her dedication is fully justified by the results.

Most Indian vocal music, even if it doesn't have a specific religious purpose, has devotional roots, and the twelve tracks on the disc open and close with a prayer. After Khan's slow, evocative introduction to **Guru Bandana,** Bhosle's voice enters low and soft, gently moving around the main note, exploring harmonic tensions before flying upwards and easing into a sunny resolution. The prayer praises the Hindu deities Brahma, Vishnu and Shiva as well as, implicitly, Ali Akbar Khan and his antecedents back to Tansen. The whole performance – five and a half minutes – just seems to hang timeless in the air. It is one of the most beautiful and sublime vocal performances on disc.

The lyrics to most of the songs are minimal: there are several taranas, which are essentially about vocal display with nonsense syllables, and a beautiful **Kheyal**, one of the more popular of classical vocal forms, in which Bhosle's soaring and swooping voice is mirrored by the sarangi, a bowed string instrument considered to be the closest to the human voice. At the heart of the disc is a **Dhrupad**, a long and stately song in the most archaic and serious of Indian vocal styles, although this rendition is unorthodox in that such songs are usually the exclusive preserve of men. It's followed by **Sadra**, in which a suitably intense sarod solo, with wonderful sliding notes, gives way to one of Bhosle's more playful songs. Overall, if you listen intently enough to this album the effect is like a form of spiritual refreshment, so it's appropriate that it ends with a prayer to Mother Sharda – the Hindu goddess of music.

> **Further listening:** On **Lata in Concert – An Era in an Evening** (Sony, India), Lata Mangeshkar, Bhosle's sister and the other great nightingale of Indian film, celebrates half a century in the business in concert in Mumbai (Bombay) in 1997.

Věra Bílá

Queen of Romany

BMG/Gig, 1999

Věra Bílá (lead vocals), Desiderius Dužda (vocals, guitar), Jan Dužda (vocals, guitar), Dezider Siška Lúčka (vocals), Emil Pupa Miko (vocals and bass) plus guests.

When you get this album go straight to the last track, **Te Me Pijav Lačhes Rosnes** (When I'm Getting Drunk), and you'll find yourself listening to one of the most extraordinary voices in Europe. After a strummed chord from the guitar, Bílá's lonely, forsaken vocal comes in; at first restrained and unemotional but then sliding and twisting with extraordinary vocal glissandi as it turns in on itself in short phrases – plaintive and long-suffering. With superb control, her voice moving from one dark tone to another, Bílá brilliantly conveys the loneliness of a man getting wasted because of his cheating wife.

Bílá is a Czech Romany, although her family originate from the Gypsy shantytowns of Slovakia. She smokes heavily and eats heartily, and her appearance (she's almost as wide as she is tall) is as formidable as her voice. She's lived a hard life – you can hear it in her voice – but has succeeded in becoming the country's best-known and most successful Gypsy performer. Although the tone is deceptively breezy, Bílá has a strength and resilience that shines through in every track of this album.

Bílá, whose surname means "white" in Czech, is supported by a band, Kale, whose name means "black" in Romany. Kale, an all-male guitar-playing quartet, write the songs with Bílá and provide close-harmony backing vocals. On this album they're joined by guest musicians on guitars, violin, piano, saxes, bass and drums.

There's a definite Latin flavour to much of the music and more than a hint of Gypsy rumba – indeed, there's a marked similarity to the music of the Gipsy Kings (see p.67), but with more grit.

Queen of Romany, drawn from Bílá's two CDs on the Czech label Ariola, *Rom-Pop* and *Kale Kaloré*, is essentially a greatest hits album. The vast majority of the fifteen tracks are fast, upbeat numbers, which fly along with hummable tunes, fizzing guitars and catchy vocal harmonies even when the lyrics are less than cheerful – the first song **E Daj Nasval'i** (My Mother is Ill) tells of a mother's illness and eventual death. As with many of these songs, the impression conveyed is that, however bad life gets, the Gypsy philosophy means that you have to make the best of things. Among the most powerful tracks are the racey **Sako Rat'i** (Every Night), a song about wife-beating whose dark subject matter is belied by an athletic walking bass and hokey violin solo, and **Čirikloro Mirikloro** (Little Bird, Little Pearls) in which the string accompaniment sounds like a Transylvanian village band.

Not every song is led by Bilá: in **Lol'i Ruže** (Red Roses), a beautiful slow love song with dark harmonies and a wistful guitar solo, the lead vocal is taken by bass player Emil Pupa Miko; in **Čhaje, Čhaje** (My Girl, My Girl), it's sung by Dezider Siška Lúčka, and on **Baron Romane Čhavore** (The Children of the Romany Grow Up) by Jan Dužda. This last song, which tells how Romany children grow up in poverty and are beaten by the gadje (white people), is a cry for unity. **Pandždženore** (Five Persons), sung by Bílá over an unstoppable bassline and a bank of guitars, is a portrait of the band: "The young men play good music. We sing for all of you and play wonderful songs." That's certainly true. When the disc finishes, with its extraordinary account of drunken depression, you just want to press "play" and be cheered up all over again.

> **Further listening**: **Gypsy Queens** (Network) is an unequalled two-CD collection of female Romany vocalists, including the glorious Esma Redžepova.

João Bosco

João Bosco

IMP, 1994

João Bosco is the smart face of samba; a musician who combines all the joy and dance of the samba rhythm but with meaningful, intelligent lyrics. Like Milton Nascimento (see p.135), he was born in the land-locked state of Minas Gerais, far from the carefree coast that produced the styles that were to dominate his sound. From an early age music was an important part of his life, and he soon discoverered samba and the tradition's greatest guitarist, Baden Powell. In his teens Bosco dreamed of becoming a musician, but by the early 1970s he had moved to Ouro Preto to study civil engineering. University holidays were spent doing what he loved: jamming and gigging in the capital of samba, Rio de Janeiro. It was here that he met Aldir Blanc, who had given up poetry to study psychiatry. The two began a correspondence that produced, "Agnus Sei", a song that captured the ears of Brazilian superstar Elis Regina, who made it a hit.

The success of "Agnus Sei" provided the platform Bosco needed to launch his own career, and in 1973 he gave up designing bridges and moved to Rio to play samba. Sung samba had always been built around guitar and percussion, and in their vintage years Bosco and Blanc never abandoned this formula, but, instead, stretched it in new, invigorating directions. Bosco's guitar playing became ever more inventive: he introduced richer harmonies, rhythms from American jazz-funk, and utilized instruments like electric bass and kit drums. Aldir Blanc made samba as lyrically respectable as the Tropicalismo of Caetano

Veloso (see p.189), adding word-play, wit and political edge. The result was a reinvented form of samba – dancey and rootsy, yet as sophisticated and innovative as any music in 1970s Brazil.

Although most Bosco compilations are worth checking out, **João Bosco** is one of the best. After initial Piña Colada crooning on *Dois Pra La Dois Pra Ca*, the samba begins in earnest on *O Bêbado e a Equilibrista* (The Drunk and the Tightrope Walker), an unforgettable groove that mixes infectious rhythm with minor cadences to create the uniquely Portuguese mood of nostalgic longing known as saudade. *O Ronco da Cuíca* (The Cuíca's Snore) kicks off with football-stadium drums and cheers, then slips into an effortlessly tight dance rhythm interspersed with shouted voices and psychedelic squeaks from the cuíca drum, its lyrics sneering sarcastically at the cruel politics of late-1970s Brazil. *Tiro da Misericordia* (the chorus of which has become a Brazilian football anthem) is a more experimental piece, mixing the rhythms of samba, jazz-funk, and the Bahian martial art dance of capoeira. *O Mestre Sala do Mares*, *Boca de Sapo* (Toad's Mouth) and *O Rancho da Goiaba* (The Goiaba Ranch) find Bosco in a lighter and more traditional vein.

The wickedly foot-tapping *Linha de Passe*, the shifting harmonies of *Casa de Marimbondo* (The Wasp's Nest), and the spare but witty *Incompatabilidade de Gěnios* (Incompatable Temperaments), are arguably the collection's strongest tracks. The first lovingly describes everyday life in Brazil's favelas, focusing on the Afro-Brazilian religion of candomblé, football and, of course, samba. In the second, samba is championed as an instrument of social protest, while in "Incompatabilidade" Bosco laments his troubled love life on an imaginary psychiatrist's couch. The popular *De Frente pro Crime* rounds off the collection.

João Bosco has yet to gain the worldwide attention enjoyed by many less talented and less influential Brazilian musicians. In Brazil, however, few performers are more highly regarded.

> **Further listening: Brazil Classics 2: O Samba** (Luaka Bop), David Byrne's tasteful overview of the samba scene, includes such artists as Clara Nunes, Alcione, Beth Carvalho and Paulinho da Viola.

La Bottine Souriante

En Spectacle

Les Productions Mille-Pattes, 1996

Yves Lambert (lead vocals, button accordion, harmonica, jew's harp), Michel Bordeleau (foot percussion, mandolin, fiddle, guitar, vocals), Martin Racine (fiddle, guitar, vocals), Denis Fréchette (piano, piano accordion, vocals), Régent Archambault (double bass, electric bass, vocals) Jean Fréchette (saxophone, flute, whistle) Robert Ellis (bass trombone), André Verreault (trombone), Jocelyn Lapointe (trumpet, flugelhorn).

Whenever you're feeling blue, when life seems full of cares and empty of sparkle – put on **En Spectacle**, good and loud, and within seconds your spirits will start inexorably to rise: such is the massive, irresistible *joie de vivre* concentrated in the music of Quebec's La Bottine Souriante.

Formed in 1976, with the aim of preserving the rich musical traditions of their venerable Acadian (French-Canadian) heritage, while placing them firmly in a contemporary context, La Bottine started out with a line-up reflecting the colourful French/Celtic blend of Acadian music, including fiddle, button accordion, mandolin and guitar. In 1990, however, they took the decisive step towards becoming the nine-man juggernaut of aural jubilation heard in action here, by adding a four-piece brass section. This union of traditional musicians with those from other genre backgrounds produced "un choc des cultures" of the most fruitful and exhilarating kind, opening up the band's sound to encompass jazz, Latin, big-band, swing, honky-tonk and soul.

Since then, La Bottine have gone on to ever-increasing international acclaim, winning numerous gold discs and industry awards at home in Canada, along with a continuing stream of critical superlatives from the world's music media. Their name, incidentally, translates as "the smiling boot" – colloquially, one whose sole is coming away from its upper. It's an allusion to the central, implacably propulsive motor behind their sound, the prodigious foot percussion of multi-instrumentalist Michel Bordeleau, who has estimated that his feet strike an approximate average of 15,000 beats during every show.

It's an explosive double report from these feet, interrupting a deep, grandly imposing introductory drone of bowed double bass and bass trombone, that – literally – kicks off the opening medley of five favourite reels, here simply entitled **Ouverture**. Around eight minutes long, it's a marvellous microcosm of La Bottine at their rumbustious best, steadily building in density, scale and dynamism as further instrumental layers are shaded into the mix, from that growling bass underlay to hot snakey sax, crystalline mandolin-picking to barrelhouse piano, configured this way and that with equal parts loose-limbed fluidity and razor-sharp precision. The next track, **Sur la Route (La Tapinie)** is one of several featuring Yves Lambert's authoritatively gruff, playful yet soulful lead vocals in a call-and-response pattern with the band's four other singers. The song in turn is artfully interwoven with a full instrumental arrangement, concluding in the first instance with the classic Québecois tune "Reel des Voyageurs".

The album's prevailing mood is headily carnivalesque, with the adrenalin cranked up several extra notches by the live setting, and reaching its peak in the final set of tunes, **La Grand' Côte**, which features a full two-minute foot solo from Bordeleau, accelerating to almost machine-gun rapidity before the rest of the band comes back for the gloriously tumultuous finale. The wryly poignant, a cappella love song **Virginie Adieu**, and the exquisite, lingeringly paced instrumental **Le Rêve Musicale**, both show that the band can do stripped-down and delicate with no less panache or finesse than their trademark manic reels.

> **Further listening**: Barachois, a highly talented and manically hilarious quartet from Canada's Prince Edward Island, mine similar traditional sources on their latest release, **Encore!** (House Party Productions).

Boukman Eksperyans

Libète (Pran Pou Pran'l!)

Mango, 1995

Theodore "Lôlô" Beaubrun Jr (vocals, keyboards, tanbou, percussion), Daniel Beaubrun (vocals, bass, lead guitar, rhythm guitar, keyboards, drum programming, percussion), Marjorie Beaubrun (vocals, percussion), Mimerose "Manze" Beaubrun (vocals), Maguy Jean-Louis (vocals, percussion), Mackel "Ti Bazol" Jean-Baptiste (lead guitar), Gary Seney (backing vocals, tanbou, katabou, percussion), Hans "Bwa Gris" Dominique (manman tanbou, Percussion), Henry Joseph Pierre (backing vocals, tanbou, katabou, percussion).

Haiti gets a pretty bad press – voodoo, violence, the tyrannical regimes of Papa and Baby Doc Duvalier and failed attempts at democracy. But it's funny how the toughest places often produce the best music. There's probably no sharper contrast in the Caribbean today than that between the vitality and exuberance of Haiti's music and its brutal and troubled history. Of course, that history has made the music sound the way it does. There's the usual Caribbean mix of African and colonial sounds, but the emphasis is strongly African. Under the French, Haiti became the richest colony in the world, exporting sugar, coffee and tobacco. To work that trade vast numbers of slaves were needed and by the turn of the nineteenth century Haiti had a slave population eight times the size of the whites and mulattos. This is why the culture is so African and why there was a slave revolution led by a voodoo priest called Boukman, after whom this band is named. Although Boukman was executed and became the country's martyr, Haiti became the first independent black nation in 1804.

Boukman Eksperyans took as their inspiration the grassroots black culture of Haiti: the voodoo religion, the rara street-carnival music and the Creole language which was banned or marginalized by the dictatorships. Their music was a very different sound to the swinging French Caribbean compas favoured by the dictators. When things changed in 1990, Boukman Eksperyans was literally the voice of the new generation. People on the streets sang their songs as they swept Prosper Avril from power and the band was at the forefront of a back-to-roots Creole-pride culture. Hopes were high as Jean Bertrand Aristide, the country's first democratically elected president, came to power. Unfortunately it didn't last. With the military coup the band found themselves again harrassed and threatened and, like Aristide, they ended up in enforced exile. They set off on tour to the UK and America, but while they were in Britain President Clinton barred non-resident Haitians from entering the US. Unable to go back to Haiti, Chris Blackwell offered them sanctuary in Jamaica, where they recorded this incredible album.

One of Boukman's strengths are their harmony vocals. **Legba**, which opens the album, is an a cappella choral invocation of voodoo deities with a gentle rattle accompaniment. Predictably, most of the band's songs have a complex rhythmic base of different types of drums with guitars, uncheesy synth and vocals always to the fore. The messages of these songs are important, but you don't need to understand a word to feel their power or get up and dance. **Libète** (Freedom) features gentle but insistent choral harmonies with a lithe falsetto solo over an insistent percussive bed; **Zani Yo Younen** (The Spirits Are Back) and **Zili** are beautiful slow, spiritual songs, the latter with a strongly African flavour. **Ganga**, one of the most impressive tracks, is about the continuing power of the ancestor spirits from Congo. Like the voodoo religion, the album calls on a syncretic combination of deities. **Rara Ti Celia** (Little Celia's Rara) inhabits the street-party atmosphere of rara, complete with carnival whistles, while the final song, **Jou Malé** (Day of the Shock), is a powerful piece about resisting tyranny and exploitation. The album is dedicated to the band's drummer and bass player, who died in 1994 from lack of medication as a result of the American embargo.

Further listening: Mini All Stars (Stern's/Earthworks) **and Coupé Cloué** are great discs of the older style of Haitian dance music – compas.

Budowitz

Mother Tongue

Koch/Schwann, 1997

Joshua Horowitz (button accordion, tsimbl), Walt Mahovlich (C-clarinet), Steven Greenman (violin), Lothar Lässer (button accordion), Géza Pénzes (cello, double bass).

Subtitled "Music of the 19th Century Klezmorim on Original Instruments", **Mother Tongue** is an attempt by Joshua Horowitz to recreate the Jewish village music of Eastern Europe before it became Americanized with jazz and swing elements. It's an approach which combines the historical research and original instruments of the classical "authentic music" movement with the living experience of village music that still exists in Eastern Europe today. It's known that Jewish and Gypsy musicians played together before World War II, and so the Gypsies – as well as keeping alive their own traditions – serve as living witnesses to the music of a world destroyed by the Holocaust.

The instruments used in the band are one reason for its particular sound. The two accordions were made in 1889 by a Galician-Czech maker called Karl Budowitz, from whom the band take their name, and were restored by Horowitz and Lässer. The natural materials from which they're made – wood, bone, brass and leather – give a mellow warmth of tone that can't be matched by modern instruments. Two accordion duets, **Bessaraber Khusidl** and **Belf's Khusidl**, show off their unique sound. The instruments demand their own particular playing style, and need special fingerings and ornamentation that you wouldn't use on a modern accordion. The tsimbl (hammer dulcimer), likewise, is a specially constructed instrument based on historical models with its string tension a fraction less than a modern concert cimbalom. Both **Horowitz's Doina**, a slow improvisatory piece, and **Freylekhs Fun der Khupe,** a fast virtuoso romp, reveal the instrument's delicate sound, as does Horowitz's wonderful playing.

While the band's fiddle player Steven Greenman is a fine klezmer violinist, Walt Mahlovich on clarinet is rather less refined – although his raw style could be said to be more "authentic". The C-clarinet is pitched higher than the regular orchestral instrument and has a piercing tone much favoured in Klezmer music. The extensive use of the cello, played by Pénzes, is justified simply because it figures in so many of the paintings and illustrations of early klezmorim. But the great strength of this disc lies in the ensemble playing, which harks back to an era when klezmer was not a big-band sound but an intimate collection of available instruments. The tracks feature a variety of instrumental combinations – sometimes just duos of violin and tsimbl or accordion, the pairings familiar from the paintings of Chagall which so evoke the shtetl (Jewish village) world from which this music comes. Budowitz succeed in stripping away the nostalgia and sentimentality which is often associated with klezmer and recreating it as great music in its own right. With a sensitive approach and a small ensemble, it's also possible to recreate the music's organic nature with its rhythmic tension and irregularities. It's not music to blow you away immediately , but music that repays attention and listening.

The first track, **Cili's Kale Bazingns**, begins with a wedding song sung by Cili Schwartz, a Moldavian Jewish lady born in 1915, remembering a tune from her youth, followed by an instrumental version of the same melody. The remaining tracks include an idiomatic selection of dances, instrumental fantasies and quasi-religious pieces that show just how rich and sublime the tradition was before it was swept away by emigration and the Holocaust.

Further listening: Budowitz's more recent **Wedding Without a Bride** (Buda) is less folksy and slightly more classical in style. The Joel Rubin Klezmer Ensemble's **Beregovski's Wedding** (Wergo) is also highly recommended.

Buena Vista Social Club

Buena Vista Social Club

World Circuit, 1997

Ry Cooder (guitars), Ibrahim Ferrer (vocals), Rubén González (piano), Orlando Lopez (bass), Manuel Mirabel (trumpet), Eliades Ochoa (vocals, guitar), Omara Portuondo (vocals), Compay Segundo (vocals, guitar), Barbarito Torres (laúd) and others.

This is one of the most talked about World Music albums of the past few years, with global sales of over four million. With its companion discs on World Circuit featuring Rubén González, Ibrahim Ferrer and the Afro-Cuban All Stars, it's put old-time Cuban music back on the map. Helped by a Grammy award and the Wim Wenders documentary of the same name, **Buena Vista Social Club** entered the album charts in Britain, Europe and America. But the reason that it's here is because it's a glorious disc in its own right.

American guitarist Ry Cooder has been hugely influential over the years in collaborating with outstanding musicians around the world, for instance, Mali's Ali Farka Toure on *Talking Timbuktu* (see p.181) or India's V.M. Bhatt on *A Meeting by the River*. For this disc, with the help of arranger and music director Juan de Marcos González and World Circuit's Nick Gold, a distinguished cast was assembled. The musicians of the Buena Vista Social Club are great old-timers of Cuban music, the musical equivalent of the glorious 1950s automobiles that, battered but proud, still cruise the streets of Havana. They include guitarist and vocalist Compay Segundo (aged 89 at the time of recording); the gentle-voiced Ibrahim Ferrer (70), who was literally called in off the streets after years of musical inactivity; guajira (country) singer and guitarist Eliades Ochoa (a youthful 49) from Santiago at the eastern end of the island; and veteran pianist Rubén González (77), who played with Arsenio Rodríguez in the 1940s.

Chan Chan, the leisurely opening guajira-style song – in a new version by Compay Segundo – immediately sets the mood. Cool but decisive guitar chords immediately lead into the beautifully balanced vocals of Ochoa, Segundo and Ferrer. Cooder unobtrusively contributes slightly ominous chords on his slide guitar, and throughout the album he takes a back seat, adding splashes of colour but leaving the Cubans to do their stuff. **El Cuarto de Tula** is an uptempo descarga (jam session) with extremely ribald lyrics (like a lot of Cuban songs) and heavier percussion. It includes a wonderful solo on the laúd (Cuban lute), a subtle instrument not so often heard these days, plus a spectacular finale from Manuel Mirabel on trumpet – a major force throughout the album. The pace eases for **Pueblo Nuevo**, Rubén González's chance to shine in a nostalgic danzon, and then **Dos Gardenias**, a romantic bolero of the sort Ibrahim Ferrer has made his own. **¿Y Tú Qué Has Hecho?** is a mischievous song with a charming guitar duet between Cooder and Compay Segundo, and **Veinte Años** includes the nostalgic vocals of Omara Portuondo, the only woman on the album.

Every track has its special qualities: other highlights include Segundo's **Amor de Loca Juventud**, the eccentric guitar solos on **Orgullecida**, and the gentle title track with an extended piano solo from Rubén González and strange siren-like guitar sounds from Cooder. The whole album is beautifully produced – a World Circuit trademark – and is a joy in its details and the sum of its parts.

The success of this album must surely be due to the warmth, sincerity and sense of fun that shines through every track. What you hear is not a bunch of musicians trying to make a best-selling CD, but a group of artists performing works they have known for decades – and doing so with real love.

Further listening: Ibrahim Ferrer (World Circuit) is the excellent follow-up album. **Casa de la Trova** (Corason) is a wonderful collection of music from regular bands at Santiago's premier music venue, including Eliades Ochoa's Cuarteto Patria.

Camarón

Calle Real

Polygram, 1983

Camarón (vocals), Paco de Lucía (guitar), Tomatito (guitar), Carlos Benavent (electric bass), Ruben Dantas and Raimundo Amador (percussion).

As a child, Camarón dreamed of becoming a bullfighter but instead developed into the greatest flamenco singer of his age. He was the epitome of an Andalucian gypsy musician and, like many musical geniuses before him, blazed rapidly through an illustrious career – astounding flamenco aficionados aged 13; recording historic sessions aged 19; and establishing one of the great flamenco partnerships with guitarist Paco de Lucía (see p.107). He also pioneered the transition from red wine to hash as favoured flamenco tipple, unfortunately moving onto harder drugs and heroin addiction, before dying of lung cancer in 1992 aged 41. He left a legacy of seventeen discs that were always good, and often sensational.

Born José Monge Cruz in 1950 in La Isla de San Fernando near Cádiz, he was nicknamed "Camarón [shrimp] de La Isla" by his uncle. Camarón and Paco always pushed the limits of flamenco, and their first discs, recorded between 1969 and 1977, changed the music for ever. Fun and anarchic, but personally unreliable, Camarón's perfect phrasing, control and pitch never failed, nor his ability to extend a vocal line over lengths of time that should have been beyond a small-chested man smoking three packs a day. These first discs were produced by Paco's father, but in the late 1970s and early 1980s Camarón and Paco's family fell out. Ricardo Pachón took over as producer and, with Tomatito as his new accompanist,

Camarón released *La Leyenda del Tiempo*, seen as the "Sergeant Pepper of flamenco" for its revolutionary impact. Suddenly there were electric guitars, drums and drugs – not Paco and his family's style. When things were patched up, **Calle Real** (Royal Street) was the second recording with Paco, on which he both plays and directs.

Although they're not flamenco virtues, there's something funky and upbeat about this record which makes it Camarón's most accessible. Paco had recently created his sextet and some of those instruments – electric bass and Latin percussion – are backing Camarón for the first time. The pioneering fretless bass of Carlos Benavent was never better and the tango **Yo Vivo Enamorao** swings so hard it became a great crowd favourite. There's a homage to Gypsy flamenco diva **La Perla de Cadiz**, with a bulerías in her name, in which he sings quotes from her repertoire. She was a big influence on Camarón and a rival for the all-time flamenco singer crown. There are other styles, too, including the fandango of **Calle Real** itself, with a chamber orchestra accompaniment – another innovation – and two other bulerías where the playing and interplaying of the guitars with the voice are sublime. If you want a classic example of how the flamenco guitar marks the rhythm while simultaneously riding it, holding it back and pushing it on in response to the singer, while the singer improvises the melody and changes it with each verse, listen to **Na Es Eterno**. Throughout, the playing of the two guitars – Paco and Tomatito – is just perfect.

Camarón's is a strange case. He is the most famous flamenco singer. His intuition and ear, perfect pitch and tuning, power and sense of rhythm, were the best. Yet in his lifetime his records sold pitifully badly (the vast majority fewer than 6000 copies each) and, while Paco de Lucía had built up a global following, Camarón hardly stepped out of Spain. In today's climate, who knows how great a star he might have been on the world stage?

> **Further listening**: For a first-class introduction to the sounds and personalities of flamenco, try **Duende** (Ellipsis Arts), a three-CD set including singers, guitarists and new explorations.

Manu Chao

Clandestino

Palm Pictures/Virgin France, 1998

Manu Chao (vocals & guitars) with Awa Touty Wade (vocals), Anouk (vocals), Angelo Mancini & Antoine Chao (trumpets), Jeff Cahours (trombone).

Born in Paris of Spanish descent, Manuel "Manu" Chao's professional history stretches back twenty years to rockabilly band Le Hot Pants, but it was with the phenomenal Mano Negra that he made his name. Like fellow French rockers Lo'jo and Les Negresses Vertes, this large and unruly band took influences from anywhere – ska, flamenco, zouk, Tex-Mex, hiphop, bal musette, rai, skiffle – then filtered them through their own peculiar mix of street-musician savvy and anarcho-punk energy. Mano Negra took their name from an anarchist cell and called this hybrid style Patchanka. Their decade together started in a blur of rebel energy and burned out in the wake of a long and disastrous tour of South America dubbed "The Cargo Tour".

Clandestino is like the reflective aftermath of the band's last chaotic years, drawing on the sounds of Mexico, Colombia, Bolivia and Chile. "Clandestinos" are those migrant workers who secretly slip across frontiers to find work and, like a clandestino, Manu surreptitiously crosses cultural and linguistic borders. Sung in French, Spanish and a little English, to a strummed guitar, with some wheezy brass and a few lo-fi samples, it evokes the sweaty cities of Latin America in a unique and extraordinary way. Manu's hoarse and throaty vocals, which sometimes sound so papery they could have been recorded on a domestic cassette, are rich with a playful melancholy and a sweet, world-weary fatigue. Few of the sixteen tracks make it beyond three minutes and they flow into one another with a lazy grace that beguiles the listener.

Overall, the album manages to be casual, catchy, cheeky and touching at the same time, with a warmth and intimacy that is at odds with the harsh life the lyrics describe. The feel of the album is established by Clandestinos, with its opening burst of distorted conversation, repeated acoustic guitar chord, bouncing two-note bass, and Manu's world-weary voice. Many of the tracks have shared elements: Desaparecido reworks a bass-line from "Clandestinos", while Mama Call and La Despedida unashamedly share an identical instrumental track complete with distinctive claves sound. Bongo Bong, an ironic comment on Mano Negra's downward career, imperceptibly becomes the lilting Je ne t'aime Plus, an appropriately skewed love song ("I don't love you – well, not every day"). The musical economy, combined with some masterful track sequencing, gives the album the feel of one long song, shifting moods in subtle and seductive ways.

The relative homogeneity of sound doesn't squeeze out the album's major set-pieces. Lagrimas de Oro is bruised but suffused with quiet dignity – an anthem for all of those who stand up under impossible pressure. The hackneyed, cod-Mexican tune of "Tequila" is misappropriated for the tired and seedy Welcome to Tijuana, a fly-blown litany of sex and drugs for sale, underscored by dusty-sounding trumpet parps, that manages to be both comic and desperate.

The arrangements are spare behind the simple powerful melodies – a ska trombone, a cheap drum-machine beat, a simple trebly guitar lick or a sweet disconnected female voice. Elsewhere in the background extraneous noise creeps in, like an answering machine message, a pirate DJ announcement, a child's electronic toy or a swell of bar-room conversation. Evocative and poignant, this album was a huge hit across Europe but sadly failed to make any impression in the UK.

> **Further listening:** Mano Negra's music is much harder and more diverse than anything on *Clandestino*. The band's two most riotous albums are **Patchanka** (Virgin) and the outstanding **Puta's Fever** (Virgin).

Hariprasad Chaurasia and Shivkumar Sharma

Call of the Valley

EMI Hemisphere, 1995

Hariprasad Chaurasia (flute), Shivkumar Sharma (santoor), Brijbushan Kabra (guitar), Manikrao Popatkar (tablas).

It seems such an obvious idea, to string together a sequence of ragas associated with different times of the day and tell a story using those ragas, but it was unprecedented when this album was made in the 1960s. Unlike Western classical music, which has a tradition of musical storytelling and scene-painting, Indian classical music is essentially an abstract art, which creates moods and emotions through the working out of a particular raga.

It's easy to imagine how the idea of this album, a Kashmiri love story stretching from dawn to dusk, would greatly appeal to a nation brought up on romantic film plots – despite the die-hard murmurings of a few classical purists. In the end **Call of the Valley** not only brought new listeners to classical music in India, but created an even larger audience round the globe, and projected its soloists into international careers.

The basic idea came from santoor player Shivkumar Sharma. He is Kashmiri-born and was trying to raise the status of the santoor, the Kashmiri hammer dulcimer, from a mere folk instrument into a respected classical one. He had already recorded a solo album, but this was something new. He mentioned the concept to G.N. Joshi, producer at the Gramophone Company of India, who developed it further. But according to flute player

Hariprasad Chaurasia, it was less of an artistic concept than a way of getting a recording out, because as young players it was almost impossible to get a contract with such a prestigious company. In the end, the story depicted a pair of lovers in the spectacular Kashmiri landscape. The guitar represents the man, the santoor the woman, and the flute evokes the natural environment, but it's unnecessary to try and link the music too literally with specific scenes and events.

The music starts at daybreak with the dawn raga, **Ahir Bhairav**. The guitar begins, followed by the flute and finally the santoor, all evoking a mood of peaceful tranquillity. With a rippling string effect the piece moves into the second scene and the awakening of the day in **Nat Bhairav**. The sun begins to rise, the tablas start a rhythmic pulse and the flute suggests birds singing and flitting around with the dawn chorus. Phrases are tossed around from one instrument to the next.

The third section is set in **Rag Piloo** and depicts the meeting of the shepherd and his lover. It's essentially a conversation between guitar and santoor (representing the man and the woman). It begins tentatively and delicately, but works up in intensity until the couple are disturbed and she flees.

Further scenes depict dusk, prayers and a late-night encounter. Finally, in the most poetic section of the piece, the moon shines down on the lake. The flute depicts the moonlight in **Rag Pahadi** and the lovers set out in a boat. There's a repeated stroking figure accompanying this section, played by the guitar and tablas, while the flute plays its solo and then is taken up by the flute in a low register to accompany the guitar melody. It's a beautiful, demure scene and you suspect that, as in the Hindi movies, the lovers will barely kiss, let alone attempt anything more.

Further listening: The solo discs of Hariprasad Chaurasia are wonderful, particularly **Venu** (Rykodisc), in which he returns to raga Ahir Bhairav with tabla player Zakir Hussein. In 1995, Shivkumar Sharma and Hariprasad teamed up again for **The Valley Recalls** (Navras).

Clifton Chenier

Bogalusa Boogie

Arhoolie, 1990

Clifton Chenier (vocals, accordion, harmonica), Cleveland Chenier (rubboard), John Hart (tenor sax), Paul Senegal (guitar), Joe Brouchet (bass), Robert St Julian (drums).

Clifton Chenier was the creator and undisputed "King of Zydeco", the black, accordion-led music of Louisiana – the Creole counterpart to Cajun. Chenier didn't hone and build his albums: he was a jobbing musician accustomed to servicing Louisiana's bars and dance halls and he just played. What he played is what you get, and this 1975 session is widely considered to be his best. It includes not only a formidable performance from the man himself, but also the Red Hot Louisiana Band, with whom he worked from the early 1970s.

Chenier was born in 1925 to a poor sharecropping family in Opelousas, Louisiana, and spent his childhood working in the cotton and rice fields. His father played button accordion and sang old-time French Creole songs, and it is his example, alongside the recordings of accordionist Amédée Ardion and the Southern Blues, which were the most important influences on Chenier's style. Chenier and his elder brother Cleveland (who appears on this album) drove oil trucks for a living and played local dances in the evenings.

They started recording in the mid-1950s, but it wasn't until the 1970s that Chenier achieved his fame and was credited with the creation of a dynamic new form of American regional music. It might not sound like the recipe for a winning musical formula, but the name "zydeco" is a corruption of "les haricots" – runner beans. It comes from an old French song, "Les Haricots sont pas salés" (The Beans Aren't Salty) which Chenier popularized as "Zydeco sont pas salés". The genre was born.

This session was recorded in 1975 in a local studio in Bogalusa, Louisiana, the sort of place that supplied discs to the jukeboxes that still provide the distinctive soundtrack to the lounges and bars of Louisiana. There's something about the slightly raw sound and steep fades that is just as much a key part of the Louisiana sound as the heavy drums and punchy accordion. Chenier was famed for his piano accordion playing, but he was also a wizard on the harmonica and it is the striking, searing sound of that instrument that pervades One Step at a Time, the opening track of the album. The harmonica squeals and screams, while the softer accordion supports and alternates with the vocal line. While most of the thirteen tracks are in Louisiana French, a handful are in English and there are a few instrumental numbers.

The Red Hot Louisiana Band was the best of Chenier's backing bands, with excellent contributions from Paul Senegal on guitar and John Hart on tenor sax. Hart provides fine solos on most of the tracks, notably M'Appel Fou and the bluesy rock'n'roll of Je me reveiller le matin. Chenier's accordion has a surprisingly soft reedy sound – light and nimble on fast tracks like the latter song, but elsewhere filled out with chords and a tremulous vibrato reminiscent of the cheesiest setting on an old electric organ.

Other highlights include the steamy blues I May Be Wrong, with excellent instrumental solos, the unusually comic and carefree instrumental romp Ride 'Em Cowboy and Allons à Grand Coteau, better known as "Allons à Lafayette", the first Cajun song ever recorded. Closing the album is the quirky Bogalusa Boogie which has playful solos on accordion, sax and guitar over a regular twelve-bar blues.

Further listening: The cream of Chenier's recordings are collected on **Zydeco Dynamite: The Clifton Chenier Anthology** (Rhino). Beau Jocque, who died in 1999, was one of the best of a new, funkier generation of zydeco accordionists. The album **Git It, Beau Jocque!** (Rounder) contains steamy live recordings from a couple of classic Lousiana dancehalls.

The Chieftains

Santiago

RCA Victor/BMG, 1996

Paddy Moloney (uilleann pipes, tin whistle), Derek Bell (harp), Martin Fay (fiddle), Seán Keane (fiddle), Kevin Conneff (bodhrán, vocals), Matt Molloy (flute), Carlos Núñez (gaita) and guests.

The Chieftains started life in 1963 and have been the catalysts for a huge revival in Irish music. The turning point came in 1975 with their music for Stanley Kubrick's film *Barry Lyndon*, a sell-out concert at the Royal Albert Hall and a signing to Island Records. *Melody Maker* named them group of the year "for making unfashionable music fashionable". Their trick was, and still is, a sophisticated, arranged sound tailored to the concert hall rather than the pub session, but without becoming sterile. Also crucial is the energy and vision of their leader, pipe and whistle player Paddy Moloney.

As the Chieftains took Irish music round the world, they began to start playing with the musicians they met on their travels. In 1983 they were one of the first Western groups to visit China (collaborating with a Chinese ensemble) and they've explored the connections between various Celtic traditions, with their 1987 album *Celtic Wedding* focusing on Breton music.

Santiago is an album about Galicia, the Celtic region of northern Spain with a landscape similar to Ireland. The Chieftains performed there in 1984, in the port of Vigo, where they heard Galician bagpiper Carlos Núñez and invited him on tour. Their long partnership with him resulted in this disc.

The title comes from the Galician city of Santiago de Compostela and the opening tracks present a gallery of some of the traditional sounds pilgrims might have encountered on the popular pilgrimage route to the city. There's ancient Basque music called txalaparta – a wooden plank struck rhythmically by two players – some magnificent trikitixa (Basque accordion) playing by Kepa Junkera (see p.83), an archaic violin called the rabel, a Portuguese cavaquinho melody (with penny-whistle additions from Paddy Moloney) and medieval hymns recorded in Santiago.

The Chieftains' approach is certainly not scholarly; instead it is driven by imaginative leaps and personal contacts. A good example is **Dueling Chanters**, a duet between Moloney on uilleann pipes and Núñez on the Galician gaita. Two tunes are played back to back, the first Irish, the second Galician: the softer, sweeter uilleann pipes opening before the slightly more reedy and raucous gaita comes in. Núñez makes sprightly, almost comic contributions to **Minho Waltz** (which highlights virtuoso playing from flautist Matt Molloy and fiddler Seán Keane) and drives **Setting Sail**, a gaita-led celebration of the ancient contacts between Ireland and Galicia. This latter builds into a dense orchestral sound which, like the **Galician Overture**, is the Chieftains in lush film-soundtrack mode.

Like the Irish, the Galicians have a history of emigration, and **Guadalupe** (with Linda Ronstadt and Los Lobos) pays homage to the Galicians in Mexico and Texas. Cuba was another popular destination (Fidel Castro, no less, comes from Galician stock) and **Santiago de Cuba** (with Ry Cooder on mandola and Cuban flute maestro Richard Egües) brings good tunes in an intricate arrangement with a distinctly Cuban swing. **Galleguita/Tutankhamen** adds a lot more Cuban musicians to the mix, including singer Pio Leiva, to create a sort of danzon party atmosphere. The album ends with a great spontaneous session in a pub called *The Dublin* in Vigo with Galicia's finest musicians proving that they can let their hair down and party just as well as the Irish.

> **Further listening:** For more classic Irish material, try **Chieftains 4** (Claddagh/Shanachie). **Tears of Stone** (RCA Victor/BMG) also contains Irish material, with guest appearances from women singers including Joni Mitchell, Sinéad O'Connor and the Corrs.

Willie Colon and Ruben Blades

Siembra

Fania/Sonodisc, 1978

Leopoldo Pineda, José Rodriguez, Angel "Papo" Vasquez, Sam Burtis (all trombones), José "Profesor" Torres (piano), Eddie Montalvo (congas), Jose Mangual Jnr (bongos), Salvador Cuevas (bass), Jimmy Delgado (timbales), Ruben Blades (acoustic guitar, vocals, percussion, lyrics), Willie Colon (solo trombone, production).

The relationship between Ruben Blades and Willie Colon was one of the most potent and original in late 1970s salsa. In a run of hit albums, the two young musicians shattered definitions of salsa for ever. They brought to New York's Fania label an even greater iconoclasm than Colon had in his previous partnership with the singer Hector Lavoe. Their new songs abandoned the older generation's almost sacred commitment to Cuban rhythms and the formulae created in Havana before the Revolution, because Blades and Colon were (and still are) pan-Latin Americans – as excited by bossa nova and folk music from Panama and Puerto Rico as by Cuban son and guajira. Significantly, they were also products of the Beatles era, and grew up during the 1960s soul explosions in Detroit and Philadelphia that transformed American music. **Siembra** (Seed) was a landmark record – the "Sergeant Pepper of Salsa" – outselling every other album in the Fania catalogue for nearly two decades. It still sounds as fresh and modern as when it was first broadcast on New York's salsa stations in 1978.

Both musicians have subsequently reinvented themselves many times, but the ideas forged together then still form a basis for their music today. Of the seven long, memorable songs (six by Blades, and one by one J. Ortiz), **Plastico** and **Pedro Navaja** are still in Blades' live repertoire.

The music on *Siembra* was shaped and polished by Colon and driven by his passion for heavy trombones. **Buscando Guayaba** and **Ojos** are the most obviously classic salsa party pieces, both exercises for Colon's solo trombone and designed to raise the dust, while **Dime** is a good old-fashioned Latin smoocher, including a mellow piano solo by José "Profesor" Torres. The other songs revel in an eclectic, rule-breaking mix of styles and frequently play down salsa's emphasis on dancing in order to lure the listener into the lyrics. Blades' sophisticated song-poems replace salsa's familiar themes of lost love, unattainable love, nostalgia for the Caribbean homeland, with stories from the streets, moral tales, allegories – and audiences lap them up.

Blades' concerns range from the explosion of consumer culture, told through a satire on a girl's obsession with shopping ("Plastico"), to street stories from Spanish Harlem as in the one about a small-time villain ("Pedro Navaja") who gets his comeuppance. On "Ojos", "the eyes of my people" are used as a metaphor for Latino culture (laughing eyes, pained eyes, eyes that look at the moon, etc), while **Maria Lionza** employs a dramatic Venezuelan two-step cumbia rhythm (backed by spoof Hollywood-Indian chants) to tell the myth of an Indian princess. The title track, **Siembra**, which closes the album, is a powerful sermon of faith in Latin unity.

Colon's fascination for the rich potential of a line of five trombones (including his own blustery lead) is one of the musical delights of this record. Another trademark Blades–Colon feature is the leap from one style to another: the introduction to the magnificent "Pedro Navaja" illustrates it perfectly in the segue from the jaggedy Chic disco strings and heavy funk bass-line to tense Afro-Cuban drumming and chants (with a background of screaming New York cop sirens). It's a novel fusion, quintessentially Blades, and linking music from two of America's most closely related communities based in Harlem and Spanish Harlem.

> **Further listening:** For the individual sound of Blades and Colon, listen to Blades' fusion of doowop, reggae and rock into salsa on **Buscando America** (Elektra/Sony) and Colon's exploration of Brazilian, Caribbean and traditional Puerto Rican music in **Criollo** (RCA).

Toumani Diabate

Djelika

Hannibal, 1995

Toumani Diabate (kora), Keletigui Diabate (balafon), Basekou Kouyate (ngoni) and others.

Like a warm breeze or a refreshing drink, the sound of the west African kora is one of the great pleasures of life. You can let the intricate plucking and subtly shifting rhythms wash over you, or you can focus in on the detailed interlocking patterns. It's a wonderful-looking instrument, made from a large calabash (gourd) soundbox, covered with cow skin and pierced with a long pole strung with 21 nylon strings. Placed upright on the ground in front of the player, it's plucked with the thumbs and forefingers of both hands to create broad-based melodic lines and delicate accompanying patterns and flourishes. Although the kora goes back at least to the eighteenth century, it's only in the latter half of the twentieth century that it's come into its own, largely thanks to the work of Toumani's father, Sidiki Diabate, who pioneered it as a solo instrument. While Sidiki was a strict traditionalist, Toumani, born in 1965 and recognized as one of the finest players in Mali and on the international circuit, has a more open and musically curious approach. While **Djelika** is not the most traditional kora-led album around, it's probably the most inviting and is still firmly rooted in tradition.

What you have here are three fantastic musicians giving an intimate acoustic recital. The other two solo instruments, the balafon (Mande xylophone) and the ngoni (skin-covered lute and ancestor of the banjo), are very ancient, going back at least as far as the great Mali Empire (1235–1469). The combination of textures which this trio of instruments provides is sublime: the delicate, feathery sound of the kora; the drier sound of the ngoni with its ability to "bend" notes on the unfretted fingerboard; and the watery, struck sound of the balafon. Contrasting sounds, but blending perfectly. The balafon player Keletigui Diabate (no immediate relation) and ngoni player Basekou Kouyate are among the very best. They're joined on several tracks by a bass (played by Danny Thompson or Javier Colina) that just fills out the sound (and implied harmony) a little and, on one track, by Dian Diarra on the kamalengoni – a darker-sounding six-string ancestor of the kora.

After an arresting opening invocation on balafon and ngoni (including, on the latter, a passing tribute to the theme tune of *The Good, the Bad and the Ugly*), **Djelika** launches into a comfortable swinging groove over which the kora starts to spin its magic with pairs of notes reaching upwards and some intricate descending patterns. After exploring the high and low registers of the instrument, there's a solo on the ngoni – with some of those bendy notes – then a sort of dialogue between the two instruments before the balafon gets a turn in the limelight. Alongside the title track, **Cheick Oumar Bah** and **Kandjoura** are the swinging numbers with some excellent solos, while **Aminata Santoro** has all the qualities of a warm, lyrical love song but without the words. **Marielle**, based on an old court song, is almost jazz-like, with a series of instrumental variations on a standard melody. **Tony Vander** starts with the darker, earthier sound of the kamalengoni and its slightly awkward melodies make a good contrast to the mellifluous streams on the kora, ngoni and balafon. The feeling you get above all from this album is that of a group of very accomplished musicians responding to each other and striking sparks. It's a privilege to be able to share it.

> **Further listening: New Ancient Strings** (Hannibal) features top-quality kora duets played by Toumani Diabate and Ballake Sissoko.

Manu Dibango and Cuarteto Patria

CubAfrica

Melodie, 1998

Manu Dibango (saxophone), Eliades Ochoa (guitar, vocals), Umberto Ochoa (guitar, vocals), William Calderon (double bass), Roberto Torres (percussion), Eglis Ochoa (maracas), Jerry Malekani (guest guitar).

Even if this book contained just ten CDs, this wonderful but undersung collaboration of saxophonist Manu Dibango with the Cuarteto Patria from Cuba would deserve its place. Dibango, born in Cameroon and leading light of the African music scene in Paris, had a huge World Music success before the term had any currency with *Soul Makossa* in 1973. While the title track has become a classic – and resurfaces as **Rumba Makossa** on this disc – the album seems somehow dated, whereas **CubAfrica** is fresh, exuberant and inventive from beginning to end. There's something inherently African about Dibango's sax playing, and it complements and contrasts wonderfully with the jangly, rural guitar style of the Cuarteto, led by the Cuban cowboy Eliades Ochoa.

Of course the musical links between Cuba and West Africa are strong. Not only does most Cuban music have West African roots, due to the slave trade, but Cuban records and bands were hugely popular in West Africa in the 1960s. The connections have continued. Dibango has played with Johnny Pacheco and with salsa supergroup the Fania All Stars (see p.61), and the recent Africando albums (on Stern's) have brought Senegalese and Cuban musicians together to produce big-band salsa that is Cuban and African at the same time. The recording of this album in France in 1996 followed closely on the heels of the

Buena Vista Social Club (see p.37) sessions in which Eliades Ochoa was also involved and which were originally going to involve a collaboration of Cuban and West African musicians.

The Cuarteto Patria are based in Santiago, the heartland of Cuban son, at the eastern end of the island. They represent the rural style of music, before it got expanded in Havana into a big-band sound. As with most traditional son numbers, it's the distinctive Cuban guitar, the tres, that starts things going with a gentle plucked introduction before the sax enters on **Cielito Lindo**, a popular Mexican tune. It is gentle, sunny and occasionally raunchy when Dibango starts playing around on it. But this is only an opener to **Carnaval**, an uptempo number sung by Eliades Ochoa, accompanied by the rural guitars of the Cuarteto. After a couple of verses Dibango enters with a nimble and unforgettable sax melody that just sweeps the song away. It's pure joy translated into music and it returns a couple of times along with a great solo on the tres. "Rumba Makossa" is the Cuarteto Patria take on Dibango's big tune, which also recounts the story of the collaboration and features Dibango's guitarist Jerry Malekani. One of the album's surprises is **Cerisiers Roses** (Pink Cherry Trees), originally a romantic French number, which manages to avoid schmaltz and get under your skin with a gorgeously lyrical melody. Similarly, **Quizas Quizas** is a beautiful, slow instrumental tune that treads a fine line between the cheeky and romantic. The rest of the disc stays very much in Cuban territory with standards like **Son de la Loma** and **El Manicero**. The closing track, **Cosita Linda**, is once again a celebration of the coming together of Cuba and Africa and gives Dibango some opportunities to really soar.

The pleasure of this disc is in its relaxed, easy-going style. It's not contrived or overambitious; it just features artists who fit perfectly together and produce a glorious whole that is much more than the sum of its parts.

> **Further listening: Africando Vol. 1** (Stern's) features a great band of Senegalese singers and Cuban musicians including stunning flute playing by Eddy Zervigon, while **Sublime Ilusion** (Virgin), Eliades Ochoa's 1999 album with the Cuarteto Patria, is first class.

Donnisulana

Per Agata

Silex, 1992

Dominique Bianconi, Gigi Casabianca, Patrizia Dau, Aline Filippi, Jacky Micaelli (vocals).

"It was like hearing a voice from the depths of the earth; a song from the dawn of time; from a beginning that one never dares believe is accessible". So wrote Dorothy Carrington in 1948, after her first encounter with Corsican polyphonies. Invited to a remote village for midnight Mass, she was enthralled when otherworldly vocal harmonies swelled through the Baroque chapel. Ten seconds into the landmark album, **Per Agata**, by the all-woman Donnisulana (from the Corsican *donna*, "woman", and *isula*, "island"), and you'll know why her reaction was par for the course.

Since its "rediscovery" by ethnomusicologists after World War II, Corsican polyphony has proved impossible to categorize. Part early Roman-Christian liturgy, Genoan madrigal, Arab wailing and pagan chant, it carries imprints of the successive invaders and settlers who have occupied this rugged, mountainous island. To northern European ears, the music sounds familiar enough most of the time, yet something wild and strange always seems to lurk close to the surface – an effect derived from the counterpoint between conventional cadences and chords (held by the bass, or bassu, and mid-range singer, secunda) with the heavily ornamented improvisations provided by the terza, or highest voice.

Bringing together the five finest living female vocalists on the island, Donnisulana was formed in 1992 to record a one-off album as a memorial to a mutual friend. This was the first time a group of women had dared venture into the normally all-male realm of polyphony. The calibre of participants, however, promised something extraordinary enough to silence even the staunchest of traditionalists.

Donnisulana's secunda vocalist, who introduces and holds the main melody line around which the others harmonize, is the famous mezzo-soprano, Jacky Micaelli. It's her impassioned singing that opens *Per Agata*. The most lyrical track on the album, **I Pricantula**, showcases the emotional intensity and rare vocal precision that has become the group's hallmark. Micaelli's lead is beautifully embraced by her four cumpagnias, whose expansive harmonies close in a series of exquisite cadences, enhanced to perfection by the natural acoustics of the monastery where the album was recorded.

Track two, a rendition of the traditional madrigal **Padre**, strikes a more austere tone, which Micaelli sustains through three minutes of solo song on track three, **Da Quì Un Cantu**. She is joined by the rest of the group for the melody's conclusion, where a sequence of unexpected chords add a darker inflection. Not until the fourth track, however, do we get a taste of Corsica's quintessential polyphonic form, the **Paghjella**. Purists on the island used to claim that female voices couldn't carry the bleak insistency of the paghjella until this album set a standard that many aficionados maintain has never been equalled. Punctuated by wonderful passing dissonances and some inspired improvisation, the first of Donnisulana's three paghjellas conjours up visions of Corsica's pre-Christian past, as well as its windswept granite mountains.

With the exception of a couple of haunting tracks for two voices, which add a welcome balance, the rest of *Per Agata* proceeds in much the same fashion, alternating between versions of traditional pieces and more fluid by the contemporary song composer Michel Raffaelli. A lament for the dead, sung solo by Jacky Micaelli, winds things up on an appropriately despairing note.

> **Further listening**: As a sampler for all-male Corsican polyphony, the compilation **Voce di Corsica** (Olivi Music), which features the island's top groups as well as a handful of older field recordings, is hard to beat. A more representative cross-section is showcased on **L'Ame Corse** (Audivis).

Cesaria Evora

Cesaria

Lusafrica, 1995

Cesaria Evora (vocals), Paulino Vieira (guitars, cavaquinho, piano, bass, vocals, etc), Toy Vieira (cavaquinho, vocals), Osvaldo Dias (guitar, vocals), Armando Tito (guitar, vocals) and other guests.

Cesaria Evora, the "barefoot diva", has a rich and smoky voice – likened to that of Billie Holiday – that has turned heads and opened ears all round the world. She is the embodiment of the music of Cape Verde and represents the classic obscurity to success story of the World Music boom. Now in her late 50s, she's recorded eight albums over the past twelve years and sold more than a million copies worldwide.

Cesaria was born on the island of São Vicente, Cape Verde – a former Portuguese colony 600 kilometres off the northwest coast of Africa. The islands were an important staging post for transatlantic trade and for slaves being taken from West Africa to the Caribbean and the Americas. With all the comings and goings, nationalities and cultures intermingled. Today, the barren volcanic islands are economically depressed and many Cape Verdeans have been forced to emigrate and there are more in diaspora communities than at home.

The most typical Cape Verdean song is the morna. Often described as the "soul of Cape Verde", it is slow and sentimental with lyrics of separation and longing. Cesaria, the "Queen of Morna", was born into a musical family: her father played the violin and guitar; her brother, the clarinet; and her uncle, B. Leza, was such a celebrated composer of mornas that the first aeroplane purchased by the national airline was named after him!

But the family was poor, and in her teens Cesaria dropped out of school to sing in the piano bars of Mindelo, where she enjoyed moderate local success.

Her lucky break came in 1987, when she was invited to Lisbon to sing in the restaurant of Bana, a well-known singer from Cape Verde, where she was heard by the founder of Lusafrica records, José de Silva, who invited her to record in Paris. Her early Lusafrica albums *Mar Azul* and *Miss Perfumado* (allegedly Cesaria's favourite) are fresher and more simple than **Cesaria**, but it was this album that really confirmed her worldwide success. It has a fine backing ensemble led by Paulino Vieira, featuring tinkling guitars, the high ukelele-like Portuguese cavaquinho, a nightclub-style piano and gentle percussion from guiro scrapers and light drum kit. Many songs also have a violin, accordion or clarinet to lend a particular colour or mood.

The album opens fittingly with Petit Pays, a lyrical morna about Cape Verde that celebrates the country and its music, the quintessential ingredient of which is *saudade*, a Portuguese term meaning "infinite nostalgia". The coladera is a more upbeat style and there's a handful here to up the pace – Tudo Tem Se Limite and D'Nhirim Reforma are good examples. Consedjo, with its duelling accordion and harmonica, evokes the mood of the more rural, accordion-led funana style. There are two desperately nostalgic songs of separation, Xandinha and Areia de Salamansa, both of which feature plangent violin solos, the latter by Bau, a celebrated violin and cavaquinho player who now leads Cesaria's band. Sadly, the mood he creates is broken by the one duff track on the album: Flor na Paul, a bland "Grandma, We Love You" sort of song with a sickly children's chorus. Thankfully, the final Doce Guerra is a fine morna carried by Cesaria's dark, late-night voice with just the lightest of accompaniments.

> **Further listening**: To see how Cesaria fits into the wider background of Cape Verdean music, much of it exquisitely beautiful, go for **The Soul of Cape Verde** (Lusafrica).

Mahmoud Fadl

Love Letter from King Tut-Ank-Amen

Piranha, 1998

Mahmoud Fadl (director, percussion), Samy El Bably (trumpet) Nagy Naoum (kanoun), Basem Darwish (oud), Mostafa Abd El Naby, Wageeh Shehata (violins), Yasser Taha (cello), Raafat Miso (alto sax), Magdi Imam (accordian), Mina Yousif (bass), Khamis Henkish (darabuka).

If there's one voice that encapsulates all that's best about Arab music it's Oum Kalthoum (1904-75). This is one thing on which virtually all Arabs agree. Born in the Nile Delta and taught by her father, a Koran singer, she moved to Cairo in 1922, where she set up a small ensemble and made her first recording in 1926. She became famous for her love songs, often performed, in live radio concerts in the 1950s and 1960s backed by a substantial studio orchestra in which swooping strings predominated. Her funeral in February 1975 was attended by Arab heads of state and over three million fans. Sono Cairo has over seventy Kalthoum albums in their catalogue. Evidently no World Music collection could be without the great Arabic diva, except that if you don't speak the language and are not partial to her exaggerated vocal style her music can be pretty hard-going. So what we have here are instrumental versions of Cairo love classics from the repertoire of Kalthoum and Mohamed Abd el-Wahaab (her male equivalent), performed by a tight eleven-piece band led by percussionist Mahmoud Fadl.

There's something about that unison string sound (here, a lean two violins and cello) – with slight slides between the notes, an incisive attack and a touch of reverb – that says Egypt. Those strings, followed by the oud (lute), open the proceedings on **Khai** (Brother), with El Bably's trumpet entering smoothly over the top. A veteran of Kalthoum's orchestras in the '50s and '60s, he's described as "the only trumpeter to master the quarter-tone intricacies of the Arabic musical modes with his horn" and he certainly delivers. These may be popular love songs, but they are composed in classical Arabic scales. Generally the trumpet takes the lead lines and the strings chip in with imitative phrases linking the phrases together – the typical pattern in Arabic popular music. Fadl provides the rich percussive groove.

Alongside the trumpet, though, there are other fine instrumental solos on offer. **Rohi** (Breath of Soul) features the kanoun, the plucked zither, which in its fragile delicacy is an excellent foil to the full-bloodied trumpet. **Ishlonak** (How Do You Do) has an insistent 6/8 rhythm, rattling percussion and the first big improvisatory trumpet solo. There's something about the sound of the trumpet throughout this disc that is reminiscent of the circus – a little brash, a little showy, sometimes clown-like and sometimes giving a high-wire performance. The spotlight then moves on to accordionist Magdi Imam, who gives a dark and intricate solo; he's followed by the alto sax and a brief percussion break before trumpet, accordion and sax join in to play in unison – except it's a somewhat notional unison because they're each doing their own thing. **Sabaht Wagdan** (I Woke up Full of Yearning) is mellow and mysterious in mood, with a lengthy violin taksim (introduction) leading into it, but it is surely in **Ana Wehabibi** (My Lover and I) that the love is consummated. This standout track is dominated by a lyrical string melody with a modicum of romantic harmony, decorated by delicate embroidery on the kanoun. With another lengthy accordion solo on **Ana Bamasi Al Haba Doll** (I Say to You Good Evening), you begin to wonder why the art of the Arabic squeeze-box isn't better known. After the darker and more intense **Llsabr Hodoud** (Patience has its limits), **El Helwa** (The Beauty) provides a suitably fast and flamboyant finale.

> **Further listening:** If you want to try the diva herself, Oum Kalthoum's **Al-Atlaal** (EMI Egypt) is among the most highly acclaimed of her discs. Alternatively, you might prefer to check out some of Mahmoud Fadl's Raks Sharki, or Belly Dance, music on **Journey of the Gypsy Dancer** (Piranha).

Fania All Stars

Live at Yankee Stadium

Charly Records, 1994

Celia Cruz, Hector Lavoe, Cheo Feliciano, Pete "El Conde" Rodriguez, Justo Betancourt, Ismael Miranda, Santos Colon, Bobby Cruz (vocalists), Ray Barretto (congas), Yomo Toro (cuatro guitar), Nicky Marrero (timbales), Roberto Roena (bongos), Larry Harlow (keyboards, synthesizers), Ricardo Ray (piano), Willie Colon (trombone), Johnny Pacheco (flute, musical director).

Imagine the scene: Yankee Stadium, 1973, the cream of New York's salsa bands joined together in one almighty supergroup, the Fania All Stars. It took Fania label boss and musical director, Johnny Pacheco weeks to plan the event and the music, and every seat was sold. Pacheco was the brains behind getting every album released by each of these band's leaders into charts all over Latin America. Now these household names were crammed onto one stage; the sheer size of the orchestra meant that the vocalists had to share microphones. Celia Cruz, the Queen of salsa, arrived teetering on stage in imprudently high-heeled shoes and a swirl of flamenco ruffles, and her first sharp, long notes triggered an explosion of cheers from audience and musicians as Pacheco's baton shaped the band into the perfect accompaniment.

Hermanidad Fania (The Fania Brotherhood) is a melodramatic introduction to the group, launched by Bobby Cruz's throaty falsetto. His equally flamboyant partner, the piano stylist Ricardo "Ritchie" Ray, raises a crazed Wurlitzer-swirl on the organ, while a tin-tray clatter of timbales from Nicky Marrero, with laser-sharp trumpets chorusing behind him, swell the sound. That fat and brassy, essentially urban, sound gives way to the softer, more nostalgic country atmosphere in the swaying Cuban guajira **Soy Guajiro** (I Am a Countryman). This ideal of peasant life evokes early rising daily routines of the cane cutters and mountain farmers of Cuba and Puerto Rico. Accompanying the orchestra and adding the key ingredient is Yomo Toro, a master of the local guitar, the cuatro, which he plays like a rock instrument, sharp, finger-picked solos and reverb effects making nods to both Hendrix and Santana.

The inclusion of **Congo Bongo** is an important reminder of the jazz in salsa. Hector Lavoe's mentor, the soulful Puerto Rican singer Cheo Feliciano uses an Afro-Spanish chant to prime Ray Barretto's conga patterns. Barretto's years spent straddling salsa and jazz are concentrated into this bubbling solo, and invites the veteran Cuban jazz drummer Mongo Santamaria into a friendly battle of the beats – a furious Cuban versus Puerto Rican descarga (jam session).

The most poignant song in the collection is Hector Lavoe's **Mi Gente** (My People). Lavoe understood how his songs reflected the audience's often tough barrio lives and drew them to him, interrupting his songs with chanted Spanglish quips, teasing other musicians and driving his partner Willie Colon into a blustery, emotional trombone solo, blown through a melee of brass and cuatro chords.

Celia Cruz sashays into **Diosa del Ritmo** (Goddess of Rhythm), singing improvised stories of her successes abroad to an adoring home crowd. Even a four-minute song reveals the secrets of her tremendous voice as she competes effortlessly with the full force of Fania's brass section. But the epic, twelve-minute **Bemba Colora** (Full Red Lips) is really unbeatable. The mistress of ad-lib reels off verses of the story, hums and chants choruses behind the instrumental breaks, and combines an extraordinary operatic performance with jazz improvisation involving sophisticated word-play within strict rhythmic rules. The Fania All Stars were always the sum of their incredible parts; this record is the Fania Family at its most functional.

Further listening: The classic disc of Salsa's greatest star is **Celia Cruz Con La Sonora Matancera** (WS LAtino), a musical postcard from pre-Castro Havana recorded in the 1950s and including great tongue-twisters like "Cao Cao Mani Picao" and the street-holler "Yerbero Moderno".

Franco

20ème Anniversaire

Sonodisc, 1989

Franco (guitar, vocals), Utu-Mayi, Dombe Opetum, Youlou and Boyibanda (all vocals) and other musicians not named.

When Franco died in October 1989, Zaire's President Mobutu ordered four days of national mourning. The guitarist and bandleader was given a state funeral, and presidents and prime ministers flew in from all over Africa to pay their final respects. Tens of thousands of ordinary Zaireans lined the streets and the radio stations played the music of his band, O.K. Jazz, 24 hours a day for almost a week. All roads in Congolese music lead back to the flamboyantly larger-than-life figure of Franco. He was the father of Congolese rumba, which in turn gave birth to the more frenetic dance rhythms of soukous, Africa's most successful musical export. His legacy lives on not merely in his own recorded output of some 150 albums and more than 1000 self-composed songs, but also in the work of the hundreds of musicians he inspired and employed. Most of the great names in Congolese music at one time or another played in his band.

Born Francis Luambo Makiadi in 1938 in a small rural village, Franco moved to the capital Kinshasa (or Leopoldville as it was then) in the late 1940s and began playing a home-made, tin-can guitar with stripped electrical wiring for strings. Local radio at the time was playing an endless diet of imported Cuban 78s. When Congolese musicians began copying the style they transformed it, using African idioms and replacing the dominant piano part of Cuban rumba with mesmerizing, circular guitar patterns. The electric guitar had just arrived in Africa and Franco's mastery of a fast, finger-picking style led to him being dubbed "the sorcerer" and created the template which virtually all African players of the instrument have since adopted. He made his recording debut in 1953 and formed the seminal O.K. Jazz from top session players three years later.

Franco maintained the group for 33 years, although it was later known as T.P.O.K. Jazz (Tout Puissant Orchestre Kinois de Jazz, or the Almighty Kinshasa Jazz Orchestra). In that time rumba developed into the modern style known as soukous but Franco remained the godfather, using his songs in later years to make sharp political and social observations. Many consider the mid-1970s as a peak in the career of Franco and O.K. Jazz, and the two discs released for his twentieth anniversary as a bandleader in 1976 are a good starting place.

Both albums are shoddily packaged with virtually no information. But the rawness of the earlier rumba has given way to a slicker production and more sophisticated sound in which Franco's guitar work is superb and the long improvisational passages (there are only eleven tracks spread across the two discs) are quite hypnotic. Volume One opens with **Liberté**, nine minutes of gently pulsating soukous rhythms. Angelically sweet harmony vocals soon give way to a mesmerizing, circular guitar pattern and a fine Franco vocal (one of only two on the album) before the motif is taken up by understated horns. **Mataya Ya Muasi Na Mobali Ekoli Kosila Te** follows a similar pattern, developing from a simple semi-acoustic introduction into denser, swirling textures and a spontaneous-sounding call-and-response vocal in which Franco takes the lead. On the thrilling **Melou**, the sweeter voice of Uta-Mayi takes over. Other featured vocalists are Dombe Opetum, Youlou and Boyibanda, but even when he's not taking the lead it is Franco's endlessly inventive guitar work that is the centre of attraction.

Further listening: Originalité (Retroafric) captures the joyousness and uninhibited charm of Franco's first recordings with O.K. Jazz, which sound as fresh today as they must have done over 40 years ago.

Ghazal

Moon Rise Over the Silk Road

Shanachie, 1998

Kayhan Kalhor (kamancheh), Shujaat Husain Khan (sitar, vocals), Swapan Chaudhuri (tabla), Sandeep Das (tabla), Pejman Hadadi (tombak), Gilad (percussion).

While there have been dozens of collaborations between Indian and Western musicians (good and bad), it's surprising that this East–West collaboration of Indian and Iranian musicians hasn't been attempted before. After all, Northern Indian classical music grew from the Iranian roots of musical traditions introduced by the Mughal Emperors. But Persian music has had a low profile on the World Music scene, probably because the classical music was always intended for an educated elite rather than mass consumption. Things are changing, thanks to the charismatic kamancheh (spike fiddle) player Kayhan Kalhor, who has succeeded in broadening the appeal of the music, not by diluting it in any way, but by the sheer artistry of his playing and his wide-ranging musical imagination.

Ghazal is a partnership of Kalhor with Indian sitar player Shujaat Husain Khan (son and disciple of leading sitar master, Vilayat Khan). Both musicians are deeply rooted in their respective traditions and follow their own solo careers, but they are also from a new generation of musicians that tours the world and is open to new ideas and collaborations. "Ghazal" refers to a musical form found both in Persian and Indian music, but which has evolved differently within each tradition. This is true, of course, with Persian and Indian music in general, although there are some common features in the importance of improvisation and the way musical structures unfold over long periods of time.

On **Moon Rise Over the Silk Road** there are two lengthy tracks over twenty minutes long, separated by a shorter, lighter interlude of eight minutes, creating a large-scale structure like a classical composition. The opening section, Fire in My Heart, begins with alternating statements from the kamancheh and sitar, a dialogue that underlines the different character of the two instruments – one bowed, the other plucked – and creates a gentle mood of exotic and languorous sensuality. After about six minutes, Shujaat Khan also reveals himself to be a wonderfully sonorous vocalist as he sings the ghazal that forms the inspiration for this first part. The kamancheh and sitar interweave and mirror the vocal line and then launch into a series of improvisations on the melody, which end with Kalhor plucking the kamancheh in imitation of the sitar, a technique not normally used on the instrument. The tabla of Swapan Chaudhari enters for the final stretch, in which the opening notes of the ghazal melody are now reversed and the music flies off into wild improvisations, with Kalhor bowing like crazy across the four strings of the kamancheh and Shujaat Khan plucking out fiery flourishes on the sitar. The piece then winds down to a gentle close.

Pari Mahal, based on an East Indian folk tune, is simpler in style, with sitar and kamancheh giving their embellishments over driving tabla rhythms. The final track, Listen to the Nay, is based on a Persian Sufi poem about the reed flute, and is sung by Shujaat Khan, but not before we've had Kalhor exploring the deep cello-like sonorities of his instrument. At the end, the instruments are joined by the higher sound of the tombak (Persian goblet drum), to reinforce the meeting of two musical cultures and two excellent musicians.

Further listening: Kayhan Kalhor's solo album **Scattering Stars Like Dust** (Traditional Crossroads) is also well worth investigating. On **Love's Deep Ocean** (Network) virtuoso singer Alim Qasimov performs Azerbaijani mugams, a form that shares many characteristics with Persian music.

Gipsy Kings

Gipsy Kings

Columbia/Sony, 1988

Nicolas Reyes (lead vocals, guitar), Andre Reyes (backing, vocals, guitar), Tonino Baliardo (solo guitar), Jacques "Max" Baliardo (guitar), Maurice "Diego" Baliardo (guitars handclaps), Tonino Baliardo (guitar), Jahloul "Chico" Bouchikhi (guitar and handclaps), Paul "Pablo" Reyes (guitar), Dominique Perrier (synthesizer), Gérard Prévost (bass guitars synthesizer), Claude Prévost (drum kit), Marc Chantereau (percussion).

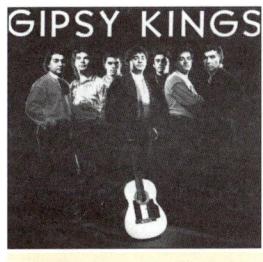

OK, so it takes you back to those hours misspent in tapas bars in the late 1980s as their mega-hit song Bamboleo rang out to the sound of another cork popping from a bottle of Rioja. But those gravelly vocals of Nicolas Reyes set against the vigorous strumming of guitars, the flamboyant guitar solos and hearty backing vocals, really take some beating. Indeed the retrospective *Best of the Gipsy Kings* (Nonesuch, available in the US only) was said to be the best-selling World Music album of all time until the Buena Vista Social Club came along (see p.37).

Hailing from the Reyes (Kings) family, three members of the band are sons of José Reyes, a celebrated flamenco singer who migrated from Spain to France during the Spanish Civil War. His children were brought up in the tradition. "There's a Gypsy legend," Nicolas Reyes recounts, "that when an old Gypsy singer or guitarist is going to die, he will sing or play for a pregnant woman. Then the child that is born will inherit his gift." It's that easy. The Reyes children formed a group called Los Reyes (The Kings) and the Gypsy Kings were formed in 1982, when the Reyes brothers (essentially singers) joined with their cousins, the Baliardos (guitarists). They were raised in the Gypsy quarters of

Arles and Montpellier and the music they play is rooted in the popular, rhythmic Gypsy Rumba style of Catalonia in southern France and northern Spain.

Legend has it that the band were busking in St Tropez when they were spotted by Brigitte Bardot, who invited them to perform at a celebrity party. Their fans have included Elton John, Peter Gabriel, Duran Duran, François Mitterrand, Princess Diana and Eric Clapton. The Gipsy Kings have now got around ten albums to their credit, some of them broadening (or diluting) the music (depending on your taste) with accordions, strings, electronics and a Latin horn section, but it's their eponymous album that truly captures that heady moment when the drama, flamboyance and occasional bad taste had its time in the sun.

After a few surprisingly tentative guitar chords, "Bamboleo" kicks in with a swinging rhythm punctuated by timbales. Nicolas Reyes' vocal sounds like it's been processed through cigarette smoke and builds up to a rhythmic climax, a dramatic silence and then the sing-along tune with backing vocal. It sounds so familiar now, but the percussive rhythmic vocals were a distinctive trademark. The song also has a rather elegant guitar solo from Tonino Baliardo and plenty of palmas (handclaps), sounding like a field of crickets. The other big hit from this album was **Djobi Djoba**, another uptempo number with seemingly nonsensical, rhythmical lyrics and lots of clapping. The same could be said of **Bem, Bem Maria**, another of their greatest hits. Much softer in texture and tending towards easy listening are **Tu Quieres Volver** and **Un Amor**, although they are saved by Nicolas Reyes' voice, with its texture of coarse-grained sandpaper. **Moorea**, **Inspiration**, **Faena** and the closing **Duende** are all instrumental tracks with a beautiful guitar solo and wistful harmonies. The supposed lapse in taste is **A Mi Manera** (otherwise known as "My Way"), which slips into semi-English on the key words, but at least the guitars and percussion have more guts than on the Frank Sinatra version.

> **Further listening: ¡Vaya Rumba!** (Nascente) is a good sampler of Catalan Gypsy rumba, while **Ida y Vuelta** (Sony France), by the Perpignan-based Tekameli, has a true authentic flavour.

Juan Luís Guerra and 4.40

Bachata Rosa

Karen, 1990

Juan Luís Guerra (guitar, vocals), Adalgisa Pantaleón (vocals), Roger Zayas-Bazán (vocals, drums), Marco Hernández (vocals, synthesizers), also Elvis Cabrera (piano, synthesizers), Osvaldo Cesa (bass), Armando Beltre (trumpet), Daniel Peña (sax), Roberto Olea (trombone), Juan de la Cruz, Rafael Guzman, Pedro Peralta, Isidro Bobadilla, Osvaldo Cesa (percussion), plus guest vocalists.

Most tropical Latin styles are a fusion of colonial (Spanish) and African sounds, all of them subtly different from one another. Salsa is based on Cuban rhythms, while merengue the Dominican Republic's main dance, is rooted in wilder folk forms. If there's one man responsible for the merengue boom of recent years, it's Juan Luís Guerra, the six-foot-four-inch son of a Dominican baseball champion. Guerra transformed it into an international sensation by mixing in with bachata, its rural grassroots cousin, played on guitar, maracas and bongos, then infusing both forms with a potent cocktail of musical ideas.

Guerra was born and educated in the Dominican Republic, but he studied jazz and composition at Boston's Berklee College of Music. In 1984 he formed his band, 4.40 (named after the tuning note A, which vibrates 440 times a second). A fan of The Beatles and Manhattan Transfer, as well as all kinds of Latin music, Guerra is also a lover of literature (including poet Pablo Neruda) and his powerful lyrics are full of colloquial language. He also added elements from the singer-songwriters of the South American "new song" movement, with its roots in the popular regional styles of bolero, guaracha and ranchera. In 1987 he wrote a song for a coffee commercial based on an anonymous peasant's poem he found in a countryside church. *Ojalá que llueva café* (May it Rain Coffee) is a campesino's prayer that the harvest will be plentiful, and food rain down from the sky. The song became the title track of the album that first brought Guerra to international attention. Three years later **Bachata Rosa** (Rose Pink Bachata) made him one of the most successful Latin musicians of all time, selling over five million copies in the first years of its release.

Almost every track on the album captures the frisson and fun of being hopelessly in love. Horn riffs burst over ricocheting percussion on the opening track, *Rosalia*, and its catchy rhythms, underpinned by those of Caribbean zouk, are guaranteed to get people onto the dance floor within seconds. Guerra possesses the key nasal quality of a salsero – he likens his voice to aguardiente (firewater) – which works just as well in outgoing, brassy numbers as it does in the slower songs. A good example of the latter is *Como Abeja al Panal*, a duet with Adalgisa Pantaleón in which Guerra openly expresses his feelings in a way which treats women as equals, never defining them in machista terms like most other Latin composers – probably one reason for the album's popularity.

In *Carta de Amor*, another slow number, he dictates a love letter, complete with punctuation; *Estrellitas y Duendes*, has something of the feel of Cuban song hero Silvio Rodríguez; while *La Bilirrubina* wittily describes the fever of passion. The Afropop song "Dede Priscilla" gets the merengue treatment on *A Pedir su Mano*, with Guerra's Spanish lyrics evoking the heady excitement of asking for someone's hand in marriage. *Burbujas de Amor* is full of frisky, double meanings, a man longing to immerse himself in a fish-tank (ie a woman's body), while *Bachata Rosa* serenades love itself. This is a soundtrack-for-life album, and if you are not in love with love when you start hearing this, you will be by the time it finishes.

Further listening: For a less sophisticated treatment of merengue try **Essential Merengue: Stripping the Parrots** (Corason). Guerra's own 1992 album, **Areito** (Karen), is both more raunchy and more political. Carlos Vives' **Clasicos de la provincia** (Philips) gave similar ground-breaking treatment to Colombian vallenato.

Hassan Hakmoun

The Fire Within: Gnawa Music of Morocco

Music of the World, 1995

Hassan Hakmoun (sintir, vocals) plus overdubbed choral refrains, qaraqab and hand claps.

Despite Brian Jones and the Rolling Stones' love affair with the Master Musicians of Jajouka, of all the sounds of Morocco it's the music of the Gnawa (also written as Gnaoua) that has most caught the imagination of the West. Many visitors to Morocco will have seen Gnawa musicians in the Djema el Fna, the vast market square in Marrakech. The Gnawa are a mystical brotherhood descended from slaves brought from sub-Saharan Africa by the Arabs, and their music fuses Arabic and Black African into a deep bluesy sound. At its most intense, it has a power and spirituality that belies its basic ingredients of chanting, sintir (lute) and qaraqab (metal clappers).

While seeing a Gnawa group with their athletic dancing can be an exhilarating experience live, recording it is rarely successful because the metal castanets drown out everything else, to the extent of almost entirely obliterating the wonderful sound of the sintir. This disc features sintir player Hassan Hakmoun in a studio recording with overdubbed clappers, and hand claps and vocals from Hakmoun himself. The incessant sound of the qaraqab is held back to let the sintir shine through. This might sound like a very artificial process, but actually in a live context the brain does a lot of that remixing for you.

Hakmoun was born in Marrakech in 1963. After a stint playing in the Djema el Fna, he travelled widely, becoming involved in various fusion projects before eventually settling in the US.

This is Hakmoun's most traditional album and the best recording there is of Gnawa music. The Gnawa lute, the sintir or gimbri, has a deep, woody cello-like sound, with a full and rounded resonance from its large camel-skin-covered body. Its four strings are pitched low, with a whiff of bass guitar about them, but the instrument is also percussive: the fingers strike and the hand slaps both the skin and the strings in a way that makes it sounds like two separate instruments. In the hands of a player like Hakmoun you can understand how the sintir is thought to have the power to control the spirits. The music on this disc is basically for sintir and voice, and originates in a ritual ceremony for healing and well-being.

On the opening track, **Sala Alla 'Alik Dima Dima**, the qaraqab and backing vocals establish a sense of ritual performance in a piece devoted to those saints descended from the Prophet Mohammed, while the ensuing track **Bu Derbala**, for sintir and solo voice, acts as a dedication to the ceremonial robes. It is these intimate tracks, for solo sintir or voice and sintir, that especially shine with the plucked strings and flexible rhythmic patterns working a peculiar magic. You can understand why the sintir, with its distinctive bendy plucked sound and spiritual power, has been co-opted by many other non-Moroccan bands. It's heard at its best here on the opening track, and in the deep and timeless sounds of the extended solo that opens **Wa Ya Ya Allah, Daim Allah**. **Sidi Musa** and **Wa Yay Yay Saadiya** (both with backing vocals) represent the more trance-inducing sounds of Gnawa music. The real sound of an authentic Gnawa ceremony at full pelt has been sacrificed here, but the gain is the elevation of the sintir into a magnificent solo instrument in its own right.

> **Further listening**: Gnawa Diffusion is the best of the contemporary bands that are fusing Gnawa music with other North African and World sounds and their **Bab El Oued Kingston** (Seven Colors) is stunning. **The Master Musicians of Jajouka** (Point Music) also bring their own variety of trance music, dynamically produced in a new recording by Talvin Singh.

Ofra Haza

Yemenite Songs

Globestyle, 1985

Ofra Haza (vocals) with orchestra and percussion arranged by Beny Nagari.

Ofra Haza died unexpectedly from AIDS-related complications in February 2000. During a thirty-year career she released a prodigious amount of music, but it is 1985's **Yemenite Songs** that is the work for which she will be best remembered. Long established as one of Israel's most popular singers, this album brought her far wider recognition, partially because of its international success but also because it led to her (sometimes unwitting) involvement in several projects at the cutting edge of the UK club dance scene.

Born in 1959 in Tel Aviv, Ofra was the daughter of Yemenite Jewish parents who had been forced to flee on foot from their native country's Muslim regime. In her early teens she joined a theatre and performance group before serving her compulsory two years in the Israeli army. Discharged in 1979 she launched her solo career and, unusually, became a star not only at home but also in neighbouring Arab nations. She even represented Israel in the 1983 Eurovision Song Contest with the classy pop song "Hai!" Over the next fifteen years she brought her voice to a host of radically different musical styles – including goth and soft disco-funk – before her unexpected early death.

Yemenite Songs was a deeply personal journey into her cultural roots, inspired by the ancient melodies taught to her by her mother. These social songs, often sung at weddings or festivals, were a rich part of the oral tradition of Yemen, one of the oldest Jewish communities on earth until almost the entire population was airlifted out in the late 1940s. Yemenite Jewish music had always comfortably combined the secular and the sacred, and Haza took many of the lyrics from the sixteenth-century devotional poetry of Rabbi Shalom Shabazi. Working closely with producers Bezalel Aloni and Beny Nagari, she used mid-1980s studio technology to present eight traditional songs in a "pop" context, forging a style that became known variously as "world beat" or "ethno-pop".

Virtually every song is punctuated by the sound of beaten metal – a clattering accompaniment to the soaring strings and the elastic bass-lines of Eli Magan. Orthodox Muslims had banned the use of conventional musical instruments, so the Yemenite Jews ingeniously used petrol cans and copper domestic trays to accompany their songs. But it is Ofra's achingly pure voice, by turns austere and sensuous, that captures the imagination. Many of the songs start with an unaccompanied statement of the melody before the small orchestra take up the tune. It is these flights of melody that have frequently worn better than some of the arrangements, which, with hindsight, can sound slightly trite.

The opening track, **Im Nin'alu**, is an intoxicating epic – both noble and earthy, and yet with a superbly catchy tune. It was this track that was to achieve fame through sampling: first as "Pump Up the Volume" by M/A/R/R/S, then through Coldcut's remix of "Paid in Full" by rappers Eric B. & Rakim. **Galbi** also became a hit, the suppressed pain of its lyric of unrequited love almost belied by the jolly tune and some particularly persistent oil-drumming. **Yachilvi Veyachali** provides one of the instrumental highlights, with a sweet horn solo underpinned by frantic hand claps and a coy vocal coda. The album closes with the sumptuous and triumphant **Ash'alech** – the aural equivalent of the beautiful cover photo of Ofra decked out in glittering traditional costume.

Further listening: Palestinian Amal Murkus reveals a haunting and powerful new voice on her album **Amal** (Hemisphere). **Al Ol** (MCI/Najema Music), by violin and oud player Yair Dalal and his ensemble, is an instrumental album which draws on a wide range of Middle Eastern musical traditions.

Huun-Huur-Tu

The Orphan's Lament

Shanachie, 1994

Kaigal-ool Khovalyg (vocals, igil, khomuz), Anatoli Kuular (vocals, bizaanchi, khomuz), Sayan Bapa (vocals, doshpulur, marinhuur, guitar), Alexander Bapa (tungur, dazhaanning khavy, etc).

Lying right at the centre of Asia, the Tuvan Republic (part of the Russian Federation) is famed for its "throat singing" (khöömei), or more correctly "overtone singing". A single performer simultaneously produces two or three vocal lines by selectively amplifying harmonics with precise movements of the lips, tongue and larynx, so they sound louder than the low drone from which they derive. Ethereal, shimmering melodies are created as if by magic, high above the deep fundamental notes. It's an absolutely extraordinary listening experience, whether performed by soloists or in groups.

Huun-Huur-Tu have been dazzling people throughout the world with their mesmerizing recordings and concerts since 1992. Having abandoned the glitzy, pseudo-folk performances of the bad old Soviet days, the group decided to revive the near-forgotten traditional songs, and travelled the country collecting repertoire from the older generations. The band's leader, Kaigal-ool Khovalyg, was born into a family of shepherds, who still maintain a traditional lifestyle with yurts and a vast herd of horses. He has an amazing deep voice, is a talented overtone singer and instrumentalist, and teaches igil (Tuvan horse-head fiddle) at the music school in the capital, Kyzyl. With all sorts of legends surrounding it, the horse-head fiddle is musically and symbolically important in Tuva (and Mongolia) and the members of Huun-Huur-Tu are as good instrumentalists as they are singers. They play a range of horse-head fiddles (igil, marinhuur and bizaanchi), the doshpulur (Tuvan banjo), the shamanistic tungur drum and dazhaanning khavy rattle made out of sheep's kneebones in a bull's scrotum. As well as reviving old repertoire (including socialist songs), the band are not afraid to experiment and have collaborated with Frank Zappa, Ry Cooder, the Chieftains and the Kronos Quartet.

Prayer, the opening track on **The Orphan's Lament**, is immensely powerful. With its deep guttural sounds, it's like a door opening onto a forgotten world, Buddhist music having been severely suppressed during the Soviet period. Performed as a vocal quartet, this track was inspired by Tibetan chant but comes with shimmering overtones on top. As the Eskimos are reputed to have dozens of words for snow, the Tuvans have hundreds of songs about horses. Tuva horses provide both rhythmic inspiration and also important metaphors. Most of Huun-Huur-Tu's uptempo numbers have subtle variations of trotting and galloping rhythms behind them, including **Aa-Shuu Dekei-Oo** (his horse clears his mind), **Kaldak Khamar** (about travelling across a mountain pass) and **Eki Attar** (linking a horse and a girlfriend). Learned from an old Tuvan singer, **Chiraa-Khoor** (describing an epic journey) is one of their most celebrated horse songs, with a continuous riding pulse and rattling sheep's bones.

The instrumental textures on this album are truly wonderful, notably the sad, yearning bowed strings that open and accompany the title track, **The Orphan's Lament,** a tragic song exquisitely performed by Kaigal-ool, with whistling overtones. There are other spectacular instrumental performances on **Steppe** and **Ödugen Taiga**, both pieces about the landscape and the animals that inhabit it. Much Tuvan music evokes the vast landscapes of the country and the natural world. It's one of the things that makes the music sound so enduringly fresh.

Further listening: Tuva, Among the Spirits (Smithsonian Folkways) is a great collection of performances and includes Kaigal-ool and Anatoli Kuular performing khöömei on horseback. **Deep in the Heart of Tuva** (Ellipsis Arts) provides a broad survey from traditional to fusion.

Istanbul Oriental Ensemble

Gypsy Rum

Network, 1995

Burhan Öçal (leader, percussion), Ekrem Bagi (percussion), Hüsyin Bitmez (ud), Ferdi Nadaz (Klarnet), Sahin Sert (kanun), Fethi Tekyaygil (keman).

Preservers of traditional music but never slaves to tradition, Gypsies are voracious and wide-reaching in their musical appetites. In Europe and the Middle East, they rank among the most important of musicians, nowhere more so than in the Balkans. **Gypsy Rum** showcases some of Turkey's magnificent Gypsy music (generally known as fasil), which, despite its slightly seedy belly-dance associations, is also a light classical music in which the refined modes (makamat) of Turkish music are treated with great expressiveness and virtuosity. Though it can be heard regularly in Istanbul nightclubs and restaurants, the quality is rarely as good as this. The Istanbul Oriental Ensemble is a top-quality outfit. If you want to treat yourself like a sultan, sit with a spread of magnificent Turkish meze, tip water into your glass of raki, and slip this disc into the CD player.

The combination of instruments a is typical one, featuring the distinctive sound of the Turkish klarnet (clarinet), keman (violin), ud (lute), kanun (plucked zither) and a percussion section dominated by the darbuka (goblet drum). The glory of this music lies in the combination of acoustic textures – the plucked sounds of the ud and kanun, the smooth, slidey melodies of the clarinet and violin, and the precise, focused sound of the percussion. The Turkish klarnet is in G (lower than regular clarinets in A or B flat) and has a particularly dark and throaty tone. The kanun, too, provides some uniquely vibrant colours: particularly impressive are the shrieks and glissandos that Sert strikes like fireworks from the instrument on **Hicaz Oyun Havasi**, and the way he seems to egg on the klarnet in **Hicazkar Oyun Havasi**.

Several numbers begin with the whole band playing together before individual instruments come to the fore for solo passages. Much of the music is fast and frenetic: "Hicazkar Oyun Havasi", **Bahriye Çiftetellisi** and **Zennube** are three particularly exciting tracks. The latter, in a more arabesk style, includes a sustained clarinet solo, spiced with squeals on the kanun, which evokes all the bustle, colour, smells and spices of the Istanbul bazaar. In contrast **Rast Balat** is much more meditative in style, with slower, intense solos on the violin, kanun, clarinet and ud in turn. The leader, Burhan Öçal on darbuka, saves himself up for track eight, the fast and intricate **Hicazkar Sahin Oyun Havasi** for extended solo percussion, and appears again in the last track, **Roman Oyun Havasi**.

The ensemble numbers are interspersed with solo improvisations (taksim), which are more reflective, but allow the players to express themselves in a different way. **Hicazkar Taksim Oud** (the disc is a bit sloppy in its spelling of "ud" which is not spelled "oud" in Turkish) is the first of these: an ud solo which begins slowly, with a lovely woody sound and explores all the microtonal details of the classical mode. Each of the melody instruments gets its solo taksim spot – the kanun track **Ussak Taksim** is extraordinary for the way Sert stresses the melody notes, which he dextrously fills in with lighter flourishes and ornaments before letting rip with some wild Debussy-like glissandi. With great solos and thrilling ensemble playing, this is powerful and exuberant musicianship at its very best.

Further listening: Mustafa Kandirali is the king of the Turkish klarnet and is well worth hearing with his ensemble on **Caz Roman** (Network). For the same instruments (plus the more mystical reed flute, the ney) in some fine classical music, try the works of **Tatyos Efendi** (Traditional Crossroads), played by the Kudsi Erguner Ensemble.

Jali Musa Jawara

Yasimika

Hannibal, 1990

Jali Musa Jawara (kora and vocals), Jali Morijan Kuyateh (balafon), Kissiman Kuyateh (guitar), Lamine Kuyateh (guitar) and Janka Jobateh, Fanta Kuyateh and Jeni Doumbia (chorus).

The music of the Mande people of West Africa is among the most appealing on the continent. It's heard across a large area including Mali, Guinea, Gambia and parts of Senegal and the Ivory Coast where this album was made. Perhaps the most distinctive instrument employed is the kora, the harp/lute with twenty-one strings, that lends its rippling textures to much of the music and is one of the main reasons for its international success. Still widely used in traditional contexts, the kora appears in intimate acoustic recordings (by Gambian musicians Dembo Konte and Kausu Kouyateh, for example), in contemporary electrified form (by Guinean Mory Kanté), and its riffs and accompaniments have been transposed onto the guitars of dance bands (like Mali's Rail Band or Guinea's Bembeya Jazz).

Music in Mande culture is generally confined to families of griots (in French) or jalis (in the Mande languages) who play it for entertainment and ritual purposes. As his prefix suggests, Jali Musa Jawara is one and so are the members of his band – the names Diabate/Jobarteh, Kouyate/Kuyateh, Kanté/Konte, Cissokho/Suso and Damba/Doumbia (for women) resonate through the history of Mande music.

Jawara was born in Guinea and is the half-brother (with the same mother) of kora and balafon player Mory Kanté. The two of them left to work in Bamako, Mali and later worked together in Abidjan.

While Kanté went on to forge an international sound with his *Yeke Yeke* recording in Paris, Jawara stayed on the Ivory Coast and his best music has always kept close to his roots. **Yasimika** was his groundbreaking disc: recorded in Abidjan and first released in France in 1983, before the big hits of Mory Kanté and Salif Keita (see p.85), it is an absolute classic. With its magical line-up of kora, guitar, balafon and female vocals, *Yasimika* exemplifies Guinean music's melodic swing which is warm, catchy and uplifting.

Opening with a kora-like guitar flourish, **Fote Mogoban**, the first track, soon gets into a mesmerising swing. The combination of balafon (Mande xylophone) with kora and guitars – the rippling, struck patterns contrasting with the plucked strings – is one of the most enchanting sounds in all music. The overall effect is repetitive and trance-like with continually varying details. There is no percussion section here – the fantastic, organic sense of rhythm comes entirely from the interaction of the instrumental ingredients.

Jawara has a strong, but not hectoring, declamatory style and the way his voice interweaves with the sweeter sound of the female chorus, is one of the great successes of this album. The first song bemoans an elusive lover; the second **Haidara** is the most convincing musical invective against the evils of drink that you'll ever hear; **Yekeke** (the same song as Kanté's *Yeke Yeke*) is about the pleasures of flirtation, and **Yasimika**, the title track, is a praise song in which the musicians pat themselves on the back along with most of the people of West Africa. Not that you need to know any of this, the joy of this disc is found in its soaring vocal melodies and beautifully sustained instrumental improvisations.

Intended for release on cassette and LP, the CD's four tracks amount to less than thirty-three-and-a-half minutes. Don't let that put you off. Yasimika's relaxing joy and sunshine (not to mention the admonitory advice) is worth anybody's money.

Further listening: Tradition (Melodie) features Mory Kanté (kora), Kanté Manfila (guitar) and vocals from Djanka Diabaté and Oumou Diabaté in a wonderful acoustic set of Guinean music.

Carlo Jones & the Surinam Kaseko Troubadours

Carlo Jones & the Surinam Kaseko Troubadours

MW Records, 1995

Carlo Jones (alto sax), André Jones (sousaphone), Erwin Brewster (banjo), Erwin Doest (trumpet), Jules Klimsop (trombone), Humphrey Vyent (skraki), Robby Krolis (snare drum).

Sometimes you stumble across a style of music that takes you by surprise and you simply can't understand why it isn't more widely known. Often it comes down to marketing or simply luck. In the case of Kaseko from Surinam it's probably due to its Dutch colonial connection that the music has failed to penetrate the Anglo, Franco, Hispanic cultural hegemony.

So a few words of introduction. Kaseko is outdoor party music from Surinam on the north-eastern coast of South America in which the predominant influences come from New Orleans jazz and marching bands, Cuban music and Calypso – perhaps an unsurprising mélange given the country's location. At the heart of the music, however, is Afro-American percussion music beaten out on the snare drum and skraki, a bass drum worn on the chest. The sound is up-beat and infectious – music to make you move your butt – and the Surinam Kaseko Troubadours playing is pretty raucous and exuberant.

Carlo Jones learned clarinet and sax as a child and then joined bands in the police force and the military. In the mid-1970s he emigrated to Holland where he formed The Surinam Kaseko Troubadours. The band got their lucky break when another

Surinam band was unable to turn up for a gig and Carlo Jones and his team were engaged to replace them. They were then invited to perform in the World Roots Festival held in Amsterdam's legendary Melkweg (Milky Way) and that's where this recording was made.

What's captivating about the band is Jones' confident, exuberant sax playing as he spices up the music with chromatic turns and swoops. The playing style on the sax and brass is open, punchy and, frankly, brassy. At the bottom, the texture is given a real lift and bounce by André Jones on the bass tuba or sousaphone with a pumping, athletic performance. The tunes are catchy and the rattling percussion lends the whole thing a real frenzy.

The album is entirely instrumental, but the tunes relate to songs such as *Todo no habi wiwiri ma' tyari loso*, which translates, we're told, as "The frog is hairless but yet full of lice"! This has some eccentric sax squeals at the beginning which could represent either the frog or the lice, or the cries of somebody who's just come across the beast somewhere. The band get a perfect balance between wild improvised solos – particularly on the sax, trumpet and sousaphone – and tight arrangements as the players come together for regular phrases.

It all gets progressively more frenetic, not least towards the end of *Na so mi yere so*, based on a song about the things women have under their skirts! Pushing at the boundaries of coherence, the music generates a real excitement which seems about to boil over, but ultimately Jones and his boys keep the whole thing under control. There are just a couple of slower, chorale-like moments, but most of this album is up-tempo, playful and unstoppably good time. The last track, *Wi de g'we, wan dey unu sa miti baka* is a traditional kaseko goodbye song which presumably is about leaving the audience wanting more. It certainly has that effect.

Further Listening: Switi: Hot Kaseko Music (MW Records) is the Kaseko compilation. For similar abandoned exuberance New Orleans style, try the **Rebirth Brass Band Live at the Glass House** (Rounder).

Kepa Junkera

Bilbao 00:00 h

Resistencia, 1999

Kepa Junkera (trikitixa, pandereta) and 51 other musicians including: Xose Manuel Budino (gaita), Phil Cunningham (accordion, piano), Alisdair Fraser (violin), Pedro Guerra (vocals), Jocelyn Lapointe (trumpet), Paddy Moloney (flute), Martin O'Connor (accordion), Liam O'Flynn (uillean pipes) and Sebastian Rubio (percussion), and the groups Hedningarna, La Bottine Souriante and Oskorri.

The world is full of great accordion-led styles, and in the global squeezebox treck it's well worth stopping off in the Basque country. This is the home of trikitixa, the rural dance music, in which lively yet elegant melodies are spurred on by the insistent fast rhythm of the pandera (tambourine). That's in its traditional form, but with this album Kepa Junkera put the music on the world stage through his own formidable technique and wide-ranging collaborations.

Junkera is among the best and most innovative of a new generation of trikitixa players to emerge over the last decade. Though a master of the form, he has never been bound by it, perhaps because he is neither from the country – he was born in Bilbao in 1965 – nor a native Baque speaker. Junkera first came to the attention of the veteran band Oskorri in the early 1980s and has played on their albums since he was 17. He was already writing and his first compositions, which sound fairly traditional, were included on *Kepa, Zabaleta eta Mutriku*, recorded in 1988. In 1992 he joined two other squeezebox greats, the Italian Ricardo Tesi and the Englishman John Kirkpatrick. Pooling their repertoire, the three formed Trans-Europe Diatonique, toured extensively and recorded an album.

Perhaps the seeds that have blossomed with **Bilbao 00.00** were sown in that collaboration, though this is an altogether more ambitious project. Setting out from Bilbao, Junkera stops off in all sorts of fascinating places – Madagascar, northern Sweden, Cape Verde, Quebec – in order to partake of their musical bio-diversity. He's like a busker playing his way round the world, except that he manages to bump into and swap tunes with the finest musicians developing the musical traditions of those places – the Madagascan valiha virtuoso Justin Vali, Irish piper Liam O'Flynn, Phil Cunningham from Scotland and the Galician piper Carlos Nuñez.

This double CD reveals Junkera's extraordinary range: **Arin Quebec** opens like a typical trikitixa piece before the trademark foot-percussion and the tight brass section of La Bottine Souriante sweep in. In **Del Hierro a Madagascar** he delicately complements the plangency of Malagasy music and achieves remarkable flourishes, as if his were a stringed rather than a free reed instrument. His sojourn with the Swedish group **Hedningarna** produced, in **Bok Espok**, a piece redolent of the frozen north: stomping-in-the-snow rhythms interspersed with tunes as melancholy and eerie as the snow-swept steppes. With Phil Cunningham and Martin O'Connor he plays **Muskerraren Balsa & La Balsa de Combouscuro**, a couple of speedy waltzes that sound as if they might have been written by Cunningham, rather than dedicated to him.

It might be argued that in his mastery – playing the accordion like a church organist and a jazz saxophonist – Junkera has sacrificed the wildness of trikitixa. Admittedly there's none of the bloodcurdling howling that urges on the dancers in the mountain villages of the Basque country. But Junkera is doing something else, listening attentively to the conversation of other people's music then contributing to the discussion thoughtfully, in his distinctly Basque accent.

Further listening: Trikitixa: Melodeon Dance Dynamite (Erde Records) is a comprehensive introduction to the rootsy form of the music featuring the finest younger players and some historical recordings. **Planet Squeezebox** (Ellipsis Arts) is a fantastic three-CD exploration of the amazing variety of accordion styles around the world.

Salif Keita

Soro

Stern's, 1987

Salif Keita (lead vocals), Brice Wouassy (drums), Michel Alibo (bass guitar), Yves Ndjock (guitar, vocals), Alain Hatot (sax), Eric Giausserand (trupet), "Bolo" Bolognesi (trombone), Jean-Philippe Rykiel (keyboards), and others.

Listen to Sina, the fourth track of this album, and you'll understand why **Soro** made such an important contribution to the growth of World Music. When it first appeared, in the late 1980s, it introduced a distinctive new voice to the world. That incantatory introduction, underpinned by a deep blast on the synthesizer, conjured up images of Mali's sub-Saharan vistas and the spectacular mud-brick mosque of Djenné, as Salif's Islamic-tinged voice echoed the call to prayer. Then with punchy trumpet and drums the piece sweeps you away. But this wasn't simply the appearance of a new voice in the person of Salif Keita; the album itself heralded a new stage in the production of African music in Paris. The man responsible was Ibrahima Sylla, subsequently to become one of the most important and influential of producers. On *Soro*, his first big success, he succeeded in finding just the right harmonious balance between electronics and a distinctly Malian sound.

Salif was born in 1949, the third in a family of thirteen children. He is not a jali – one of the hereditary musical families that dominate music-making in West Africa – but of royal stock, a descendant of Mali's great thirteenth-century warrior king Sundjata Keita. This meant that he had to overcome family resistance to becoming a "lowly" musician. He's also albino – a "white" son of black parents – which itself carries a stigma. Salif has spoken of how as a boy he would go out into the fields around his village to sing to the monkeys, simply in order to overcome his loneliness. When bad eyesight prevented him from taking up his chosen profession as a teacher, he started singing for a living in Bamako.

In the early 1970s he became a member of Mali's famous Rail Band (government employees based at the Buffet Hotel de la Gare in Bamako), as did Guinean singer Mory Kanté, who also went on to a similar international career. Salif then joined Les Ambassadeurs du Motel, who played a more international repertoire with strong influences from Cuban and French music. The band transposed to Abidjan in 1978 and Salif's international reputation was underway. By the mid-1980s he was working in Paris, as was Kanté, his former colleague and sometime rival. Salif, working with Senegalese producer Sylla came up with *Soro* and Mory Kanté, with producer Nick Patrick, recorded *Akwaba Beach* (with its hit song "Yeke Yeke"). Both albums catapulted modern Mande music onto the world stage.

Soro is bold and brassy, its distinctive sounds created by the interaction of Salif with the female backing vocals, the prominent trumpet (a Cuban music influence), the athletic bass guitar of Michel Alibo, and the keyboard splashes of Jean-Philippe Rykiel. The opening track, Wamba, an uptempo dance number, is followed by the title track which, at nearly ten minutes, is much more ambitious. The dry keyboard accompaniment surely harks back to the sound of the balafon (the ancient Malian xylophone) and the piece ends with an exciting sequence of drums and metallic percussion combined with the backing vocals and Salif's soaring voice. The lyrics and vocal style of Souareba also evokes the traditional jali repertoire, despite the heavy synth and drums. Ironically, it's the more traditionally rooted songs that have the most electronics, but it's all brilliantly done and this must stand as one of the great African music albums of all time.

> **Further listening:** Mory Kanté's **Akwaba Beach** (Barclay) is another popular classic that could well have been an entry in its own right. **Musiques du Mali: Banzoumana** (Melodie) is a fantastic two-CD compilation of Malian music, both traditional and modern.

Khaled

Khaled

Barclay/Universal, 1992

Khaled (vocals, keyboards, accordion, oud, bendir), Musatapaha Kada (keyboards), Randy Jacons (guitar, bass), Don Was (bass, keyboards), David Coleman (oud, cello), Mosen Chentouf (debouka, bendir), Michael Brook (guitar, bass, percussion), Afid Saidi (drums), Willy N'For (bass).

The emergence of modern rai from the urban backstreets of Algeria into a major international musical force has been one of the success stories of World Music over the past ten years and more. Synonymous with its rise has been Khaled, the official, undisputed and ever-smiling king of the genre. It's difficult to single out just one release from the four groundbreaking studio albums he has made since signing to the French label Barclay in the early 1990s. All are highly recommendable, but it is almost impossible to find fault with his 1992 album, simply entitled **Khaled**, which played a key role in spreading the rai gospel far beyond the Maghreb and its outposts-in-exile around the port of Marseilles and the Bobigny and Barbes districts of Paris.

The son of a mechanic from Oran in western Algeria, the precocious "Cheb" Khaled made his first record at the age of 14 in 1974. Almost iimmediately he ran into trouble with the Islamic authorities, who disapproved of the Western pop influence in his music and the celebration of the hedonistic pleasures of youth in his lyrics. But the fact that he was soon banned from Algerian television and radio did little to stop the rebellious spirit of rai sweeping the Maghreb and empowering disaffected Arab youth. At the first official festival of the new music in Oran in 1985, Khaled was crowned "King of Rai", a title he has never lost. By the following year he had relocated to France, where his *Hada Raykoum* became the first internationally released rai album the following year. Dropping the "Cheb" from his name (it means "young" or "charming"), he began ambitiously incorporating more sophisticated elements of funk, jazz, reggae and rock into the exciting but essentially cheap sound of 1980s rai-pop

Of course, there are those who claim that once he left Algeria he lost touch with his roots, and with it some of his emotional intensity, but such attitudes are short-sighted. His accessible and innovative approach achieved the remarkable feat of selling working-class Arabic music to a white bourgeois audience for the first time, particularly in France, where he swiftly became a superstar. But his pop success and his obvious enjoyment of the trappings of fame were anathema to the doctrinal forces of Islamic fundamentalism, which were growing ever more militant and violent back in Algeria. There were death threats and he decided it was unsafe to return home. Yet the political turmoil, which was to lead to the assassination of fellow rai star Cheb Hasni in 1994, does not appear to have affected the exuberance of his music.

Khaled was produced by Don Was and Michael Brook and remains his most important release. **Didi**, the opening track, with its rattling Arabic percussion, pumping bass-line and catchy instrumental hook, was a huge dance hit and probably remains Khaled's best-known number. **Wahrane** features some inspired guitar playing and Khaled showing his prowess on French-style accordion, while **Ragda** is Arab-style reggae. **Liah Liah**, a heartfelt jazz-blues number, shows off the expressive power of Khaled's voice to fine effect. Two tracks that underline the difference between Was's rock-based production and Brook's more traditional approach are the rai-funk of **Braya** and gentle, even wistful inflections of **Harai Harai**, with Khaled now on the Arabic oud, which rounds off the album.

> **Further listening**: Cheb Mami, who has long played crown prince of rai to Khaled's king, can be heard at his best on **Meli Meli** (Totem/Virgin). On the live double album, **1, 2, 3 Soleils** (Barclay), Khaled links up with Rachid Taha (see p.171) and Faudel, two of the other biggest names in rai.

Nusrat Fateh Ali Khan

Musst Musst

Real World, 1990

Nusrat Fateh Ali Khan (vocals), Michael Brook (guitar, bass), Robert Ahwal (guitar), Farrukh Fateh Ali Khan (harmonium), Darryl Johnson (synthesizer, bass), plus guests including Massive Attack.

The late Nusrat Fateh Ali Khan is a good example of an artist whose name became internationally known as a result of the growth in World Music. And **Musst Musst** is perhaps the best example of the fusion of cultures and musical styles that has been such an important part of the genre. Nusrat was already a superstar in the Indian subcontinent as the leading exponent of qawwali, the Sufi devotional music performed at holy shrines in Pakistan and India. The great Muslim devotional singer embraced electronic dance culture – it seems an unlikely combination, but it was one that Nusrat was happy with and saw as part of his mission to spread the word in his music. And spread it he did. *Musst Musst* was a huge hit and demonstrably drew people to Nusrat's more traditional qawwali in concert and on disc.

Sufis believe in music as a tool to achieve nearness to God. It's intended to inspire awe and transport the listener into another world. In a traditional performance Nusrat's voice would simply shriek and soar above the secondary singers, harmonium, hand claps and percussion on tablas or dholak drums. The poetic lyrics are often about love – both sacred and worldly – often mystical and often fragmentary, repeated over and over again. Indeed a lot of qawwali performances are composed of rhythmic syllables and scales where the meaning is less important than the trance-like effect produced. Audiences who understand nothing of the lyrics or the philosophy are simply overcome by the sonic and magical power of the music.

Peter Gabriel first invited Nusrat to sing on the soundtrack for the film *The Last Temptation of Christ*, and *Musst Musst* followed soon after. Although Nusrat was a devout man, the tolerance of Sufi beliefs meant that he was open to new ideas. His music subsequently appeared on the soundtracks of several films, including *Natural Born Killers*, *Dead Man Walking* and *Bandit Queen*.

The opening track, **Musst Musst**, takes its lyrics from a song in praise of the Sufi saint Lal Shahbaz Qalandar, but here it's transformed into a pop song with a catchy hook. With a squelchy bass and snatched guitar chords alongside the harmonium, it takes on a dance groove and Nusrat does exuberant improvisations over the top. But it was the Massive Attack dance remix which closes the album that really took Nusrat's voice to places it had never been before (notably, when it was used for a Coca-Cola ad), although Nusrat's voice – which normally dominates – is pretty low down in the mix. The second track, **Nothing Without You**, is an anthemic love song with harmonium and tablas to the fore and Nusrat's vocals soaring over the top. The one drawback to this album is that the unrestrained vocal power of Nusrat at full throttle is lost in the production, but here the visceral but sensitive quality of his voice comes through without interference.

The remaining tracks exploit the meaningless tarana syllables of qawwali with Nusrat using his voice like an instrument. **Tracery**, one of the more poetic tracks, uses these tarana – multitracked like the decorative tracery the title suggests – over gentle guitar strumming and backing vocals. A more traditional feel prevails on **Taa Deem**, with its muscular vocal melody and exciting microtones, and Nusrat's unique ground power is also retained on **Shadow**. All in all, this a ground-breaking album that reveals more and more layers with every listen.

Further listening: For traditional Nusrat, try the recently released archive recordings, **Dust to Gold** (Real World), while **Hommage à Nusrat Fateh Ali Khan** (Network) is a collection of tributes from Sufi singers around the globe.

The Klezmatics

Rhythm + Jews

Piranha, 1991

Frank London (trumpet, cornet, keyboards, vocals), David Krakauer (clarinet, bass clarinet), Alicia Svigals (violin, vocals), Lorin Sklamberg (accordion, keyboards, lead vocals), Paul Morrissett (bass, vocals), David Licht (drums), plus guests.

This is New York klezmer with attitude – bold, sophisticated and, when it needs to be, raw. There are klezmer groups that are more radical, but none match the Klezmatics in their energy, inventiveness and daring musicality, which they combine with a real understanding of the tradition. This is their second album and there isn't a dud track on it. They've made several fine ones since and collaborated with superstar violinist Itzhak Perlman, but **Rhythm + Jews** will take some beating. The love and respect the band has for their material allows them to be incredibly free with it, pulling tunes apart and reassembling them in new forms.

Klezmer music originated in the Jewish communities of Eastern Europe, where it was played principally at weddings. It shares district characteristics with Ukrainian and Romanian music, with some inflections from Jewish liturgical chant. It can be gloriously exuberant – with fast uptempo freylekh and bulgar dances – and sometimes deeply soulful, with slow, introspective, improvised solo doinas. The music travelled to the US with mass emigration from Eastern Europe in the late nineteenth and early twentieth centuries. In America early recordings were made by clarinettists like the legendary Naftule Brandwein (1889–1963), which have been seized on as source material for the dynamic klezmer revival, which includes groups like the Klezmatics.

The opening track, **Fun Tashlikh**, takes its tune from a 1926 recording by Brandwein, but transforms it with Arabic percussion from Mahmoud Fadl (see p.59), growling bass clarinet and ghostly screams. It's a powerful opening and an understated political comment in the way it combines Jewish and Arabic sounds. The **Araber Tants** (Arab Dance) is also a Brandwein tune and an example of the Klezmatics at their most inventive. It begins with Alicia Svigal's evocative, arabesque-like violin solo throwing off distinctive ornaments and colours and moves into a hot and sultry instrumental stew from which the Brandwein tune has to burst out.

One of the band's hallmarks is the slow, relentless building up of tension and dissonance through an improvised solo until it boils over and the whole band falls into a frenzy of unstoppable foot-tapping melody. A great example of this is the **Bulgar à la Klezmatics** (another Brandwein tune) which features solos from Svigals on violin, David Krakauer on clarinet, Frank London on trumpet and David Licht on drums. There are also spectacular instrumental improvisations in the **Clarinet Yontev**, with Krakauer bending hell out of the notes, and Svigals contributing an introspective doina and driving dance for electric violin.

Rhythm + Jews also has four songs featuring Lorin Sklamberg, one of the best Yiddish vocalists. These include **Di Sapozhkelekh** (My Boots) – a staple amongst klezmer bands – and the Hasidic anthem **Shnirele Perele** (String of Pearls). Typically Klezmatics is **Honikzaft** (Honeyjuice), bringing a homoerotic flavour to the Land of Milk and Honey. The last track, a medley of four tunes, brings the trumpet of leader Frank London to the fore.

This is an album of great music in a tradition that is continually reinventing itself. With its sensation of steaming streets teeming with people, screaming sirens and urban angst, this CD is a reminder that New York is the largest Jewish city in the world. Welcome to the urban shtetl.

> **Further listening**: The magnificent recordings made by Naftule Brandwein between 1922 and 1941, the source of several tracks on *Rhythm + Jews*, can be heard on **King of the Klezmer Clarinet** (Rounder).

Euis Komariah and Yus Wiradiredja

The Sound of Sunda

Globestyle, 1990

Euis Komariah (vocals), Yus Wiradiredja (vocals), plus Pateraman Dasentra Group and Jugala Group.

It's a sultry and languorous Javanese evening at dusk. Over the warm sound of gongs and drums, a shrill bamboo flute cuts like a twist of lemon. The voices of Euis Komariah and Yus Wiradiredja appear – sometimes playful, sometimes caressing, sometimes full of longing. We're in a world of romance and, as the sleeve notes of this disc recommend: "This CD should be played only after 6pm in a peaceful environment, while your guests are arriving for dinner or when your love-object has left you." In other words, this is music that could break the ice or enhance the ambience at your dinner parties, or even help console you with wistful melancholy at times of trouble.

The Indonesian islands of Java and Bali are well-known for their gamelan music featuring large ensembles of gongs and metal xylophones. This has been widely recorded, but what is less well-known to Western audiences is the extraordinary variety of Indonesian popular music, much of which is very approachable and makes enchanting listening – notably styles like dangdut, kroncong, jaipongan and, what we have here, degung. Sadly there is very little on international labels, while in Indonesia it's largely an ephemeral cassette market. So congratulations to Globestyle for releasing this entrancing collection of degung music from a 1989 release on the Jugala label in Bandung.

Degung is the gamelan-based style of music from Sunda, the large western region of Java. It its traditional from it's played on a small ensemble of hanging gongs, a set of pot gongs, a kecapi (plucked zither) and – lending a particular nuance to the music – the suling (bamboo flute). In 1960 Indonesian President Sukarno tried to counter the growing influence of Western music by launching a campaign to promote indigenous styles. A ban on performing Western pop lasted until his downfall in 1965. Whatever the ethical drawbacks of such a policy, it certainly played a large part in the revival of older forms like degung, the creation of new characteristically Indonesian styles like jaipongan and the pop-Sunda scene which successfully fuses Western and indigenous styles.

All nine tracks on **Sound of Sunda** are vocal numbers, mostly solos from the ethereal, breathy-toned female singer Euis Komariah plus a few duets with the richer tones of vocalist Yus Wiradiredja. Large sections of each song are instrumental, and the minimal vocals are sparsely scattered within the subtle texture of Sundanese gongs and metallophones plus two zithers, a two-stringed bass fiddle and suling flute. The ensemble mirrors the vocal line, punctuates it and also sets off on its own magical flights of fancy. Most of the songs are about love lost and longed for, with the duet **Duh Ieung** standing out for its swooping harmony vocals and shimmering gongs. On **Asa Tos Tepang** (the title track of the original cassette release) the zithers lend a touch of warmth to this song of potential romance, while the delicious **Pengkolan** is notable for Komariah's deeply lovelorn vocal as she waits for her lover who doesn't come. Her voice creates a sense of consolation by entwining itself with the wistful sounds of the flute. The closing **Campaka Kambar** is the album's most dramatic track, with a loud outburst on the gamelan, strummed zithers and a growling bass fiddle. It's a poetic text about a dream of two white flowers, but the instrumental picture hints at a deeper drama. This is beautiful music that can get dangerously addictive.

Further listening: Coyor Panyon (Wave, Japan), a landmark album of pop-Sunda by Detty Kurnia, is quite hard to track down but well worth the effort. **Indonesian Popular Music: Kroncong, Dangdut & Langgam Jawa** (Smithsonian Folkways) is a great introduction to other popular Javanese styles.

Kronos Quartet

Pieces Of Africa

Nonesuch, 1992

David Harrington (violin), John Sherba (violin), Hank Dutt (viola), Joan Jeanrenaud (cello), and guests.

Kronos are a string quartet with a difference. Formed in 1973, its members have been dedicated to performing contemporary music from the very beginning. Over the last 25 years, the enthusiasm of leader David Harrington for the world's music has led to collaborations with quite a number of musicians from the World Music scene – including tango master Astor Piazzolla, Tuvan throat-singers Huun-Huur-Tu and Romanian Gypsy band the Taraf de Haidouks – all of whom have their own entries in this book. There might be those that think a Kronos Quartet album doesn't belong here, but just as Paul Simon brought a new audience to Ladysmith Black Mambazo with *Graceland* (see p.165), so Kronos introduced a classical music audience to African music. **Pieces of Africa** is their best-selling recording and has sold over 250,000 copies worldwide.

Kronos commissioned seven African-born composers to write for them. Apart from Kevin Volans, none of them were raised with Western classical music, although several had collaborated with Western musicians – Hamza el-Din with the Grateful Dead, for example. On most of the tracks the composers are also involved as performers on their own instruments.

The Zimbabwean Dumisani Maraire, a leading mbira (thumb piano) master, built his piece, Mai Nozipo (Mother Nozipo), out of Shona melodies. With a classical fast-, slow-fast structure, it comes with a glorious rhythmic swing. Saade (I'm Happy), by

Hassan Hakmoun (see p.71), an international star of Moroccan Gnawa music, provides one of the best fusions of quartet and African sounds on the album its opening phrases on the sintir (Gnawa lute) offset Hakmoun's powerful vocals. Foday Musa Suso is a celebrated kora player from Gambia and a US resident for many years. His piece, **Tilliboyo** (Sunset), is a restrained composition using mostly pizzicato strings to tie into some rather uneventful kora playing. Justinian Tamusuza is Ugandan and **Ekitundu Ekisooka** (First Movement), which was written while he was studying with Kevin Volans in Belfast, relates back to the Kiganda music of his childhood. It is for the quartet alone and brilliantly creates its own distinctive sound, world, with percussive sounds, pizzicato and capricious melodic fragments.

Escalay (Waterwheel), by Nubian oud player Hamza el Din, is a version of a piece he wrote in 1969. The title may have a certain ironic intent, since much of the Sudan had been submerged by the building of the Aswan dam. The music is repetitive and cyclical with a regular organic pulse with woody plucked strings (inspired by the sound of the lute), soft, elliptical bowed melodies and Din's own contributions on the tar (lute). **Wawshishijay** (Our Beginning), by Ghanaian Obo Addy, springs directly from an indigenous tradition, with the quartet playing music built out of a sequence of short melodic fragments accompanied by a tapestry of drums and percussion. Kevin Volans, born in South Africa, is the only white composer represented here and his music grows out of his reaction to the environment around him. In **White Man Sleeps**, Volans doesn't draw on specific traditions, but shows his fascination with free-flowing musical structures. To end, there's an exuberant finale from Maraire. **Kutambarara** (Spreading), an anthemic sing-along with gospel choir, loses some of the intimacy the album had created up to this point, but it neatly makes a musical link between Africa and the US.

> **Further listening: Missa Luba** (Philips) is a powerful setting of the Mass derived from Congolese religious music, while David Fanshawe's **African Sanctus** (Silva Classics), premiered in 1972, is an impressive fusion of African tapes with a Western choir

Fela Kuti

The Best Best Of Fela Kuti: The Black President

Universal/Talkin Loud, 1999

Fela Kuti (vocals, sax, keyboards, drums) and a cast of thousands.

One of the most important artists to emerge from the vibrant West African scene, Fela Kuti was a musical visionary who invented a sound and inspired a generation. It was called Afro-beat, a fecund and intoxicating mix of thundering percussion, call and response vocals sung in pidgin English, riffing brass and radical politics which often led him into trouble with the authorities. But it made him the voice of the dispossessed in his native Nigeria and, like Bob Marley, a spokesmen for black resistance around the globe.

Born in 1938 into the Yoruba tribe, Fela's father was a Protestant minister who hoped that his son would become a doctor. Instead he came to London to study music, returning to Nigeria in 1963 to front a band playing high-life and jazz. It was only after a stay in America in the late 1960s, where he came under the influence of the militant Black Panthers and assimilated elements of funk, that Fela's Afro-beat took on it's distinctive style. With his huge band Africa 70 which incorporated some 20 female dancers and singers, he proceeded to make a prolific string of albums, frequently attacking the Nigerian regime for it's incompetence and corruption. His songs, had a wide appeal thanks to their satire and humour, but this brought constant harassment from the government and in 1977 some 1,000 soldiers attacked and burnt his home and threw his 82 year old mother out of a first-floor window. He refused to moderate his stance and continued to use his music as a political weapon. In

1984 he was sentenced to a prison term for what were widely regarded as trumped-up charges of currency smuggling. When he died of an AIDS-related illness in 1997, an estimated one million mourners attended his funeral in Lagos.

Yet despite Fela's undoubted greatness, his recordings have always been something of a minefield, covering 50 or more albums, characterised by long improvisations which frequently covered both sides of a vinyl LP. Sometimes the results were inspired, sometimes they were self-indulgent. When Afro-beat enjoyed a dancefloor-based revival in the late 1990s, much of Fela Kuti's best work was collected together in two expensive vinyl box sets and a selection of his albums from the 1970s and early 1980s was released on ten "two-for-one" CDs. Fine for the committed fan, but the newcomer needed something more digestible. Fortunately, Femi Kuti, Fela's son and the most exciting contemporary practitioner of Afro-beat, was at hand to compile this double CD. With over two and a half hours of music there are still only 13 tracks – and several of those are edited from longer versions. Yet they genuinely represent the best introduction to Fela's uncompromising legacy.

Lady, later covered by Hugh Masekela, is a simmering, hypnotic brew of keyboards and horns led by Kuti's incendiary sax, topped by a beautifully lilting melody. **Gentleman** is a funkier variation on a similar theme. **Coffin For Head Of State** and **Shuffering and Shmiling** are edited versions of stoned tracks which originally consumed entire albums. **Zombie** is Kuti at his most polemical, a powerfully satirical attack on militarism recorded during a brief exile in Ghana which contains some of his most potent sax playing. **Army Arrangement** is a similarly stinging indictment of the corruption of Nigeria's military regime. Fela Kuti's free-range style contains a built-in resistance to the compilation treatment, and yet probably no performer has ever needed such a collection more. **The Black President** is the perfect compromise between those two imperatives.

Further listening: Femi Kuti's **Shoki Shoki** (Talkin Loud) continues the Afro-beat tradition but with a more contemporary dancefloor sensibility.

Ladysmith Black Mambazo

The Star and the Wiseman

Polygram TV, 1998

Joseph Shabalala (vocals), and others.

That an a cappella South African choir singing in Zulu can fly in the face of pop fashion and sell a million albums is one of the most heartening stories of recent times – and it's all down to a television baked beans commercial. In 1997 Heinz chose the song **Inkanyezi Nezazi** for a high-profile advertising campaign. Released as a single, it gave Ladysmith Black Mambazo an improbable Top 20 hit. **The Star and the Wiseman** is an intelligently chosen compilation of their finest moments, hand-picked by the group's leader Joseph Shabalala to exploit the advert's popularity.

Their rich but softly modulated vocal harmonies are known as iscathamiya, a Zulu word meaning "to step softly" or "tip-toe". The name derives from the dances and songs which men took with them when they migrated from their villages to work in the factories and gold mines. Forced to stay in all-male hostels where their rowdy singing and stomping was banned, they developed the tip-toe style.

Ladysmith Black Mambazo was formed by Shabalala in the early 1960s. Although the composition of the group has varied over the years, it has always been based around two or three closely linked families from the town of Ladysmith (the present line-up includes four of Shabalala's sons). The name means "black axe", a reference to early singing competitions, when their voices cut down all rivals. They were catapulted to international fame by their appearance on Paul Simon's *Graceland* (see p.165), contributing the magical *Homeless* and singing on Simon's own composition *Diamonds on the Soles of Her Shoes*. Both songs appear on this compilation, although "Homeless" is a slightly later version, recorded without the American singer.

Despite the political controversy which surrounded *Graceland* (Simon simply ignored the cultural boycott of South Africa), Ladysmith Black Mambazo's involvement with the project brought them great benefits. The group toured with Simon (the first time they had ever played to racially mixed audiences) and in 1988 he produced their album *Shaku Zulu*. It won a Grammy and is represented here by the captivating *Rain Rain Beautiful Rain*.

The earliest recording here, *Ngelekele*, comes from the group's 1973 debut album, *Amabutho*. It has a rawer sound, but the style in which Shabalala's lead voice weaves through the swelling harmonies has remained characteristic. Mixing songs sung in Zulu and English, the material reflects both Shabalala's strong religious faith and his sense of humour. *Sisesiqhingini* ("we are sitting on top of our own islands") is a witty look at the divide between old and young, with the chorus "everything is so stupid". *Akehlulek'ubaba* ("with God everything is possible") serves the dual purpose of praising both God and the miracle of the new post-apartheid South Africa. The choice of covers, such as *Swing Low Sweet Chariot* and *Knockin' on Heaven's Door*, also reflect Shabalala's faith, although the version of Sam Cooke's *Chain Gang* is horribly lame.

In an attempt to sustain the commercial success of *The Star and the Wiseman*, in 1999 the group recorded *In Harmony*, a pop crossover album that included ill-advised collaborations with the likes of Des'ree and the Lighthouse Family. Yet, at their unadulterated best, Ladysmith's complex vocal harmonies remain one of the most uplifting sounds in World Music.

Further listening: Shaku Zulu (Warners), the Ladysmith album produced by Paul Simon, makes an excellent follow-up. Black Umfolosi, from Zimbabwe, who perform in a similar a cappella style, can be heard to good effect on **Unity** (World Circuit).

Famille Lela de Permet

Polyphonies Vocales et Instrumentales d'Albanie

Indigo/Label Bleu, 1992

Remzi Lela (clarinet, vocals), Myslym Lela (clarinet, vocals), Shqiponja Lela (vocals), Ahmet Lela (accordion, vocals), Fatmir Lela (lute, vocals), Mentor Gega (vocals), Bilali Lela (percussion, vocals), Xhinani Xhihan (percussion, vocals), Čerçiz Mehmeti (violin).

Albanian music doesn't often feature high on the World Music charts. For political reasons it's a country that's been sidelined for years and nowadays only makes news as a result of Balkan conflicts or economic problems. From a musical point of view, it's a great shame because the country is home to some of the most beautiful music in Europe. In the north of the country it's rugged and sinewy – lots of heroic epics and the like, but in the south it is soft, sweet and deeply emotional. In Albania there is a saying that when one person travels he's alone, when two travel they quarrel, but if three travel they sing.

As the title suggests, this music is often a family affair, and the Lela family (now resident in the capital Tirana) comes from the southern town of Përmet, deep in the mountainous south of the country on the Vijosë River and one of its musical centres. At the time of the recording, the leader of the group was clarinettist Remzi Lela, but since his death a couple of years ago Myslym has taken over, although this is essentially ensemble music rather than a vehicle for individual display, with the most fantastic interplay between the gentle sounds of the clarinets, violin, accordion and lute. Bands like this are booked for weddings and parties, and the music is for feasting and dancing. However, despite the celebratory nature of the occasion there's a melancholy feeling to this music which makes it sound very different from the good-time sounds of neighbouring countries like Macedonia, Bulgaria or Greece.

The opening track, **N'Pensheremne e Zotrise Sate** (At the Window of Your House), whisks us straight into the soundworld of this disc. A wailing clarinet invocation, like a human cry, is echoed by the violin supported by a gently plucked lute (llautë) and sighing accordion. A solo voice enters and then the other vocal parts surround it. Vocal sections alternate with short instrumental interludes. What gives the music its character are the wonderful falling intervals on the clarinet, violin and voice that slide from the upper note to the lower one with an emotional sigh.

The following track, **C'u Mgrita Menate** (A Rock Falls from the Mountain), shows its origins in Turkish music with slow, rhapsodic improvisations (kaba) on breathy clarinets and violin before the clarinet gruffly launches into a slow, weaving dance tune with gentle drum and tambourine accompaniment. The music continues with romantic songs and rustic dances, in which the clarinets and violin imitate and tumble around each other with fast, vociferous melodies. Just revel in the poise and seething emotional restraint of **Leskoviqare**, another slow kaba (from Leskoviku), before it slips into the midtempo dance of **Mora Perpjete Čarshine** (I'm Heading for the Woods). This is one of the album's most memorable melodies, sung by smoky-voiced female vocalist Shqiponja.

In the last of the eleven tracks, **Labrishte** (Lament from Laberia), a slow, intense and wistful instrumental introduction leads into an unaccompanied clarinet solo, intoned like a prayer, before the other instruments re-enter while the clarinet, klezmer-like, yelps and screams with passionate outbursts. This is a glorious album of profound music-making, which ends – like the future of the country that produced it – in the air like an unanswered question.

Further listening: Music from Albania (Rounder) is the best all-round introduction to the rich variety of Albanian music-making.

Oscar D'Leon

Los Oscares de Oscar

Top Hits Records, 1996

Oscar Emilio Leon Samoza, better known as Oscar D'Leon, is one of salsa's most lastingly charismatic and dynamic performers and one of its most versatile and talented singers. For over twenty years, "El Sonero Del Mundo" (the world's great salsa singer) has led a magnificent show-band from his hometown Caracas, Venezuela, all around the Americas and into Europe and Asia. Now aged over 50, and with sons Yorman and Jorge Luis frequently on stage with him, his performances still drive female fans to swooning point but the sexy, hip-swivelling dancing and deadpan double-entendres are just a fraction of his attraction. The tall, handsome D'Leon holds audiences rapt with his dynamic, agile voice and his powerful brass-led orchestra. Although his own double-bass playing is nowadays restricted to solos, when he hugs the instrument towards him and dances with it like a long-lost lover, the audience swoons with delight.

Oscar D'Leon took up bass playing and singing when already in his 20s and working as a school bus driver. His passion for Cuban music led him to performing covers of the songs he heard on the radio and in bars and clubs in Caracas. He was a natural sonero from the start, particularly influenced by the Cuban supremo, Beny Moré (see p.123) but also by the trumpet-led Sonora Matancera, the violins-and-flute charanga Orquesta Aragon (see p.141) and the salsa bands who burst onto Latin America from New York in the 1970s. With each of his successive bands, in particular the sensational Dimension Latina, trombones were the key to his unique sound, but he has always experimented with other flavours, usually matching trombones with trumpets and occasionally adding violins, a Cuban tres guitar and even a saxophone. Soaring over the top were his clear, precise vocals.

This 1996 compilation (typically containing no clues as to dates or personnel) includes his first hit, **Lloraras** (You Are Crying), and tributes to the Cubans in **Calculadora**, made famous by Orquesta Aragon and by Beny Moré, **Rumba Rumbero**, written and sung by Miguelito Valdes, and the spicy **Los Tamalitos de Olga** (Olga's Little Buns), by flautist Jose Fajardo. In the latter, D'Leon toughened Fajardo's sweet version with trumpets and trombones and employed his split-chorus trademark – the first half, "los tamalitos", a straight unison between Humberto "Tigre" Becerra and Victor Mendoza and "de Olga" in the quaint nasal old-lady voice (voz de vieja) of traditional son groups. Quintessential late 1980s salsa is provided by **Detalles, Liberate** (Let Yourself Go!), **Poco a Poco** (Little by Little) and **Que Se Sienta** (How She Feels), their smooth, circular rhythms woven by trebly percussion and a tinkly lead cowbell, as D'Leon's tenor flies over trombone choruses and piping trumpets. On the softer salsa numbers, **Lloras** and **Yo La Vi** (I Saw Her), D'Leon's fast, precise tenor and playful scatting are on full show while the flattened trombones recall the sound of Willie Colon (see p.49). **Detalles** is quintessential D'Leon, driven by a jumpy beat, changing mode between the sections, a big joyful salsa rush.

"Calculadora" (the Calculator) must be the fastest chachachá in history: with a snakey rhythm laid down by the guiro scraper, it possesses an irresistible swing an itchy brassiness. D'Leon switches the strings from light, bassy, bobbing pizzicato introduction to fast, unison bowing, while trumpets and trombones harmonies come and go in punchy solos. There is only one thing better than an Oscar D'Leon compilation – a live show. His brilliant control and flair for improvisation mean anything can happen – and usually does.

> **Further listening:** José "El Canario" Alberto's **Herido** (Ryko/Latin) epitomizes the classic sound of New York City. Africando is a supergroup of Senegalese vocalists and top New York-based salseros, with a shared passion for Cuban songs. **Vol. 1 – Trovador** (Stern's Africa) is a compelling variation on the salsa theme.

Cheikh Lô

Né La Thiass

World Circuit, 1996

Cheikh Lô (lead vocals, rhythm guitar), Omar Sow (guitar), N'Deye Marie Ndiaye (vocals), Habib Faye (bass, keyboards), Pathe Diassy (double bass), Mbaye Dieye Faye (percussion), Assane Thiam (talking drum), Thierno Kouyate (saxes), Thomas Vahle (flute), and guests.

Unusually for an African artist, Cheikh Lô is probably better known outside Senegal than he is at home. That he has built his reputation abroad but does not enjoy the same fame or recognition on the streets of Dakar as Youssou N'Dour (see p.129) or Baaba Maal (see p.109) is down to local tastes. The current demand is for pumped-up electric dance grooves and Lô offers a gentler acoustic take on the Senegalese tradition, characterized by rhythmic subtlety and a reflective spirituality based on his adherence to the Baye Fall, a laid-back sect of African Sufis. His long dreadlocks and colourful patchwork clothing are both trademarks of his faith.

Born in Burkina Faso, he grew up speaking the tribal languages of Wolof and Bambara and listening to traditional African music. But at an early age he fell in love with imported Cuban records, an experience that was later to colour his own music. "We didn't understand what they were singing about but we related to the swing and the rhythm. We heard it and we said that is African," he recalls.

Yet Lô had to wait until he was in his forties to taste success. Moving to Senegal in 1978 at the age of 23, he joined the house band at Dakar's most upmarket hotel, the *Savana*, playing drums and singing varieté, bland pop for overseas tourists. By 1985 he had migrated to Paris, where he worked for two years as a studio musician. He finally got to make his first record back in Senegal in 1990, a low-cost cassette of the kind which dominates the West African market. Eventually Youssou heard him playing in a Dakar club and offered to produce an album intended to launch Lô on the world stage. Due to Youssou's own busy schedule, they were unable to begin recording until 1995. **Né La Thiass** was released the following year on Youssou's Jololi label in Senegal and licensed internationally to World Circuit.

To say the album caught the public by surprise is an understatement. Youssou's name on the production credits generated expectations of the pulsating, high-octane grooves of mbalax, the dominant strand of modern Senegalese dance music. Instead, from the opening bars of the first track, **Boul di Tagale** (Let Lovers Be), it is clear that something quite different is going on. A syncopated acoustic guitar is accompanied by tama (talking drum) and flute before Lô's high, soulful vocal enters and they embark upon a six-minute jazzy improvisation rippling with both African and Cuban inflexions.

The title track, **Né La Thiass** (Gone in a Flash), is even better, with an almost flamenco-style acoustic guitar and an infectiously swaying rhythm. **Doxandeme** (The Immigrant), with its impassioned vocal and unobtrusive sax, is a song about Lô's less than happy Parisian experiences, but the undoubted highlight is **Set** (Cleanliness), on which Lô's high, sweet voice duets with Youssou's deeper baritone soaring above a rippling accompaniment as the song builds to its extraordinarily hypnotic climax. The album closes with a trio of songs about Lô's faith, the best of which is **Guiss Guiss** (Take a Good Look), a mesmerizing hymn-like dedication to his personal marabout, or holy man, that is pure African gospel.

The album's appeal lies in its unique but accessible marriage of a warm and intimate spirituality with a groove that defies you to keep your feet still – a dance album for the soul.

> **Further listening:** Cheikh Lô's **Bambay Gueej** (World Circuit) is a worthy follow-up to *Né La Thiass*. For another beautifully mellow Senegalese album, try **Iso** (Barclay) from Ismael Lô, no relation.

Paco de Lucía

Siroco

Mercury, 1987

Paco de Lucía (guitar, production), José Maria Bandera (second guitar), Ramon de Algeciras (second guitar), Ruben Dantas (cajon, second guitar), Pepe de Lucia (palmas), Juan Ramirez (dancer).

Paco de Lucía is the most important figure in modern flamenco guitar and, since flamenco is the most technically and emotionally demanding of all guitar styles, this makes him one of the greatest guitarists of all time. Flamenco, as both music and dance, springs so directly from the heart and soul that it is unsurprising that Paco finds it impossible to describe what he does or how he does it: "I don't know how to define music because I'm not a schooled musician. I have entered it and I live with the music through an intuitive perception."

Born in Algeciras in 1947 into a payo (or non-Gypsy) family, Paco has been setting new standards for flamenco guitar ever since his first teenage performances in the early 1960s. He has always been innovative and pioneering in his approach, elaborating the finger and thumb techniques of the right hand, for instance, and dispensing with the capo to play the different toques or flamenco styles, which are each set in a certain key. The resulting use of the whole fingerboard introduced dramatic new harmonic and chordal possibilities, which in turn led the singers he was accompanying, notably Camarón (see p.39), to reinvent their own approach.

Every one of Paco's recordings and collaborations has had both his admirers and competitors hanging on his latest move. In the early 1980s he created his sextet (adding electric bass, Latin percussion, flute and sax, most of which were quite new to flamenco). He wrote film scores for director Carlos Saura, including reworkings of Bizet's *Carmen* and Manuel de Falla's *El Amor Brujo* (rearranging the orchestra for guitar), and was the first flamenco guitarist to record Rodrigo's famous *Concierto de Aranjuez*. However Paco is a man conscious of his standing and place in history, and was aware these were creating a distance between himself and his purer flamenco path and audience. In 1987 he set himself to record, apart from a little percussion and *palmas* (hand claps), his first solo disc in a decade.

The resulting **Siroco** is astoundingly good. You're hit first by the power of the playing – Paco has the large thick hands, and build, of a farm labourer, which makes his right hand immensely strong in the rhythm. The ferocity of the tangos La Cañada, the alegrias La Barrosa or the bulerías El Pañuelo suggests a man out to prove a point. The sound just cracks, pounds and explodes from the instrument. Yet a tender, human element in his work is never far away – listen to the poignant delicacy of the minera Callejón del Muro, or the closing soleá, Gloria al Niño Ricardo, a tribute to flamenco guitarist Niño Ricardo, one of Paco's greatest influences. With hindsight one can now hear how many of Paco's stylistic innovations, such as the octave soloing on the rumba Caña de Azuca, have found their way into the flamenco guitar repertoire.

No other single disc of flamenco guitar contains such a panorama of skill and emotion as *Siroco*: Paco tears himself apart right in front of you. To perform at this level of demonic intensity on a regular basis would be untenable, and playing live Paco prefers to let his band take a lot of the weight off his shoulders. He has nothing left to prove. The sirocco is known as an ill wind and whatever devils Paco was wrestling with at the time he recorded *Siroco* resulted in a session as quintessentially flamenco as you will find.

> **Further listening:** The Paco de Lucía Sextet can be heard on **Live One Summer Night** (Philips). All younger flamenco guitarists are influenced by Paco, but the brilliant Rafael Riqueni, heard at his best on **Mi Tiempo** (Nuevos Medios), has managed to take his own path.

Baaba Maal

Nomad Soul

Palm Pictures, 1998

Baaba Maal (vocals, guitar), Kawding Cissokho (kora), Assane Ndoye Cisse (guitars), Hilaire Chaby Hagy (keyboards), Alione Diouf (drums), Elhadj Niang (bass), Massamba Diop (tama), Barou Sali (hoddu), Mansour Seck (backing vocals), and guests.

The charismatic and flamboyant Baaba Maal is the only rival to Youssou N'Dour as Senegal's biggest star, but in truth the two men have very different musical styles. Maal comes from the country's remote northern region, on the edge of the Sahel, across the shallow and crocodile-infested Niger River from Mauritania. As a northener, his voice has a more intense Islamic flavour and he sings in the Pulaar language rather than the main Senegalese tongue of Wolof favoured by N'Dour. His band is tellingly called Daande Lenõl ("voice of the race") and he is a keen preserver of ethnic and linguistic identity. Yet, like his friend and rival, Maal has also courted international success in collaboration with Western artists and the atmospheric **Nomad Soul** finds him working with Brian Eno, Howie B and Sinéad O'Connor among others.

Born into a noble family, Maal is not a griot (one of the ancient caste of singers and storytellers) and his parents hoped he would become a doctor or lawyer. Instead, after university in Dakar and Paris, he embarked on a tour of West Africa researching traditional music with his friend, the blind griot Mansour Seck. After a series of cassette-only, local acoustic releases, the best of which has since been re-released on CD (see below), he finally began to make an international impact when he moved to Chris Blackwell's Mango label in 1991.

Baayo, his first album for Mango, was strongly acoustic and traditional in flavour but Maal spread his wings dramatically on the more eclectic *Lam Toro* (produced by Simon Emmerson) and grew progressively more adventurous with each subsequent release. *Firin' in Fouta* in 1994 was a thrilling mix of ancient and modern with jazz, salsa, rap and reggae beats, alongside the traditional African influences. Interestingly, Maal claims reggae as a cousin of yela, a beat characteristic of his region. "It is an imitation of the pounding of the grain. The structure is the same as reggae. The rhythm between the calabash and the clapping of the hands is the same as between the kick drum and the guitar in Jamaican music."

Nomad Soul is easily Maal's most complete release to date. Recorded in Dakar, London, Kingston and New York, it is a truly global mix that still manages to remain deeply rooted in tradition. It opens with **Souka Nayo** (I Will Follow You), which marries Celtic voices with Maal's own high wail, like the muezzin calling the faithful to prayer, before a hypnotic bass-line kicks in and his kora player Kawding Cissokho begins to weave his magic alongside the sound of an Irish harp. The track is produced by Emmerson, whose Afro Celt Sound System (see p.3) made an entire career out of exploring the musical trade routes between Dakar and Dublin. **Africans Unite (Yolela)** is a charged-up slice of African reggae on which the deep voice of the Jamaican star Luciano combines sensuously with Maal's higher register. **Mbolo**, **Iawa** and **Guelel** are perfect examples of how traditional instrumentation – talking drums, kora and hoddu (lute) – can be seamlessly integrated with contemporary programmed grooves. **Douwayra** is a percussive storm which fuses traditional and modern beats, and the album reaches an explosive climax with **Lam Lam**, a long and magnificently shimmering soundscape produced by Brian Eno, Howie B and Jon Hassell, with haunting vocals by Maal. Here past and future seem to collide somewhere between outer space and an ancient Saharan village to create a new African music for the 21st century.

> **Further listening**: The marvellous 1984 acoustic album, **Djam Leeli** (Yoff/Palm Pictures), made by Maal and his mentor Mansour Seck, is now re-released on CD with added tracks.

Miriam Makeba and the Skylarks

The Best of Miriam Makeba and the Skylarks

BMG Camden, 1998

Miriam Makeba (vocals), Abigail Kubeka, Sam Ngakane, Mummy Girl Nketle, Mary Rabotapi, Nomonde Suhawu (all vocals), and studio musicians.

Arguably the best-loved singer ever to come out Africa, Miriam Makeba – like so many victims of apartheid – has led a tragic life that forced her to spend more than three decades in exile. During those years she made dozens of albums, yet it is her early recordings (sung in Xhosa and Zulu) made in Johannesburg, before she was cruelly cut off from her roots, that remain her most powerfully enduring work. Today she is "Mama Africa", but when she came out of township poverty in 1953 to sing with Nelson Mandela's favourite group, the Manhattan Brothers, she was still a wide-eyed girl. From there she went on to front her own all-female vocal group, the Skylarks, with whom she made her greatest recordings between 1957 and 1959, the cream of which are collected on this mid-price compilation.

Before she left her homeland, Makeba made an appearance in *Come Back Africa*, an American documentary which had been shot covertly about conditions under apartheid. In 1959 she attended the film's premiere at the Venice Film Festival without the permission of the South African authorities and travelled on to America, where she was befriended by Harry Belafonte. Prevented from returning home again until after Mandela was released from prison in 1990, she was even refused permission to attend her mother's funeral. When in 1963 she made an impassioned testimony about the evils of apartheid before a United Nations committee, the apartheid government banned all her records. Newsreel footage of the speech turns up in television documentaries from time to time and the simple and moving directness of her oratory still brings a lump to the throat. Yet, primarily, Makeba was not a politician but a singer. It was the power of her music that turned her into a spokeswoman for her people and it often seemed that South Africa's tragedy was echoed in her own sacrifice and turbulent personal life – during her exile her daughter Bongi died in tragic circumstances, and Miriam had five (not always happy) marriages with husbands including the South African trumpeter Hugh Masekela and Black Panther activist Stokely Carmichael.

There is a timeless quality about her early South African recordings that will never age. The version here of her most famous song, Phatha Phatha, possesses a gently swaying grace and beauty, her voice full of simple emotion against a simply strummed guitar, bass and drums accompaniment and Spokes Mashiyane's pennywhistle – the "kwela" sound then enjoying a craze in the townships. The same session produced Inkomo Zodwa and Ekoneni, both by the talented South African song writer Gibson Kente and also featuring Spokes' extraordinary whistle. Recorded in August 1959, less than two weeks before Makeba was to leave her country and her daughter knowing she might never return, it is not fanciful to believe that the intensity in her voice – which somehow expresses both hope for a better future and deep sorrow – was directly related to her personal circumstances.

Elsewhere her talents as a composer as well as a singer are evident, both on her arrangements of traditional material such as Kutheni Sithandwa (which Belafonte was to adapt for his "Banana Boat Song") and her own melodic compositions such as Vula Aamsango and Owakho. Backed by the exquisite harmonies of the Skylarks and the pick of the studio musicians at Gallo, South Africa's oldest record label, these recordings have a rare emotional directness that resonates to this day.

Further listening: Township Jazz and Jive (Nascente) is a fine collection of the best of 1950s township music, while **The Very Best of the Manhattan Brothers** (Gallo) captures South Africa's first black supergroup at their height.

Samba Mapangala and Orchestre Virunga

Virunga Volcano

Earthworks 1990

Samba Mapangala (vocals), Fataki Lokassa (second vocal), Lawi Somana (lead guitar), Bansilu wa Bansilu (bass), Rodie and Atei (sax), Shaban Onyango (drums), Kalvin and Loboko (second guitar); also features Sammy Mansita (lead guitar), Siama Matuzungidi (second guitar), Diabanza Walengo (bass), Lover "Machine" (drums).

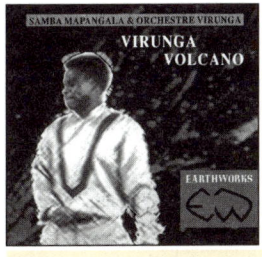

This is one of the great guitar discs in the history of African music. In the late 1970s and early 1980s, the Nigerian capital, Nairobi, offered a range of opportunities that drew musicians from throughout East and Central Africa and made it one of the most exciting musical environments in Africa. This was the situation in 1977, when Samba Mapangala first rolled into Nairobi with his group Les Kinois. The Congolese-born musician had spent the previous year performing at a club in Kampala (Uganda) and, in the year prior to that, had toured throughout eastern Zaire. Unfortunately, the combination of Kenyan visa problems and an ill-fated engagement in Kampala (in which soldiers attacked members of the band) led to the break-up of the group in 1980. Samba wanted to return to Kinshasa (Congo) to recruit new band members but needed money. To raise the cash, he made a deal with Nairobi's Polygram studio to record four songs for an album. Since he no longer had a band, he rounded up some of his musician friends, recorded the songs, and named his scratch ensemble Orchestre Virunga – after a range of volcanic mountains in the eastern Congo.

The four songs recorded in 1981 were released as an LP entitled *Malako*. **Virunga Volcano** combines those four tracks with two additional songs recorded in 1983 by the performing Orchestre Virunga. The disc was important for the way it incorporated common elements of Congolese and East African music in a completely new way. The sound is lean but with complex, interlocking guitar lines, a percussive and rhythmic bass, fast-paced percussion and with a sax duo providing solos and embellishment. Another notable quality of the Samba/Virunga sound was the sheer quality of the product: in particular, each of the songs is propelled by Samba's voice with its tremendous range, power and perfect intonation.

The opening song, Malako, immediately sets the tone for the whole album. Samba introduces it with a slow, powerful vocal solo before the song breaks into an uptempo dance beat with streaks of pulsing bass and the rich intertwining of rhythm and lead guitar. The track's remaining eight minutes take us on a slowly evolving journey in which Samba (singing in the Lingala language) tells of his mother's dying wish that he should take care of his younger brothers after she is gone. Solo verses are contrasted with three-part harmonies, followed by delicate guitar solos, sweet sax duets with rhythmic bass streaming from low to high registers. Ahmet Sabit opens with a smooth and flowing sax duet over a choppy, syncopated rhythm. Two minutes later, we're listening to a light fluffy guitar interlude that suddenly breaks into a brilliant, flowing, high-energy guitar solo. Virunga, the band's calling card, is rather restrained at its opening, but soon breaks into a fast dance with alternating solo and harmony vocals, and choppy sax and tingling guitar breaks set against a ringing high-hat. Yembele, with its complex moralizing lyrics, is a more subdued song, although there is still room for a nimble guitar solo. Neliya and Mansita, from the 1983 session, return to the high-energy mould that characterizes most of this album: both start with a mid-tempo song that then breaks into an extended uptempo dance section. Although Samba Mapangala and Virunga have gone on to record several other albums, their debut has a sunny warmth that makes it a classic.

Further listening: Guitar Paradise of East Africa (Earthworks/Sterns) a delightful collection of '80s material that includes the classic Congolese East African hit by Orchestra Super Mazembe, "Shauri Yako".

Thomas Mapfumo

The Best of Thomas Mapfumo

EMI Hemisphere, 1995

Thomas Mapfumo (vocals, mbira), Chartwell Dutiro, Choruwa Benjura, Basil Makombe, Ngoni Makombe (all mbiras), Jonah Sithole, Ephraim Karimaura (both guitars), Ashton Sugar Chiweshe (guitar), Charles Makokova (keyboards, bass), Washington Kavhayi (bass), Chartwell Sutiro (sax), Everson Chibhami (trumpet), Ernest Ncube (trumpet), Canaan Kamoyo (trombone), Sabastian Mbata (drums), Lancelot Mapfumo (congas).

Thomas Mapfumo, the legendary Lion of Zimbabwe, has been his country's most famous musician for more than twenty years. A virtuoso on the mbira (thumb piano), an instrument strongly associated with his Shona people of Zimbabwe, Mapfumo has also adopted a strongly political stance, having forged the chimurenga ("struggle") style of resistance songs "to encourage the boys who were fighting in the bush".

Born in 1945, he began his career in the 1960s by covering American rock'n'roll and soul hits. By the mid-1970s, as Rhodesia worked its painful way towards independence, he had dropped the covers and embraced Shona culture. Singing in his own language, he placed the electrified mbira at the heart of the new sound, a symbolic reclaiming of indigenous traditions in the face of a regime that had taught its black population that its own culture was worthless. The music became a crucial tool in the liberation war as Mapfumo formed first the Acid Band and then, in 1978, Blacks Unlimited. The mbira has always been a spiritual tool, used for summoning the spirits of the ancestors and Mapfumo became simultaneously both traditionalist and modernizer: he took the country's most ancient and sacred instrument and made it the main vehicle for a new form of popular music, drawing on contemporary

African sounds to reinterpret his own traditions. He also transposed the mbira's slowly shifting cyclical rhythms onto the guitar. The result was a uniquely Zimbabwean guitar sound of which the great Jonah Sithole, a mainstay of Blacks Unlimited, until his death in the mid-1990s, was a master.

Chimurenga inevitably attracted the disapproval of Ian Smith's regime. Mapfumo's records were banned from the radio and in 1977 he was held in detention for ninety days without trial. He continued to write overtly political songs, at times disguising their message in Shona proverbs and metaphor. Although his musical switch was initially greeted with incomprehension, the style was soon widely influential on a new generation of artists.

This compilation is drawn from Mapfumo's work between the years 1977 and 1993. At the heart of the music is the mbira, often used in threes to create meshing, trance-like harmonic patterns that are surprisingly subtle in their complexity. The drum beat has much in common with the kick drum of mbaqana, the South African township style: guitars spin and chatter, adding their own hypnotic patterns, and Mapfumo's rough but appealing voice sings of both the political struggle and the commonplace events of African life. **Shuma** is typical chimurenga, Sithole's deceptively simple guitar driving the track while Mapfumo warns of spies who are out to undermine the liberation struggle. **Vanhu Vatema** contains a simple but powerful message delivered in prophet-like tones, while **Zvenyika** uses a more upbeat rhythm to recall a time before politics turned life into a trial. Even after the birth of independent Zimbabwe in 1980, Mapfumo kept his political edge and **Ndavekuenda** warns the country's leaders to remain humble and stay in touch with the people, using a traditional call-and-response chant. Other songs, however, have no agenda, and **Nyarara Mukadzi Wangu** and **Hanzvadzi** are based on ancient allegorical folk tales.

> **Further listening**: Oliver "Tuku" Mtukudzi, the second giant of Zimbabwean music, has a soulful voice and accessible style. A selection of his best work can be heard on **Shoko** (Piranha).

Maurice El Médioni

Café Oran

Piranha, 1996

Maurice El Médioni (piano), Michel Rebibo (vocals), David Krakauer (clarinet), Frank London (trumpet), Sabah Habas Mustapha (bass guitar), Mahmoud Fadl (percussion), Marco Maimaran (kit drum).

Alongside the famous names of World Music and the landmark recordings, there are many less well-known artists who simply have a magic that is irresistible. The Algerian-Jewish piano player Maurice El Médioni is one of them. He may not be a major figure in the history of his country's music, but in the Berlin studio where this album was made, the right people came together to create something special – with a quirky, understated sense of humour all its own.

Whether Café Oran was a real place isn't clear. But if it was, it might have been located a couple of streets back from the waterfront of the bustling port of Oran – the city which gave birth to rai. In the 1940s such a café would have been frequented by sophisticated Arab and Jewish Oranais, colonial French, Americans who had liberated the city in 1942, not to mention the diverse and sleazy clientele that pass through any port. Or perhaps it was in Marseilles (where Médioni now lives), a meeting place for Algerian expats nostalgically savouring the atmosphere of the city they had left behind.

Médioni was born in 1928, taught himself the piano at an early age and frequented Oran's American bars in the 1940s. His big loves were boogie-woogie and Cuban music, and his style is born of the fusing of these distinct influences with Arabic music. The piano is, of course, a European instrument, but in Médioni's hands the melodies take on a middle eastern character, subtly decorated and turning round on themselves in modal arabesques. On **Café Oran** he is joined by the Moroccan-born singer Michel Rebibo (who sings in Arabic and French), master-percussionist Mahmoud Fadl (see p.59) and by two members of The Klezmatics (see p.91) on clarinet and trumpet.

Médioni's infectious, jazzy rhythms are apparent from the first few bars of Bienvenue/Abiadi. It's a welcome song, sung in French with a catchy tune that doesn't let go of you. Médioni adds light, ornamental twists around the melody and the whole thing is driven along by delicate percussion on a goblet drum. The next track Taktouk Andalou/Ghazalati is based on an Egyptian rhythm, over which Médioni weaves his gently arching melodic lines. His piano technique generally consists of florid phrases which are given a harmonic context by the occasional chord. Rai Rock Rumba is more robust, an Arabic boogie-woogie with dark murmurings on clarinet and a restless bassline. Ma Testahalchi begins with a slow wistful piano solo, which then slips into an uptempo number in which Médioni switches from one melody to another and one rhythm to the next. It's like a journey through a souk, with a tempting trinket here, a wafting aroma there; sometimes a phrase that's loud and assertive, then another that's tantalizingly elusive. It's followed by one of the album's highlights, Ya Maalem/Kelbi Razahi. Opening with a bold and brassy trumpet melody in a rumba rhythm, it's a song in praise of Médioni and an invitation to party. There's a great clarinet solo, twisting the notes high up on the instrument, a prayer-like vocal incantation and a rhythmic finish. The final track, Cocktail Andalou, is a strange melancholy solo – Médioni's improvisation is like a lament for a world lost forever and a life nearing its close but, like the old pro that he is, he prefers to end with a smile and the song concludes with a lighthearted coda.

> **Further listening:** The late Reinette l'Oranaise, a pupil of Médioni's uncle, was a marvellous singer and oud player. The retrospective **Mémoires** (Blue Silver) was recorded shortly before her death in 1998.

Mighty Sparrow

25th Anniversary

Charlie's, 1980

Mighty Sparrow (vocals) Professor Art De Coteau (arranger, conductor).

It's been said that the whole history of Trinidad can be told through calypso and it's true that nowhere else in the world has quite such a lively and potent tradition of musical comment and satire. Calypso was first recorded in 1914 and throughout the twentieth century calypsonians strove to represent the voice of the people in matters of everyday life and politics. Over the last 25 years or so there's been a shift of emphasis as soca, a newer form of dance-led party-style music, has emerged, but still the wit of the calypso voice lives on. What's more, the lyrics are in English – or at least a colourful and poetic form of it.

Calypso music is centred on the annual carnival in Trinidad and Tobago when normal life stops for days of revelry, otherwise know as mas. The Calypso Monarch prize is given by a panel of judges to the best calypso, and the Road March title goes to the most-played calypso – the people's choice. The leading postwar calypsonian is Slinger Francisco, better known as Mighty Sparrow. Born in 1935 in Grenada, he moved to Trinidad at an early age. Initially, senior calypsonians ridiculed him for jumping around like a little sparrow when he sang. Sparrow confidently used the slight to his own advantage by adding the prefix "Mighty" and going on to become the most successful calypsonian of all time. He first won the Monarch prize in 1956 with "Jean and Dinah", a song about the effect of the closure of the American base on the country's prostitutes, and then formally resigned from the competition in 1974 to give others a chance.

Calypso isn't a form that lends itself naturally to an album – although there are great individual songs. Every year compilations are released of the best carnival songs, but, as a lot of the music is topical or just intended for partying, they tend to have a sell-by date. This disc is an exception, commemorating Sparrow's **25th Anniversary**, it has all the ingredients that make him the leader in the field – the outgoing rhythmic energy, the melodic gift, the sexual explicitness (an important element in calypso) and the verbal wit.

Highlights include the tingling and exuberant Love African Style ("When she settle down to romance, you won't stand a chance without injurance. Her loving is like sugar, it's part of her own culture that comes from she grandmother in Africa"), Save De World ("Stop searching strife, stop taking life, stop making bombs"), which tries to get beyond the parochialism of calypso and address global issues, and London Bridge, which blames Britain's decline on its female monarch and the recently elected Margaret Thatcher ("In a land that used to be strong there's a women boss in the town and the next one wearing the crown, London bridge is fallin' down").

In You Mad he addresses the local housing problems and in Rum is Macho urges people to drink local rum rather than imported whisky. He also serves up several excellent party tracks, Play You Mas, Mas in Caracas and Don't Drop the Tempo, showing that Sparrow has no problems turning his hand to soca. Art de Couteau's arrangements generally include exuberant horns, a throbby bass, rattling percussion and assorted effects – computer-game-style gunfire on Dead or Alive, and whistles, squeals and assorted electronic good-time noises for the carnival songs. The only drawback to this disc is that, as with most releases on calypso labels, there's no personnel information, recording dates or lyrics.

> **Further listening: 16 Carnival Hits** (Ice) includes the best recordings of two veteran postwar calypsonians, Mighty Sparrow and the carnival-loving Lord Kitchener. **The Rough Guide to Calypso and Soca** (World Music Network) makes an excellent introduction to the music.

Mila na Utamaduni

Spices of Zanzibar

Network, 1996

Mila na Utamaduni/Culture Musical Club taarab orchestra and singers.

Should Ry Cooder ever wish to work his Buena Vista magic elsewhere, he should head to the spice islands of Zanzibar off the east coast of Africa. Not only are there great old-time musicians, both instrumentalists and singers, but there are ready-made "social clubs" playing seductive taarab music on a regular basis.

The sounds of a taarab orchestra in the whitewashed streets of Stone Town, the capital, are just as evocative as the beautiful dhow boats with their elegant triangular sails that transport the fruits and spices on which its reputation was built. The taarab melodies really swing as they're sawn out by a bank of nine violins (in this band) in the manner of an Egyptian film orchestra with swoops and slides between the notes. There are splashes of colour from Arabic instruments like the oud (lute) and qanun (plucked zither); a couple of accordions, which take important solos, and supporting it all is a bed of percussion from dumbak (goblet drum), bongos and rika (tambourine) playing essentially African rhythms.

The word taarab comes from the Arabic tariba, "to be moved or agitated", and legend has it that the music had its origins when a Zanzibari was sent to Cairo in the 1870s to learn the qanun. In Stone Town the Ikhwani Safaa Social Club members were so impressed that in 1905 they ordered more instruments from Egypt and formed the first taarab orchestra. In those days the orchestras played for the Oman Sultans who controlled the islands and for the cultured elite. Since independence in 1964, the music has become more democratic, with a preference for songs over instrumental music. Mila na Utamaduni (Culture Musical Club) is one of two big taarab orchestras that dominate the Zanzibar music scene, the other is the still-thriving Ikhwani Safaa Musical Club, which celebrated its ninetieth birthday in 1995. Culture's roots go back to 1958, but it adopted its current name in 1964, when it became something like the national taraab orchestra under the Ministry of Culture. Since 1981 it has been an autonomous club where the musicians meet and practise for concerts and performances at weddings and Islamic holidays.

This disc is a great selection of nine catchy tracks ranging through the band's typical repertoire. It opens with an instrumental number – a bashraf (a word which surely derives from the Arabic peshrev, an instrumental prelude) – which is typically played as wedding guests arrive. We hear the rich string sound of the orchestra – nine violins (played under the chin rather than upright, in true Arabic style), cello and double bass – in a langourous, repeated melody interspersed with solo spots for accordion, followed by orchestra leader and first violinist Khamis Shehes and then Maulidi Haj on qanun.

What follows is a series of vocal numbers, including performances by top singers Makame Faki, Fatma Issa and Saada Mohamed. Some of these songs are romantic, others venture into social criticism. Taarab is sung poetry so the words are important. They are always audible, lightly accompanied by percussion and violin, oud or qanun, and one of the attractions is the way the orchestra bursts in and moves things along between the vocal lines. There's also a second instrumental bashraf with reflective solos on oud, played by Said Nassor, accordion and violin.

> **Further listening: Bashraf** (Dizim) features newly recorded instrumental music from Mila na Utamaduni. GlobeStyle have released four excellent discs from Zanzibar, including **Nyota: Classic Taarab from Tanga**, which highlights a more dance-oriented style from the northern coast of Tanzania.

Beny Moré

Cuban Originals – Beny Moré

RCA Original Masters/BMG

Uncredited performances, but almost certainly featuring pianist Damaso "Perez" Prado and trumpeter Alfredo "Chocolate" Armenteros.

Nearly fifty years since his death in 1963, Beny Moré's reputation as Cuba's most beloved singer shows no sign of diminishing. Records like this near-perfect compilation of songs recorded between 1949 and 1958 will convert new generations to the magic of his romantic boleros and life-enhancing, big-band mambos and son songs.

Beny Moré's stage shows, on Cuban television and in the swankiest and most exotic Havana nightclubs, are remembered for the intricate precision and superb musicianship of his Banda Gigante and for the singer's highly personal appearance and performances. A straw hat, a walking stick and the baggiest zoot suits were his uniform; an intricate set of improvised dance steps were an entertaining reminder of the moves he learned as a child in the African ceremonies of his country village.

But Beny Moré's greatest appeal was his voice. In quintessential boleros like Como Fue (How it Used to Be) and Tu Me Sabes Comprender (You Know How to Understand Me), he soars to a high note and settles there, warbling across whole bars like a bird of prey gliding across thermals. The tone is molten gold and at times reminiscent of Nat King Cole – a regular visitor to the *Tropicana*, where Moré also sang. For the brassy dancing frenzy of mambos and uptempo son montunos like Bonito y Sabroso (Pretty and Tasty), Santa Isabel de las Lajas, Que Bueno Baila Usted (How Well You Dance) and Francisco Guayabal, he adopts the rougher, cruder pitch associated with the country traditions.

Moré's themes include romantic love, tributes to friends and musicians and also dancing. The smouldering smoocher "Como Fue" finds Beny boosting the lyrics ("It was your lips or your mouth, your hands or your voice…") with a tremolo effect, while a muted trumpet chorus enhances the sense of desperation. In Hoy Como Ayer (Today Like Yesterday) the convincing vocal emotion is undermined by the slapstick melodrama of La Banda's rattling, crashing drum breaks and dramatic stop-start effects.

The relaxed, choppy pace of Beny Moré's tribute to his birthplace, "Santa Isabel de las Lajas", is broken by sharp solo trumpet phrases, against which he delivers a long, slow, rap-like chant. Nostalgia for the rural life he deserted in 1940 also figures in Compay José (My Mate, José), a sharp, brassy transformation of acoustic country son in which the wistful lyrics (about a thatched hut and eating chicken and rice by the riverside) are countered by the unmistakably urban backing. Rumberos de Ayer (Yesterday's Rumba Musicians) is a melancholy tribute to the great African-Cuban drummers, most particularly to conga player Chano Pozo, who was murdered in New York in 1948. There are many songs about dancing. Bonito y Sabroso is an exuberant debate about the relative sexiness and dancing merits of Cubans and Mexicans – Moré lived in Mexico City for several years in the 1940s – endorsed by shudderingly erotic conga beats and repetitive, sizzling trumpet choruses. The chorus of the evergreen people-mover, "Que Bueno Baila Usted", praises Beny's dancing skills.

With the absence of personnel lists on any Beny Moré records, one is forced to make guesses. Pachito E'Che, recorded in 1950 (Moré's last year in Mexico City was spent performing with the ultimate mambonik, Perez Prado), features all the Prado trademarks – screeching trumpets, an anarchic, free-jazz piano solo and his unmistakable grunts and groans. It is a fabulous reminder of a magical partnership between two wild Cuban geniuses.

> **Further listening:** The four-CD box set, **Cuba: I Am Time** (Blue Jackal Records), is a comprehensive account of twentieth-century Cuban music, from earliest acoustic trios to the brashest salsa big bands nearly a hundred years later.

Muzsikás and Márta Sebestyén

Morning Star

Hannibal, 1997

Márta Sebestyén (lead vocals), Mihály Sipos (fiddle), László Porteleki (fiddle), Péter Éri (kontra, mandolin), Dániel Hamar (bass, gardon, cimbalom), plus guests.

Hungarian vocalist Márta Sebestyén has one of those natural voices that is arresting and expressive whether you understand the language or not. Her mother was a music teacher (and student of Hungary's celebrated composer and ethnomusicologist Zoltán Kodály) and although Márta grew up in Budapest she convincingly emulates a peasant style of singing with a rawness of tone. The same is true of Muzsikás, the band with whom she regularly works.

The Hungarian roots revival, known as the táncház (dancehouse) movement, took off in the 1970s largely as a reaction to the sanitized folklore groups favoured by the Communist regime. Musicians, singers and dancers went to rural districts to learn genuine folk music, then reproduced it in the táncház clubs back home. Most of these musicians (Márta Sebestyén and Muzsikás included) flocked to the Hungarian communities of Transylvania in neighbouring Romania, where there is a flourishing village music tradition to this day. Many have formed alliances with great Gypsy musicians of the region and learned directly from them. Muzsikás have successfully married an authentic, village-style approach to professional concert and recording techniques and have become the leading representatives of their music on tour and on disc.

Morning Star's nine tracks are virtually all from Transylvania – the music Muzsikás love most and do best. The disc opens with a fabulous nine-and-a-half-minute medley of wedding dances and songs from Füzes, played as they might be at a wedding party, with one dance neatly segueing into the next as the tempo is jacked up a notch. Here is the typical Transylvanian sound – a couple of fiddles playing sprightly tunes over a rhythmic bed of sawing bass and off-beat chords played on the kontra, an accompanying viola with three strings. Márta Sebestyén contributes some great songs, notably **My Mother's Rosebush**, a touching allegorical lyric often sung as a farewell to the bride at weddings. Péter Éri takes over the idiomatic fiddle playing.

Muzsikás generate variety by picking material from three regions of Transylvania, each with its own musical style. Most distinctive is the wild music from Gyimes (**Round Dance of Gyimes**, **Cry Only on Sundays**) in the Carpathian mountains, where the typical ensemble is a duo of fiddle and gardon, a percussive cello struck with a stick. Less traditional is **If I Were a Rose**, the juxtaposition of a Hungarian song and a Bashkirian song from Siberia with khöömei (throat singing) from András Berecz to underline the connections to the Hungarians' ancestral origins in the Siberian steppe. The title track (which closes the album) is a song that was sung before soldiers were called away to the army as they waited for the rising of the "morning star" that signalled their departure. It was learned from Sándor (Neti) Fodor, one of the great fiddlers of Transylvania.

This album demonstrates the enduring beauty and power of traditional Transylvanian music. Although some may find the playing style rough-edged at first hearing, that roughness is an intrinsic part of the music and real village bands are even grittier. Muzsikás and Márta Sebestyén don't pretty things up too much for the international market – they quite rightly trust in the quality of the material itself.

> **Further listening:** For those wanting to sample the real thing, Sándor Fodor's **Hungarian Folk Music from Transylvania** (Hungaroton) can't be recommended too highly. If you want more of Márta Sebestyén, try **Kismet** (Hannibal), a solo album featuring songs from several different traditions including Bosnian, Hindi and Irish.

Le Mystère des Voix Bulgares

Le Mystère des Voix Bulgares

4AD, 1986

Choir of the Bulgarian Radio and Television, with soloists Yanka Rupkina, Kalinka Vatcheva and Stefka Sabotinova.

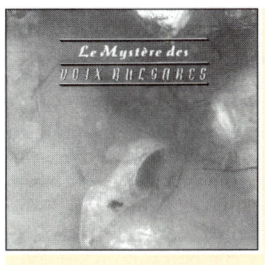

It's no exaggeration to say that this disc kick-started a whole surge of interest in Bulgarian music and in particular the striking, dissonant, "open-throated" style of women's singing. It's not so much the melody, or even the harmony, but the timbre of the voices that attracts attention – powerful, elemental and heart-rending. The music has been used in films and adverts, and there are three further volumes in the French version of this series (on Philips France) alone. The British version, on indie rock label 4AD, comes with a cover image of a suitably mysterious ladies' shoe lying underwater, an account by label founder Ivo Watts-Russell of the "nape hair rigid" effect the music had, and precious little else. But there was no ethnographic intent behind this release or any interest in Bulgarian music, just the sheer enthusiasm of Watts-Russell, who had never before been "so intensely subjugated by the human voice".

It's worth dispelling some misconceptions, first off – this is not Bulgarian traditional music, although the distinctive timbre does come from the villages. It is a style developed by a number of important composers and arrangers, foremost among them Philip Kutev (1903–82), who used traditional melodies and singing styles and reworked them into a "national" art form for State Ensembles in the Soviet model set up after World War II. This is carefully arranged music performed by professional choirs and *Le Mystère des Voix Bulgares* is a canny compilation put together by Marcel Cellier who licensed the tracks from Bulgarian Radio and Television and first released them in France in 1975.

According to Dora Hristova, who's conducted one of the Radio and Television choirs for years, this distinctively Bulgarian style of singing was once heard throughout Europe, but evolved into the more refined bel canto style with which we're familiar today. Bulgaria, thanks to five hundred years of Ottoman occupation, lost touch with European vocal developments and preserved this older style of singing, which resonates only in the chest, rather than the head and chest of European bel canto. The vocal range is limited and the harmony seems to come from an archaic sound-world in which a drone voice (like a bagpipe, an instrument regularly heard in Bulgarian folk music) is often a major component. One of the things that makes this music so fascinating for outsiders is the way that dissonances (clashing notes) are employed so regularly. There are striking chords and tensions – and often surprising resolutions.

Many of the thirteen songs here feature clashing harmonies – for instance the opening track **Pilentze Pee** and **Pritouritze Planinata and Schopska Pesen**. Other numbers play on the complex, irregular rhythms for which Bulgarian music is also famous, including the wedding song **Svatba**, **Erghen Diado** and dance song **Brei Yvane**, which alternates irregular choral sequences with pungent instrumental outbursts. Three of the songs feature a solo voice over the choral background, most strikingly in **Kalimankou Denkou**, the album's "hit song". Yanka Rupkina's voice, like a Russian icebreaker, surges implacably onward, carrying the beautifully ornamented rising and falling melody through dangerous harmonic waters. All the voices are very sharply focused, as they need to be for harmony like this. There's ornamentation, but no wobble. After these beautiful (but sometimes strident) sounds, the concluding lullaby-like love song, **Polegnala e Todora**, with its soft and gentle harmonies, is as soothing as a warm bath.

Further listening: The Bisserov Sisters are one of Bulgaria's best family ensembles from the Pirin region. **Three Generations** (Pan) features them with a great group of instrumentalists. **Village Music of Bulgaria** (Nonesuch) is an excellent collection of field recordings made in the 1970s.

Najma

Qareeb

Triple Earth, 1987

Najma Akhtar (vocals), Naushad Sheikh (tabla, dholak, madhal, percussion), Navazish Ali Khan (violin), Ray Carless (saxes), Kiran Pal Singh (santoor), Lazar Der Gregorian (fretless bass), Ian Terry (keyboards).

Imagine a candlelit dinner with your loved one, in an Indian restaurant sumptuously decorated with carved wooden arches, devotional statues, and miniature paintings depicting lovers wistfully longing for each other. This is the album that should be playing on the music system and prolonging those romantic feelings. Najma's ardent, languorous voice performs intensely memorable melodies spiced with surprising turns and chord changes. The arrangements are immaculately conceived: Indian percussion, santoor (hammered dulcimer), a warm violin that alternates and interweaves with the vocal line, plus some cool soprano and tenor saxophones.

Najma Akhtar was born in Chelmsford in the UK, and was in her early 20s when **Qareeb** was recorded. It is one of the most memorable releases in the flowering of British Asian music in the 1980s, with the use of the track Dil Laga Ya Tha on the soundtrack of the film *Sammy and Rosie Get Laid* undoubtedly aiding its success. *Qareeb* certainly proved that contemporary ghazals could be popular outside the south Asian community, given the right music and voice. Although ghazals originated in Persia, they have been sung in the subcontinent since the eighteenth century. While in their archaic form they are artful and refined, today's versions (often used in films) shade into the area of sophisticated pop song. *Qareeb* is the Urdu word for "nearness" or "closeness", and the texts on this disc (mostly by contemporary Urdu poets) are primarily concerned with romantic love, longing, desire and regret – in other words, the conventional territory of the genre.

A gentle synthesizer chord, like the tinkling of sparkling water, and Najma's voice enters twisting in flight like a soaring bird. Navazish Ali Khan's violin mimics the voice and then the tabla launches us into *Neend Koyi*, a song of lost love with a melody that sounds typically Indian. Najma's voice has the slightly childlike quality favoured by Indian film singers, while the staccato punctuations of the accompaniment and the lively bass are more Western in style. All seven tracks here are magical, but the two hit songs, *Dil Laga Ya Tha* and *Apne Hathon*, are especially beautiful. The first has an unforgettable melody, exquisite two-voice vocal harmony (by Najma), and a distinctive harmonic shift in the third phrase that brings a touch of brightness and joy. Instrumental spots are taken by Ray Carless on sax. On "Apne Hathon", the violin takes the lead with an ornamented improvisatory introduction before Najma enters with a more reflective vocal line, which also has some beguiling harmonic shifts as it moves up and down, circling around and in on itself – pure melodic poetry. If the lyricism and emotion of these songs sometimes sound oversentimental, the music and arrangements have a concentration and restraint that keep it all brilliantly in check.

A more upbeat mood is established by *Zikar Hai Apna Mehfil Mehfil*, with its folk-like bhangra flavour, and by the most free-form song on the album, *Karoon Na Yad Magar*, on which a double-tracked sax weaves positively Oriental lines around the voice. The final track, *Har Sitam Aap Ka*, with its splashes of jangling santoor and long lyrical lines on the violin, suggests the sounds of the heart strings. Time for the heated facecloth and mouth-freshening seeds.

> **Further listening:** Hariharan is one of the star names of the pop ghazal in India. His album **Hazir** (Magnasound) is notable for its excellent arrangements and the presence of the outstanding tabla player, Zakir Hussain.

Milton Nascimento/Lô Borges

Clube da Esquina

EMI, 1995

Milton Nascimento (vocals & guitar) and a band including Lô Borges (vocals & piano), Wagner Tiso (organ), Beto Gedes (bass & vocals), Toninho Horna (bass & guitar) Robertinho Silva (drums), Tavito (guitar), Eumir Deodato (orchestral arrangements).

There are few singers anywhere with a voice like Milton Nascimento's, and few composers outside jazz and classical music who can match either his harmonic depth or his ear for melody. To those used to the light sophistication of bossa nova or the festive riot of samba, his music is not obviously Brazilian. But Brazil's music is as diverse as its landscapes, and Milton hails not from Rio but from Minas Gerais, a state whose back lands are famous as the inspiration for the mystical novels of writers like João Guimarães Rosa. Minas music is similarly melancholy and reflective and often socially and politically aware. Milton is its most sophisticated exponent.

From his teenage years in the Minas capital, Belo Horizonte, Milton was closely connected with a group of poets, writers and musicians called the Corner Club, or *Clube da Esquina*. After the young singer shot to fame in the late 1960s – when he toured Mexico and the US with Art Blakey and João Gilberto – he was embraced by the US jazz community. But, rather than choosing to find fame abroad, as others like Sergio Mendes had done before him, he returned to his friends and his Minas roots to record his finest album of the decade. He named the record after them, credited it to himself and fellow Corner Club singer-songwriter Lô Borges, and put a picture representing the two of them as children on the front cover.

Both Borges and Nascimento contribute songs to **Clube da Esquina** and, though the album is strong throughout, Milton has all the best tunes. At first listen, the Lô Borges tracks like Um Girassol da Cor de Seu Cabelo (A Sunflower the Shade of Your Hair) or Trem de Doido (Weird Stuff) sound as good as any of the others, but after the tenth play they begin to feel less substantial and a little bit dated.

By contrast, Milton does not yield all his riches on first listen. Classics like the epic protest lament Os Povos (The People) are initially quite inaccessible, while apparently simple songs like Cais (Quays), or the exquisitely sung Um Gosto de Sol, seem effortlessly to fuse the melodic sleight of hand of a McCartney with the harmonic complexity of jazz composer Joe Zawinul.

Milton shifts in mood throughout *Clube da Esquina*, through light, gentle instrumental tracks like Clube da Esquina 2 to the bitter, angry Pelo Amor de Deus (For the Love of God), and reaches his emotional peak on Dos Cruces, a Carmelo Larrea love song of tragic intensity which Milton sings in Spanish. The song begins with a whispered voice and guitar, and builds in tension, through a second verse (with a wonderfully subtle counterpoint melody), to a final, towering chorus rich with a multilayered vocal harmonies and syncopated percussion.

Those who understand Portuguese will find the lyrics, by Milton and his co-writer Fernando Brant, as rich as the music. Their overriding themes are a search for spiritual reality, social injustice and Brazil's racial divide. But these are rarely explored overtly – Milton is no Billy Bragg – instead, they are alluded to in an oblique and poetic way that is often difficult to translate. Outside music, Milton is a committed social activist, and has worked closely with liberation theologians such as Pedro Casaldaglia to bring the plight of the Latin Americas poor and indigenous to the world.

Further listening: Brazil Classics 1: Beleza Tropical (Luaka Bop) is a great compilation by David Byrne introducing some of the top artists of MPB (Música Popular Brasileira), including Jorge Ben, Gilberto Gil, Caetano Veloso, Chico Buarque, Maria Bethania and Gal Costa.

Youssou N'Dour

The Guide (Wommat)

Columbia/Sony, 1994

Youssou N'Dour (lead vocals) and band, including Jean-Philippe Rykiel (keyboards), Brad Wheeler (sax) and The Super Etoile.

Youssou N'Dour is one of the few African artists to have become familiar to those with no particular interest in World Music, even if they find pronouncing his name a bit of an obstacle. This is largely due to high-profile concerts, Grammy nominations and 7 Seconds, the hit single with Neneh Cherry from this disc. It's also because he has a powerful and distinctive voice – if not a beautiful one – and masses of energy and vision. He's one of the leading African musicians creating modern pop that draws on indigenous styles. But he's also an example of the dangers of the global music industry, and the way African artists can be seized on by the major labels in the search of the Next Big Thing and then quickly dropped when it doesn't happen. *The Lion*, Youssou's album with Peter Gabriel for Virgin, was widely seen as too Westernized and the label dropped him after his second Virgin album, *Set*.

Born in 1959 into Senegal's griot (gawulo) caste, Youssou took on griot responsibilities at an early age, singing at circumcisions and other rituals. He still sees himself as an urban griot and his songs frequently tell stories and offer advice or admonition. Youssou started his own band, Etoile de Dakar, in 1979 and was one of the creators of Senegal's contemporary sound, mbalax – a Wolof word for a traditional rhythm. At the heart of Youssou's mbalax are rhythmic patterns, with the garrulous talking drum (tama) of Assane Thiam to the fore, and his characteristic sound has a light, lean feel to it, even with the addition of Cuban-style brass. Already a big name in Senegal, Youssou attracted the attention of Paul Simon (he guested on *Graceland*) and Peter Gabriel, with whom he also recorded. He joined the Human Rights Now! tour in 1988 and his international career took off. After his Virgin albums, which re-recorded material from his Senegalese releases for the Western market, Youssou set up his own studio in Dakar and declared that his international releases would be the same as those at home, although this hasn't turned out to be the case.

The Guide (Wommat), with arrangements by Habib Faye and Jean-Philippe Rykiel, was the first of his albums to be made almost entirely in Senegal. Just one track, "7 Seconds", was recorded in New York, but it is, frankly, a rather bland pop ballad. The opening track, Leaving, is a more upbeat number, despite the lyrics about emigration, with a lightweight rhythmic accompaniment which shows Youssou's muscular voice off well. It's followed by Old Man, a good example of Youssou's fusion of traditional and modern, African and Western, with some wild, disruptive drumming. Bamba is a lively praise song with some good sax and brass flourishes, and is dedicated to Cheikh Amadou Bamba, the Muslim saint who is hugely important in Senegal, while How You Are lists the independence dates of various African countries. My People is one of the most beautiful numbers on the album, a soft intimate ballad addressed to his fans. Ironically, the love song Silence begins with a splendid flourish on the talking drum, which keeps up a stimulating chatter throughout and is echoed by the brass. Bob Dylan's Chimes of Freedom is an anthemic finale, underpinned by magnificent percussion.

One of the less celebrated aspects of this album is the way its success, and that of Youssou's studio in Dakar, has made it possible to foster Senegal's own music industry and to bring new names like Cheikh Lô (see p.105) into the limelight.

> **Further listening**: For more classic Youssou and Super Etoile, but with a rootsier feel, try **Best of the 80s** (Celluloid/Melodie).

NG La Banda

The Best of NG La Banda

EMI Hemisphere, 2000

José Luis Cortés (flute), Tony Calá and Jény Valdés (vocals) Feliciano Arango (bass), Perez Perez (saxophone).

Papa Chango is a stomping entry point for these ten key songs by Cuba's leading progressive new wave salsa band, NG La Banda. Even for the rule-breaking José Luis Cortés, invoking the Yoruba warrior god Chango in a live session in the bandleader's back yard is an unconventional way of recording a salsa album. Having paid their homage to Chango, the musicians settle into the twisting, turning rhythms of Cortés's radical new salsa (which he calls timba) and demonstrate why his music has travelled so fast around the Latin world.

In these songs, Cortés the musicologist, virtuoso flautist and composer also pays homage to Cuba's legendary sonero Beny Moré (see p.123), and to the post-revolutionary Afro-Cuban salsa and jazz of his previous employers, Los Van Van and Irakere. NG La Banda was founded in 1988, when Cortés left Irakere and pulled together a gang of like-minded young Turks, fellow futurists who wanted to develop Cuban dance music – hence the "NG" which stands for "Nueva Generacion". Their home crowd comes from Havana's noisy streets and Cortés borrows their slang for his song titles and subject matter, while they take his invented words back into their street talk.

The album includes two classics by Beny Moré – **Bonito y Sabroso** and **Cienfuegos**, both showcases for the impressively mature singer Tony Calá. The fusion-jazz-chachacha version of "Cienfuegos" is a soft groove compared to Moré's trumpet-led version, and it includes Calá's gentle scat-vocals and a knotty Irakere-inspired saxophone solo by Perez Perez. "Bonito y Sabroso" (Lovely and Sweet) is musically and harmonically more complex than Moré's original 1950s mambo, and Cortés breaks the brass domination with a long, inspired, improvised flute solo.

The inspiration for many La Banda songs are the goings-on at street level in Havana. **Verano Habanero** (Havana Summer) is a guided musical stroll through the capital's neighbourhoods to typical bucking timba rhythms. **Cara Guante** (Mask Face) describes the kind of trickster character who could feature in a Ruben Blades song; **La Bruja** (The Witch) tells about a woman who drives away in a sex-taxi – a direct criticism of the city's sex tourism. Cortés calls it "salsa-rock" but it feels like racy, ensemble salsa-jazz, revolving around Arango's funky, angular bass and pretty piano melodies. **Veneno** (Poison), the title track from a 1997 album, is mature Cortés, sung with a jazz voicing by Jény Valdes, and more romantic and smoother than many of his turbulent timbas. It features a surprising brass chorus playing Ravel's *Bolero*. **La Apretadora** (The Predator), one of their greatest hits, is a brassy salsa feast, with radiant blasting trumpets, and vocally fluid improvised verses filled with word-play that includes rhyming references to Beny Moré's "Calculadora" and merengue master Wilfrido Vargas's "Abusadora". **No Me Molestas Mas** (Don't Touch Me) is pure New York – bright, brassy, uplifting salsa with a twist. Tony Calá, sounding uncannily like Oscar D'Leon, breaks into comic caricatures in mock argument.

NG La Banda close the alfresco party with Congo de los Refranes (Conga of Proverbs) a carnival street party with a lilt of soca in the brass, propelled by Feliciano Arango's burrowing, thumb-picked bass-lines, which gives the rhythm the vertebral strength of a sidewinder snake.

> **Further listening: No.1 en Cuba** (Magic Music) is a classy introduction to the new-wavers, including former NG La Banda singer Paulito FG. For New York's response to timba, try **Swing on** (Sony) by Dark Latin Groove, a salsa-rap-timba trio who dominated the Latin charts in the late 1990s.

Orchestra Baobab

Pirates Choice

World Circuit, 1989

Issa Cissako (tenor sax), Barthelemy Attisso (lead guitar), Papa Ba (rhythm guitar), Adama Sarr (guitar), Charle Antoine N'Biay (bass guitar), Balla Sidibe (vocals, timbales), Mountaga Kouyate (percussion) Radolphe Gomis, Nbjanga Dieng, Medoune Diallo, Mapenda Seck (vocals).

It's late in the evening. You want to relax and chill out. Keep this by your CD player at the ready. It is soothing and mellow, but also interesting and quirky. The disc is subtitled "the legendary 1982 session" but quite why it was legendary is unclear, unless it was simply that this Senegalese band were at the height of their powers and produced a set that fully deserves immortality. What makes the disc so special is equally hard to define. It certainly sounds a lot older than 1982, the sound is very "unproduced", with the amplifiers sounding decidedly clapped-out, but it's precisely the boxy, rough-and-ready tone that somehow makes it a classic. And what a great name – Orchestra Baobab, named after that strange, unlikely looking tree (as seen on the cover) with its great fat trunk and root-like branches.

The Orchestra Baobab was formed in 1970 and grew out of the Star Band, Senegal's first great popular band, which had emerged ten years earlier with the country's independence. After decades of strong Cuban influence, it was a time when a new African sound was being created – although there are plenty of Latin flavours in **Pirates Choice**. The instrumentalists who most define the band's distinctive sound are Barthelemy Attisso, whose hypnotic, slightly nasal electric guitar solos strike out on idiosyncratic paths but with an unswerving authority and just the right reverb, and Issa Cissako, whose sax melodies are gravelly and bold. Too bad that the big-name vocalist associated with Baobab, Thione Seck, wasn't present on this recording, but has since gone on to an illustrious career with his own band.

Utru Horas opens the album with a Cuban flavour. A guitar solo coolly sets things going, the timbales rattle in preparation and then the meaty, rough-edged sax comes in with a glorious melody, full of longing. Lyrics are sung in a mixture of Wolof (the dominant language in Senegal) and Spanish, and there are earthy interjections on sax and a heavenly guitar solo. The mood lightens for **Coumba**, another catchy tune with a distinctly Cuban rhythm, although the lyrics – in French, this time – are about the loss of a girl and how his life hasn't (for "hasn't" read "has") changed since she left him. Cue sultry guitar solos. **Ledi Ndieme M'Bodj**, in Wolof, is apparently a praise song for the wife of the Gambian president – uptempo with a swinging rhythm rattled out on the timbales, call-and-response vocals and the distortion effect turned well up. **Werente Serigne**, again in Wolof, with a call-and-response style, is driven hard by percussion and features interweaving guitar and sax, plus solos on guitar, bass and, wait for it, the kitchen department.

With **Ray Mbele**, we're back to the Cuban sunshine with a cheery sax solo and Latin-styled vocals (although not in Spanish). The whole track seems to get more and more eccentric and ends up as a Cuban-style jam. The Latin feel stays in super-mellow form on **Soldadi**, another melody from Baobab's top tunesmith, Radolphe Gomis. With Cissako giving really smooth sax, this is seriously languid and as it fades away into the sunset you're just praying for there to be more . . . and there is! Just to save you disturbing your reverie and having to press the start button again, World Circuit have kindly provided alternative takes of the first two tracks at the end of the album.

> **Further listening: The Music in My Head** (Stern's) is a very fine compilation of golden-age, mainly Senegalese, popular music which, includes Thione Seck.

Geoffrey Oreyma

Exile

Real World 1990

Geoffrey Oreyma (vocals, guitar, nanga, lukeme), David Bottrill (percussion), David Rhodes (guitars), Brian Eno (piano, synth and backing vocals) and Peter Gabriel (fake organ and backing vocals).

Alongside Nusrat Fateh Sali Khan's *Musst Musst* (see p.89) and the Afro Celt Sound System (see p.3), Geoffrey Oreyma's **Exile** has been one of Real World's top sellers It's an example of the phenomenon – not uncommon in World Music – of an artist establishing a far greater reputation outside their country than at home. In Oreyma's case this is because he was forced to leave his native Uganda in 1977, after his father was killed by Idi Amin's government. He's now a resident of France which is why his debut album was released on an international label.

Oreyma grew up in Kampala, the capital of Uganda, where as a child he became familiar both with the traditional music played by his father and with groups like The Beatles and the Rolling Stones (Uganda was a British colony). Both these ingredients fuse in the music of this album which strikes just the right balance between tradition and innovation and includes some very beautiful ballads. As the title suggests, the songs largely focus on the experience of exile and nostalgia for home.

Broadly speaking the ten tracks fall into two alternating styles: the more traditional feature Oreyma on the nanga (seven-string harp) and lukeme (thumb piano), while the lyrical, generally melancholy, ballads are closer to the Western singer-songwriter tradition. The album was produced by Brian Eno and it's easy to understand how Oreyma's repetitive, circular patterns and motifs must have attracted him. Oreyma was afraid his initial demo tapes were too rootsy, but the more traditional tracks, like the opening *Piny Runa Woko* are hugely appealing. The interlocking patterns of nanga and lukeme set up a springy, repetitive pattern over which Oreyma sings. He often uses both high and low pitched vocals as if in dialogue with each other. He does this, for instance, in *Piri Wango Iya*, a song about the excitement of love set against a lightly rhythmic background dominated by a high-pitched thumb piano. There's a similar dialogue in *Lacan Woto Kumub*, a more reflective and mellow number, and *Jok Omako Nyako*, a dramatic song about spirit possession with intricate rhythmic patterns. These pieces have an organic energy all their own.

The ballads adopt a more Western approach, using guitar accompaniment and addressing Oreyma's personal history and the experience of exile. *Land of Anaka*, a hymn to the place where his father is buried, is the album's standout song. It suggests that Oreyma grew up listening to Dylan as well as The Beatles and the Stones and in particular "The Land of the Rising Sun". It's presumably a conscious homage, as the melody and chord progressions are so similar they can be virtually sung alongside each other. Still, this is recognisably Oreyma with the soulful tin whistle of Richard Evans adding a haunting strain. The song is gentle and melancholy, suggesting feelings of love and dignity rather than anger – and much the stronger for it. *Makambo* is a similarly restrained meditation on the pain of leaving home. The refrain is a repeated descending phrase – resigned and inevitable – supported by a soft guitar. *Solitude* also develops a personal theme and is Oreyma's song of mourning to his widowed mother, while *Exile*, the album's title track, calls for an end to violence and suggests the stunned realisation of the after effects of war. Oreyma's is a beautiful and distinctive voice that gently understates its message.

Further listening: Uganda has had a relatively low profile in World Music terms but **Music from Uganda 3: Modern Kampala** (Caprice) is a compelling selection of 1990s Ugandan popular music.

Orquesta Aragon

Cuban Originals – Orquesta Aragon

BMG/RCA, 1999

Rafael Lay (violin, leader), Richard Egues (flute), Rafael "Felo" Bacallao (lead vocals), Pepe Olmo (vocals), José Beltran (double bass), Orestes Varona (timbales), Pepe Palma (piano).

Cuba is famous for the longevity of its musicians and of its dance orchestras, but Orquesta Aragon – "The Eternal Charanga"– is in a league of its own. Founded in 1939 by double-bass player Orestes Aragon in the town of Cienfuegos, Orquesta Aragon is still on the road, featuring descendants of the original line-up. After making a local name with their romantic, instrumental danzons, the band moved to Havana in 1948, where Aragon handed over to violinist Rafael Lay, who reigned until 1984. In the early 1950s, chachachá was captivating the city's dancers and Lay's band took to it like rum to Coca Cola. Their records on RCA Victor spread their fame to New York, where musicians like the young flautist Johnny Pacheco launched their own charanga craze in the 1960s, while in parts of Africa and Latin America the name "Aragon" is virtually synonymous with Cuban music.

Orquesta Aragon represents the classic charanga formula. The searing, trilling, joyful – and occasionally spiky – flute of Richard Egues holds its own above a full line of flowing, and sometimes rhythmically tempestuous, violins. Sharp interplay between percussion and piano keep the romantic rhythms clear of any soppy pitfalls. The elegant Aragon personnel lull and seduce and also dance – every soloist is also a nifty mover.

Aragon's trademark chachachá appears here in many guises. Their first hit, Egues's **La Bodeguero** (The Grocer), about a man who dances chachachá in his shop surrounded by beans, potatoes and chillis, was also a hit for Nat King Cole in 1956. **No te Vuelvas Loco** (Don't Go Mad) warns about the dangers of getting hooked, and the hilarious **Senor Juez** (Mister Judge) proves that the chachachá obsession can lead to the courts – a defendant pleads not guilty for dancing it (the infectious backing music surely satisfies the court).

Several of these songs are established Cuban favourites, reworked and sometimes retitled as upbeat salsa. **Al Vaiven de Mi Caretta** (They're Rocking in My Cart) is a nostalgic country guajira song, moving to an appropriately rolling cartwheel rhythm, with background whistles and shouts to the farm animals. Felo Bacallao's gorgeous high vocals recall the Andalucian ancestors of the guajiros. The measured, elegant chachachá **Calculadora** (The Calculator), one of Aragon's most covered hits, prompted a brisk, upbeat version by Oscar D'Leon. **Yo Tengo una Muneca** (I've Got a Doll) uses a simple music-box theme played on triangle and picked up by piano, to tell this *Giselle*-like story. **Sabrosona** (Tasty Girl) crops up in many guises in Cuba and the US; Aragon used a jaunty, whistled chorus following the flowing violins, to lend it an air of Hollywood.

Away from the versatile cha-cha-cha, Aragon reverts to the slower danzon in **Ritmo de Azucar** (Rhythm of Sugar), which opens on a surprisingly unsyncopated American–Latin cocktail-bar piano motif backed by brushed cymbals. It avoids excess sugar by shifting the piano solo into a spacious, complex Afro-Cuban solo and winding the flute to a sharp pitch. The potential for schmaltz in these songs is always there, but the band mostly avoid it. **La Gloria Eres Tu** (You Are the Glory) comes dangerously close but its high falsetto, recalling 50s American doowops, redeems it and is irresistible proof of Orquesta Aragon's place in the wider American dance history.

> **Further listening**: To follow the Aragon legacy, turn to bass player Juan Formell's Los Van Van **The Best of Los Van Van** (EMI Hemisphere), which evolved via the Beatles and the Cuban Revolution. The modern charanga-plus of singer Candido Fabre, **Candido Fabre y Su Banda – Son de Cuba** (TUMI), is a current favourite in Cuba.

The Gabby Pahinui Hawaiian Band

The Gabby Pahinui Hawaiian Band

Edsel, 2000

Gabby Pahinui (twelve-string guitar, steel guitar, traditional Hawaiian percussion, vocals), Atta Isaacs (guitar, vocals), Bla Pahinui (guitar, vocals), Cyril Pahinui (guitar, vocals), Sonny Chillingworth (guitar, vocals), Manuel Kupaha (bass), Randy Lorenzo (bass), Ry Cooder (mandolin, tiple).

When Ry Cooder visited Hawaii for a concert in April 1974, he was already familiar with the music of Gabby Pahinui, and made a point of seeking him out at his home in Waimanalo. As a result of their meeting, a house was rented on Big Island, portable recording equipment (including generators) was imported, and two albums' worth of music was recorded.

At the time, the 53-year-old Gabby was already a virtual living legend, and an inspirational figure for many Hawaiians. He inspired a renaissance of interest in Hawaiian slack-key guitar, which takes its name from the fact that it is retuned, away from standard guitar tuning, into "open" chords. These tunings have been explored and developed by Hawaiian musicians and are closely guarded family secrets of an almost mystical significance.

The band on this record includes two other major figures of Hawaiian music, slack-key guitarists Sonny Chillingworth and Atta Isaacs, as well as two of Gabby's sons, Bla and Cyril. The instrumental mix of five acoustic guitars, mandolin and electric steel guitar (all in different tunings) produces waves of silvery overtones and wide-ranging rhythms – as mellow as a warm Pacific breeze or as vital as the driving surf. The 1970s was a period which saw a major revival of the Hawaiian language, and nine of the eleven songs are sung in Hawaiian (the remaining two are in English). They date from all periods of the country's musical history and include three songs written by the prolific Hawaiian royal family. **Moani Ke' Ala**, by Prince Leleiohoku, is a song in which the singer calls for the swift return of a loved one. Arranged by Gabby as an uptempo party hula, it has a central section on which everyone gets to solo, culminating with Gabby himself on twelve-string.

E Nihi Ka Hele is by King David Kalakaua, the most influential of the royal composers, who initiated the Hawaiian cultural renaissance of the late nineteenth century by rescuing ancient Hawaiian chants (mele) and the hula dance from the threat of obliteration by Christian missionaries. The third royal piece, **Ipo Lei Manu**, a mele written by Queen Kapi'olani for her husband King David Kalakaua, after his death in San Francisco, is a classic of the genre.

Gabby, with his distinctive falsetto voice, takes the lead vocal on most of the songs. Strings accompany **Pu'uanahulu**, **Moonlight Lady** and **Wahini U'i**, a fact which some Hawaiian music purists find disturbing. However, Gabby was always the complete musician, with a very broad musical vision and an eclectic taste: he loved film music and there are often musical quotations in his arrangements. Ry Cooder takes a characteristically back-seat role, playing mandolin on four tracks and tiple, a small ten-stringed instrument, on another.

The album was recorded for the Hawaii-based Panini label but was released by Warners in mainland America and Europe, thus becoming the first real Hawaiian music since the 1930s to be widely distributed. It remains as sparklingly fresh today as when it was first released, and it has helped (along with the music on George Winston's Dancing Cat label) to pave the way for a whole new interest in acoustic slack-key and string-band music in Hawaii and mainland America.

> **Further listening:** An alternative version of "Pu'uanahulu" can be heard on **Hui Aloha** (Dancing Cat), a disc which showcases a more modern version of the Hawaiian string band featuring Martin Pahinui, another of Gabby's sons.

Ivo Papasov and His Bulgarian Wedding Band

Orpheus Ascending

Hannibal, 1989

Ivo Papasov (clarinet), Maria Karafizieva (vocals), Yuri Yunakov (saxophone), Nechko Neshev (accordion), Andrey Kamzamalov (guitar), Radi Kazakov (bass), Stefan Angelov (drums).

With his huge gut and unwieldy frame, Bulgarian clarinettist Ivo Papasov seems an unlikely vehicle for some of the most nimble music anywhere in the world. As king of the Bulgarian wedding scene, his band commanded huge fees and was in heavy demand across the country. Bulgarian wedding music involves frenetic dances in fiendishly complicated time signatures – although it's only musicologists that worry about that, since the musicians themselves just feel them, and when you're high on firewater (the other essential ingredient at a wedding) they feel just right. If you thought Bulgarian music was all about female choirs in folk costume, then make way for the fat clarinettist.

Ivo was born in Kardzali close to the Greek and Turkish borders. As he likes to point out, this is Thrace where Orpheus was born (hence the album title) and it's an area rich in music. Much of the music in the Balkans is in the hands of the Gypsies, and Ivo was born Ibrahim into a Turkish Gypsy family. During the 1980s, Todor Zhivkov's Communist regime forced members of the large Turkish minority to Bulgarianize their names, and several times Ivo and other musicians were arrested, beaten by the police and imprisoned for playing Gypsy and Turkish music. In 1994 Yuri Yunakov, the saxophonist in Papasov's band, sought asylum in the US and has formed his own band in New York. The "wedding music" developed in the 1970s, when musicians like Ivo took Bulgarian songs and folk tunes and arranged them for ensembles including synthesizers, electric guitars and drum kits. This was something of an "underground" sound, as the regime favoured purer Bulgarian music and disapproved of Western influence. The official disapproval doubtless encouraged the growth of the music which became hugely popular in the 1980s.

Orpheus Ascending begins with a slow, ornamented improvisation from Ivo, underpinned by electric bass, before the band burst in with the **Bulchenska Ratchenitsa**, an infectiously catchy tune in ratchenitsa rhythm (a fast seven beats to the bar). As the pace increases, fantastic clarinet improvisations weave their way over guitar and percussion. Ivo cites some of the greatest jazz clarinettists and saxophonists as influences – Benny Goodman and Charlie Parker – but alongside them is Petko Radev, an outstanding traditional clarinettist from Thrace. However wild he gets, Ivo's playing is always grounded in its Bulgarian roots with echoes of traditional instruments like the kaval (end-blown flute) and gaida (bagpipes).

The pace lets up for **Mamo Marie Mamo**, one of three vocal tracks on the album, sung by Maria Karafizieva, Ivo's wife, in ornamented Bulgarian style with Ivo adding some sweetly expressive passages on the clarinet between the vocals. **Marika Duma Prom Duma** contains wild instrumental improvisations as Ivo slides up and down his instrument in a virtuoso display. **Ivo's Dream** is an intense clarinet solo, over eight minutes long, exploiting the varied tone colour of the instrument. After another slow, lyrical vocal number, **Kopanitsa** is yet another of those foot-tapping Bulgarian dances (this time in 11/8). The band play together incredibly tightly and then let rip for their own spectacular solo passages. The gentle **Na Trapesa** – music to listen to at a feast – provides a welcome chance to get your breath back.

Further listening: Ivo's **Balkanology** (Hannibal) spreads the net even wider by including Turkish, Greek and Macedonian tunes. The album **King Ferus** (GlobeStyle), by Macedonia's Gypsy clarinet and sax maestro, Ferus Mustafov, features a selection of wedding tunes.

Astor Piazzolla

Tango: Zero Hour

Nonesuch, 1986

Astor Piazzolla (bandoneon), Fernando Suárez Paz (violin), Horacio Malvicino (guitarist) Héctor Console (bass), Pablo Ziegler (piano).

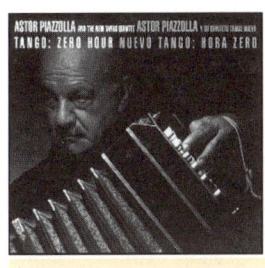

Astor Piazzolla revolutionized tango. Taking this seductive dance of pimps and whorehouses – described by George Bernard Shaw as the "vertical expression of a horizontal desire" – he transformed it into one of the most dazzling musics of the late twentieth century. For Piazzolla, "tango was always for the ears rather than the feet", and while he introduced modern classical and jazz ideas his "new tango" remained what he called "danger music", mapping the experiences and atmospheres of the "zero hour" following midnight – "an hour of absolute end and absolute beginning" that stretched until dawn.

Piazzolla was attacked by many of his fellow Argentines – he was even called a "tango assassin" – because they thought that he was killing off the old tradition. Today, many of the works he wrote are an essential part of any tango concert or stage show. Piazzolla knew exactly what he was doing: he had played with the great tangueros since boyhood, notably a brief period with Carlos Gardel and the band of Aníbal Troilo, and his music never moved far away from tango's dark core. Indeed he opened it up, taking tango's sense of hopeless love and unfulfilled dreams, and reworking it in a way that exteriorizes feelings and experiences, searching for moments of emotional truth. A "musician's musician", his influence was enormous and his fans include many ground-breaking musicians, from classical violinist Gidon Kremer to the Kronos Quartet.

Close your eyes when you hear the seven pieces of **Tango:**

Zero Hour, let its filmic dimensions unfold: walk Buenos Aires by night, pass through backstreets and main thoroughfares, visit the bars and clubs, shadowed by the ghosts of tango's turbulent history. Recorded in 1986 in New York (where he had lived for a time as a child) chanting voices, snatches of crazy conversations and wild laughter preface the opening Tanguedia III, evoking the raw, exuberant urban world quintessential to his music. Piazzolla's instrument is the great diatonic 71-button bandoneon, a particular kind of accordion, held splayed across the knee. His rhythms are bold with unusual emphases; his harmonies often dissonant; his melodies full of Argentine-Italian melancholy rooted in pathos and quixotic, often violent, emotion.

The tone of the second piece, Milonga del Angel, is languorous and infinitely nostalgic, but by the third piece, Concierto Para Quinteto, upbeat percussive timbres – the key to Piazzolla's sound – become part of the musical conversations while bass and piano drop in heavy chords and the violin screeches high above. It's as if Piazzolla's own complex personality – passionate, argumentative, black humoured, playful – infuses the whole work. The fourth piece, Milonga Loca, seems to confront a busy thoroughfare – jerky movement mirroring the hurly-burly of urban life.

Each instrument tells their part of a story, as if recalling different memories: one minute it's the violin, the bass, then guitar, then piano, who take you into their fragmented worlds. Passionate and sad, angry and joyous by turn – it's as if melodic shapes drawn by instruments are individuals speaking out their desires and fears, looking for wisdom. Finally in Mumuki, a piece that seems to challenge mortality, exquisite instrumental solos dovetail into each other, until the bandoneón enters proud and tragic finally resolving the mood into one of resignation mixed with triumph which gradually fades into the final lovely wail of a police siren.

Further Listening: The Rough Guide to Tango (World Music Network) sets Piazzolla in the context of the music's historic development. **Raúl Barboza** (ADD/ND) is a showcase for accordionist Raúl Barboza, the leading player of chamamé, the Guarani Indian-inflected country cousin of tango.

Tito Puente

50 Years of Swing

RMM, 1997

Tito Puente (timbales, vibes, bandleader, arranger, composer), plus vocalists including Celia Cruz, Graciela, India, Tito Rodríguez, Cheo Feliciano and others, Israel "Cachao" Lopez (bass), Ray Barretto, Willie Bobo, Candido, Mongo Santamaria, Giovanni Hidalgo (Cuban percussion), Johnny Pacheco, Dave Valentin (flute), Jose Curbelo, Charlie Palmieri, Hilton Ruiz, George Shearing (piano).

Ernesto "Tito" Puente, who died in 2000 aged 77, was one of Latin music's most legendary figures. Known as "El Rey del Timbal" (King of the Timbales), "The Mambo King", "King of Latin Jazz", or simply "TP", he was a silver-haired, grimacing showman who used to clown around with his timbales sticks but who pulled no punches when it came to serious music-making. Audiences in five continents thrilled to the fusillades of syncopated melodies, ricocheting pulses spraying from all surfaces of his drum kit and the sparkling notes exploding from his vibraphone.

The 50 tracks on this lovingly conceived three-CD box set recall every era since 1946 when the handsome 23-year old percussionist (newly demobbed from the US Marines) first whipped up a storm in New York's clubs with Cuban pianist José Curbelo's band. The opening fast and tricky rumba track, **Que No, Que No!**, recorded in 1946, is significant for the presence of the 23-year-old Puerto Rican singer, Tito Rodríguez – Puente's future rival for the title of "Mambo King".

The set divides into three stylistic eras. The brassy, raucous, Americanized versions of the Cuban rumbas, congas and mambos best illustrate his brilliant arrangements for a brass band with a heart of percussion. In the Latin-jazz numbers he brings together both Latin and American "names", including many of the pioneers of Afro-Cuban Jazz. The third disc is devoted to the leading figures of four decades of New York salsa. The title song from the 1999 tribute album *El #100* is a starry parade of the relative vocal styles of the top salseros, led by José Alberto, Oscar D'Leon and Tito's Queen, Celia Cruz.

Puente was always drawn to the female singers who excelled in improvisation. Here are the ruby-voiced Graciela ("the Sarah Vaughan of Latin Jazz"), in a raunchy rumba banter with Vicentico Valdes's El Yoyo, recorded in 1949; the tempestuous La Lupe, her vocal passion temporarily calmed by the bolero Que te Pedi from 1963; the dynamic Hollywood exotic, Abbe Lane, in a funky ode to the Cuban saint, Babalu (1958); and Celia Cruz telling an upbeat, tongue-twisting tale of their lives together, Celia & Tito (1991).

TP the soloist is best heard on the jazz selection of disc two. The original Ran Kan Kan revolves around his unrestrained, sparkling vibes solo and a bouncy double bass-line; in Mambo Herd, saxophonist Woody Herman's snorting, bucking saxophone lines make way for TP's reckless timbales showpiece; Tito on Timbales is a master-class of extraordinarily delicate "rim-shot" work; his trio with Mongo Santamaria (congas) and Willie Bobo (bongos) builds a sinuous, finger-clicking groove, Ti Mon Bo. The cover of Shadow of Your Smile is unforgettable for Cachao's glorious, bowed double-bass solo, while at the other extreme is James Moody's sultry late-night ode to a young beauty Moody's Mood for Love.

Oye Como Va is now a byword for Latin music – and for Puente himself – and it makes a fitting closing number. This 1992 recording with Puente's Golden Latin Jazz All Stars includes a crystalline flute solo by Dave Valentin, which draws rapturous responses from the delighted New York home crowd who sing all the choruses.

Further listening: **Paquito D'Rivera Presents Cuban Jazz – 90 Miles To Cuba** (Tropi-Jazz/RMM) is a broad swathe of Afro-Cuban Jazz from a reunion of scattered Cubans. **Live from Soundscape, Latin Jazz** (DIW) records early '80s jam sessions which blew apart existing Latin jazz certainties.

Purna Das Baul

Bauls of Bengal

Cram World, 1994

Purna Das Baul (vocals, khamak, ektara, nupur, baaya), Subhendu Das (vocals, khamak, dhol, baaya, dupki), Dibyendu Das (dotara, banjo, mandira), Nanda Dulal Das (khol, percussion), Gour Pal (flutes).

It's the classical music of India that gets nearly all the attention in the West. But there are countless other musical forms in the subcontinent, and the music of the Bauls of Bengal is, in many ways, more approachable than the lengthy ragas of the classical players. Found in Bangladesh and the state of Bengal in India, the Bauls are a mystical brotherhood of wandering musicians who express a refreshingly unorthodox and undogmatic faith of love for humanity. Like the Sufis, they believe that music is a way to contact the divine. Their name comes from the Sanskrit word for "mad" and the Bauls describe themselves as "madmen of God". That air of madness, craziness and unpredictability is one of the things that makes their performances and music so compelling.

While the Bauls may often seem little more than buskers performing at bus stations or on trains, they attracted the attention and admiration of Nobel prize-winning poet Rabindranath Tagore (1861–1941), who began to champion their ideas and cause. More recent admirers have included Allen Ginsberg and Bob Dylan, and Purna Das Baul featured on the cover of Dylan's 1968 album *John Wesley Harding*.

Purna Das represents the seventh generation in an unbroken line of Baul musicians. His father, Nabani Das Baul, was the singer who inspired Tagore, and his sons are carrying on the tradition. This lively and joyous album features the family band, plus guests. At the heart of the Baul ensemble is the mystical sound of the ektara, a single-stringed instrument symbolising the union between mankind and God. While this might be the most important instrument symbolically, the sound is dominated by the high bamboo flute, dotara lute and khamak drum which has strings attached to it which change the pitch and give it its distinctive springy timbre.

There are nine vocal and three instrumental tracks on this disc. The opening song, **Agun Pani**, takes us straight into the ecstatic world of the music with a sprightly flute tune over the lean, but virile percussive sound. There's no fat in this music, the textures are open and clear, the pace energetic. The vocals, which tell of the elements that make up the human body, are a spiritual incantation, the two singers sometimes singing together, sometimes firing off each other in turn. This is a leaner cousin of Sufi qawwali music. On **Ja Lolite Ange Kushum Tule** (Lolite, Go Pick the Kushun Flowers), one of several songs on this album inspired by Krishna, the pace relaxes. The flute and lute weave a dream-like web around the vocal line, sung by Paban Das, and mirror its contours. It's like an evocation of paradise: an idealized world of idyllic landscapes, flowers and love. **Kalkatou Mon Heshekeley** (Spend Your Life Full of Joy) says don't waste time pursuing material wealth, because in the end "Everything is left behind." **Ananda Lahari** is a gorgeous instrumental track where you really get to hear the squelchy sound of the khamak drum. Over the busy chattering percussion the flute soars like a free spirit as if symbolising a spiritual liberation from the mundane cares of the world. In **Amar Aei Rudir Dhara** its the vocal line which soars while the flute explores those magic microtonal spaces between the notes. This an album that will make you feel purified and refreshed.

Further Listening: On Real Sugar (Real World) **Paban Das Baul collaborates with British guitarist Sam Mills. Ganga** (Virgin France), a musical journey down the Ganges, includes a couple of Baul tracks.

Ismael Rivera

El Sonero Mayor

WS Latino/Sony, 1999

Ismael Rivera (vocals), Rafael Cortijo (percussion, leader), Rafael Ithier (piano), Roberto Roena (bongos), Kito Velez (trumpet), Eddie Perez (tenor saxophone), plus uncredited band members.

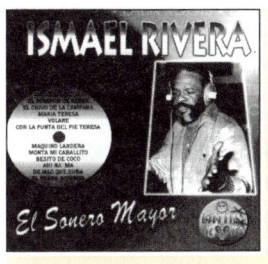

Puerto Rico's home-grown salsa is too often overlooked in the rush for fresh treasures from Cuba's archives and new teen-fodder from New York and Havana. For decades, however, the neighbouring country has been quietly producing great stars of its own. Since his first appearances in the early 1950s in the port-side dives of the capital San Juan, Ismael Rivera has stood out above the rest and, nearly twenty years after his death in 1982, he still occupies a special place in the hearts of Puerto Ricans. Rivera's reputation was such that Beny Moré, Cuba's own salsa supremo (see p.123), bestowed on him the weighty title of "El Sonero Mayor".

These thirteen songs, recorded between 1955 and 1959, chronicle the peak years of Rivera's partnership with timbales player and bandleader Rafael Cortijo. The two first attracted attention while still at school, playing percussion in neighbourhood Afro-Rican street bands. Their perfect partnership ended tragically in 1962, when Rivera's drug habit landed him in an American jail. On **El Sonero Mayor** Rivera is at his most flowing and huskily soulful. The album provides a showcase for his sophisticated rhythmic scatting and onomatopoeic, tongue-twisting way with words. He's backed by a trumpet-and-saxophone-led combo in which Cortijo's timbales help to keep the melodies sharp.

What distinguished Rivera and Cortijo from the scores of

other late 50s dance bands in the mambo era was their choice of the bubbling rhythms descended from Puerto Rico's slave traditions, the bombas and plenas. Cortijo injected these distinctive, upbeat rhythms into the brassy big-band formula and created a racy background for Rivera's emotive voice, which was less bluesy than the Cuban equivalent.

The album begins at a tearing pace with Cucala, Cucala, its bass-line and congas anticipating the beat just enough to give it a sexy lurch. Rivera punctuates the song with trademark goat-cries, which reappear throughout the record in bleats and cackles and are echoed in some riotous braying trumpet choruses. On Besito de Coco, Rivera's vocals are accompanied by a throbbing bomba beat, the Puerto Rican equivalent to Cuban rumba, while he cracks the words along their syllable joins and tosses them across the rhythms like a concrete poet. In Maria Teresa conga drums bubble to a bomba beat behind the "old-lady" chorus style borrowed from the Cuban son, punctuated by an occasional curling saxophone solo. The delightful Con la Punta del Pie Teresa is an erotic, jumpy dance tribute in triple-beat rhythm. El Bombon de Elena, from 1955, was the Cortijo Combo's first hit, booming out of every jukebox in San Juan, and subsequently carrying the band's reputation to New York. This is quintessential plena, opening to a jumpy pandereta (frame drum) solo, before the rattlesnake hiss of a guiro (scraper) leads to a fluttering chorus of saxophones and another "old-lady" chorus. Rivera enters seductively, playing with the simple lyrics to tell a typically risqué story. El Negro Bembon comes closest to Puerto Rico's modern salsa style, led by a clanking cowbell and Rafael Ithier's flowing piano breaks. The most surprising appearance is Volare, usually a sun, sex and sangria sing-along, but here transformed into something more substantial by its trumpet arrangements and a chorus of children's voices.

> **Further listening**: For the sax, trumpet and trombone-led sound created by Rafael Ithier for El Gran Combo, try the compilation **Gracias, 30 Anos De Sabor** (Combo). **Los Soneros De Hoy** (Sony Tropical) is a showcase of today's leading Puerto Rican salseros, including Victor Manuelle and Luis Enrique.

Abdel Gadir Salim All-Stars

The Merdoum Kings Play Songs of Love

World Circuit, 1991

Abdel Gadir Salim (vocals, oud), Hamid Osman Abdalla (tenor sax), Mohammed Abdalla Mohomidia (solo violin), Ahmed El Mubarak Ahmed (violin), Adil Awab Hassab Seido (keyboards, bass), and others.

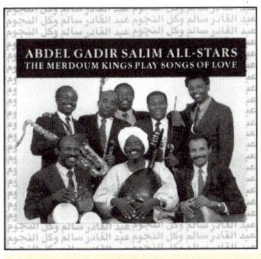

Since 1989 and the coup by the National Islamic Front, Sudan has suffered a fundamentalist clampdown and civil war. So it's not the first place you'd associate with exuberant good-time music and songs of love – indeed, several of Sudan's most prominent musicians have been intimidated, and others, like the celebrated singer and oud (lute) player Mohamed Wardi, have fled into exile. Abdel Gadir Salim himself was injured in an attack which killed fellow performer Khogali Osman in 1994.

The irony is that it's Sudan's pivotal position at the meeting point of the Middle East and Africa which is behind both its political strife and its potent music. Salim has described his music as an African sound, Arabic words and international instruments. He's an accomplished oud player – the one in the turban on the cover photo – while his All-Star band, all dressed like bank clerks, play violins, sax, guitar, keyboards and various percussion.

Abdel Gadir Salim was born in Dilling, right in the centre of the country in southern Kordofan. He was educated in Arabic and European music in Khartoum, and his instrument, is the leading instrument of classical Arabic music. What is especially distinctive about his music is his use of the local folk styles of the Kordofan region – typified by his signature song Umri Ma Bansa (I Will Never Forget You), which he made popular on the radio in the 1970s and which opens this album. It begins with violin and oud solos, as if preceding a long Arabic improvisation solo, but then inexorably Salim calls out "Umri Ma Bansa", the band punch a couple of chords and we're into a swinging Kordofan rhythm called merdoum, with lyrical phrases alternating between vocals and the band.

Every language has key words which tend to recur in songs: in Spanish it's corazon (heart) and sueño (dream); in Arabic it's habibi (darling), and we're in habibi territory here. These are love songs, after all, but you don't need to understand the lyrics to enjoy the melodies and fine sax playing by Hamid Osman Abdalla (who also plays with Sudan's other big-name male vocalist, Abdel Aziz el-Mubarak).

The songs here express not only love for women, but also for Sudan and its people, for nature and for things of the spirit. **Mal Wa Ihtagab** is a solo song for voice and lute, with a wonderful introduction showing off Salim's oud playing to great effect with a warm, throbbing sound. **Almaryood** is an intimate duo for voice with oud and saxophone and **A'Abirsikkah** is a good example of Sudanese reggae with its distinctive off-beat guitar strums.

The "hit song", though, must be **Bassama**, in which stabbing string chords lead into a swinging melody which spills over into into a catchy tune falling and then rising with Arabic twists and turns. It's a beautiful song and a glorious example of the big-band sound – featuring swirling strings and sax – which, though largely unknown outside the Arab world, is typically Sudanese. Felicitously recorded while Abdel Gadir Salim was touring the UK with his band, the album ends with a live version of "Mal Wa Ihtagab", performed in concert in London, which, in fact, adds little to the studio version heard earlier.

> **Further listening:** For the more urban sound of Sudan, listen to Salim's "rival" **Abdel Aziz el-Mubarak** (GlobeStyle), with many of the same instrumentalists and, for the new generation, the young female vocalist in exile, Rasha, on **Sudaniyat** (Nubenegra).

Nitin Sawhney

Beyond Skin

Outcaste, 1999

Nitin Sawhney (guitars, keyboards, synthesizers, programming, samples), Shri (bass), Aref Durvesh (tabla), Steve Shehan (percussion), Rjendra Singh (swalin), Marque Gilmore (percussion), Andy Hamill (double bass), Ronu Majamba (flute), Chandru Shekar (karnatic violin). Jayanta Bose, Devinder Vikyat Singh, Sanchita Farruque, Tina Grace, Rizwan Muazam Qawwali Group, Nina Miranda, Spek, Swati Natekar, Sushmita Ghosh (vocals).

Released to a cascade of critical acclaim, **Beyond Skin** marks the emergence of Nitin Sawhney as a major talent. Taken as a whole, this suite of songs stands as a remarkable fusion of the rhythmically complex music of India and the harmonically complex music of the West – all with a cool club sensibility. Trying to summarize Nitin's "tabla juxtaposed with techno bass and beats" approach, *The Face* magazine came up with the phrase "Asian Modernist" and Nitin's musical vocabulary bears this out. Drawing on the experience of being a second-generation Indian in Britain – listening to Indian music at home, yet exposed to contemporary Western sounds outside – has given him the confidence to blend flamenco, Latin rhythms, jazz and drum'n'bass with the traditional and classical music of music of the Indian subcontinent.

Nitin isn't afraid of big themes. His previous album, *Displacing the Priest*, used a field recording of an ancient Hindu evocation to introduce an exploration of modern spirituality. This album opens very differently – here the prelude to the album's big theme is Indian prime minister Vajpayee proudly announcing the testing of three nuclear bombs in 1998. From this chilling opening, *Broken Skin* slides into a sophisticated Soul II Soul groove with strings and electric piano underpinning co-lyricist Sanchita Farruque's emotive vocal, "Broken . . . distant . . . silent . . .", which weaves in and out of Bombay-based singer Jayanta Bose's impassioned **Bengali Song**. Although this is not a concept album as such, the atmospheric use of evocative spoken word samples opens the album up to a series of deep questions: "Am I less Indian if I wasn't born in India? Am I English because of my upbringing? Who decides?"

Nitin's choice of vocalists is superb – from Tina Grace's sleepy Björk-ish murmur on the seductive **Letting Go** to Spek's insidious rap on the wry **The Pilgrim**. **Homelands** combines Hindi strings with sublime qawwali vocals and Nitin's flamenco guitar stylings. With **Immigrant**, Nitin returns to the theme of the British Asian's search for self with a quote from his father, remembering the promises of a new life that enticed him to emigrate to the UK, turning into a soulful folk song.

Profound but still funky, Nitin has a gift for a good groove. The human voices are swathed in crystal-clear textures of instrumental colour that speak out over chattering percussive beats. Nitin's virtuosity with guitar and keyboards is as muscularly graceful as it was when he played with the late 1980s "acid-jazz" incarnation of the James Taylor Quartet. **Tides** is acoustic piano in a dinner-jazz style. **Serpents** is as block-rocking as any of Talvin Singh's work – the snicker and purr of drum'n'bass shrouded in Indian flute and filtered wordless vocals. Although Nitin plays many of the instruments himself – from white-noise generator to Wurlitzer piano – there are sublime contributions from specialists like tabla player Aref Durvesh and dubby bass-player Shri.

The album closes with the floating, fragile voice of Swati Natekar, on the acoustic half of the title track, following on from a techno wasteland, complete with quote from the *Bhagavad Gita* about Shiva as "Death, the destroyer of worlds". If the traditional rock-concept album pompously sought to provide "answers", then this CD is humble enough to try and pose the questions.

Further listening: Sawhney's 1995 album, **Migration** (Outcaste), addresses the themes of journey, transition and adjustment and features stunning vocals by Natacha Atlas.

Shakti

The Best of Shakti

Moment, 1994

John McLaughlin (guitar, vocals), L. Shankar (violin, viola, vocals), Zakir Hussain (tabla and other percussion), T.H. "Vikku" Vinayakram (ghatam and other percussion), R. Raghavan (mridangam).

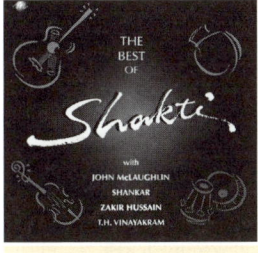

"Good evening friends," says John McLaughlin at the outset, "thank you for that warm welcome." His gentle, diffident tone doesn't prepare you for the fire that follows. In unison the band tear away at an incredible pace through a frenetic melody that seems unstoppable, rising and falling in breathless surges until a couple of minutes later it momentarily pauses before McLaughlin launches into a spectacular guitar solo.

There have been many East–West collaborations, but somehow Shakti was in a class of its own. The seed for the project was sown when British-born McLaughlin was a boy and heard a BBC radio broadcast of south Indian temple music. The best jazz guitarist of his generation, he left for America in 1969, worked with Miles Davis and suggested collaborating with Indian musicians on the *Bitches Brew* album. McLaughlin started to study the south Indian veena (the stringed instrument from which the sitar developed), but, feeling unable to master two instruments, ended up applying aspects of the veena to the guitar. He developed a custom-built instrument with sympathetic strings and a scalloped fingerboard so he could play the notes of Indian ragas. He first met tabla player Zakir Hussain in California in 1970 and they founded Shakti together in 1974. The group was not only a meeting of East and West, but of north and south India. Hussain comes from the northern Hindustani tradition and violinist L. Shankar and ghatam (clay pot) player T. H. "Vikku" Vinayakram come from the southern Karnatic tradition. Of course jazz and Indian music share the art of improvisation, and in this case the imaginative power and virtuoso abilities of the players were perfectly matched.

The quartet recorded three albums in New York, London and Geneva, and this disc is compiled from those three albums. That opening track, **Joy** is a virtuoso Karnatic ragam transformed into a sensational eighteen minutes of tight ensemble jazz with McLaughlin and Shankar alternating solos. It's like a volcano erupting and the sparks fly as both soloists work their way up to the very heights of their fingerboards. Tabla and mridangam punch the proceedings along and egg the soloists into an increasingly competitive display. It's one of the most extraordinary performances of any sort on disc and, not surprisingly, the audience erupts when it reaches its finish in perfect unison.

The remaining eight superb tracks bring contrasting moods and textures. The second piece, **Bridge of Sighs**, is mellow and reflective and gives an opportunity to hear the extended range and expression of McLaughlin's guitar. **India** too begins with an extended guitar solo in which McLaughlin emulates the sound of the veena. Accompanied by soft strumming on the upper strings, a slow, stately melody moves gradually downwards, getting deeper and darker as McLaughlin bends and modulates the notes by sliding on the fingerboard. **Happiness is Being Together** is an exuberant track that features a soaring Gypsy-style violin solo that leaps around, occasionally spinning off into the stratosphere – another incredible feat of playing. On **Isis** there are extended solos on the tabla and ghatam, and throughout the album it's incredible the way Hussain (right) and Vikku (left) work so well together, and complement each other in the very complex rhythmic patterns. The final **Two Sisters** is a gentle winding-down after a mesmerizing and astonishing set.

Further listening: A decade after the Shakti experience, John McLaughlin and Zakir Hussain joined forces with Indian flautist Hariprasad Chaurasia and Norwegian saxophonist Jan Garbarek to record **Making Music** (ECM), another landmark in East-West fusion.

Ravi Shankar

LIVE: Ravi Shankar at the Monterey International Pop Festival

Angel, 1998

Ravi Shankar (sitar), Alla Rakha (tablas), Kamala (tamboura).

Now that he has become, arguably, the most famous Indian alive, Ravi Shankar's credentials as an ambassador for the subcontinent's culture are common property. What took him there is a little more subtle. Connoisseurs may argue over the relative achievements of fellow sitarists Vilayat Khan or Nikhil Banerjee. As a creative spirit, however, Shankar is in a world of his own. He developed the sitar, extended its technique, perfected the gayaki (singing) style of playing, and achieved an astonishing pace and brilliance of articulation. In partnership with tabla players, notably the late Alla Rakha, Shankar made a feature of "question and answer" exchanges (in which the players create excitement by imitating each other's rhythms) that have become a standard feature of most classical Indian instrumental performances. And he made links with other musical forms that are the foundation of several lines of contemporary fusion music.

Strangely, Shankar's current discography doesn't do justice to his achievements. A raga, which is both the melodic scale that forms the basis of an extended piece and the piece itself, can unfold over hours. Full-length performances are, therefore, difficult to record and Shankar can more frequently be heard in the cleverly condensed raga elaborations which, in his hands, have become an art form in their own right. A slightly more expansive recording comes from Shankar's historic appearance at the 1967 Monterey International Pop Festival with Alla Rakha. This concert was a major landmark in the popularizing of Indian music to Westerners, with a huge audience who, for the most part, is being knocked flat by this music for the first time. In response, the sitar playing just gets more and more focused and exciting. No recording can catch the immediacy of the relationship between Indian musicians and their audience, but on this disc, the concert's atmosphere, which seems to heighten in a rapidly escalating spiral, is palpably communicated to the listener.

The opening piece, **Raga Bhimpalasi**, is a late-afternoon raga associated with devotion and joy. Like most ragas, it begins with an alap, a slow rhythmically free statement of the melody, which feels restless at first, as though Shankar is a little nervous. As he settles, his playing becomes more exploratory and the mood more contemplative. After about ten minutes, the raga starts to pick up speed and the rhythm becomes more complex. The playing steadily grows increasingly impulsive and resourceful and, as a fixed pulse sets in, more brilliant and intense. Reaching a fast pace, Shankar sustains it several minutes longer than you might expect, before suddenly slowing down for the raga's conclusion.

All this while Alla Rakha has remained silent. Ravi Shankar now introduces him and explains that he will play a **Tabla Solo in Ektal**, ektal being a rhythmic cycle of twelve beats – though the flying fingers of the next five minutes speak for themselves in a characteristic Alla Rakha combination of flair and fire. At the end he recites a couple of short verbal compositions in the traditional rapid mnemonic style before playing them on the drum. Finally the two players join together for a light-classical **Dhun** in two parts; the first section at a moderate pace, the second, featuring some of the duo's most staggering quick-response exchanges, really flying. The crowd goes wild. So will you.

> **Further listening:** The combination of Shankar and sarod player Ali Akbar Khan on **Ragas** (Fantasy) is a profound and unalloyed pleasure. Vilayat Khan, another great sitarist, can be heard displaying his lyrical genius on two (tabla-free) ragas on the album **Ustad Vilayat Khan** (Fantasy).

Shooglenifty

Venus in Tweeds

Greentrax, 1994

Angus R. Grant (fiddle), Iain MacLeod (mandolin), Garry Finlayson (banjo, banjax), Malcolm Crosbie (guitar, whistling), Conrad Ivitsky (bass), James Mackintosh (drums, percussion).

"Hypnofolkadelia" and "acid croft" are two of the more memorable attempts that have been made at summing up the mad, bad and dangerous sound of Shooglenifty, an instrumental Scottish six-piece who've done more than any other current outfit to change the face of their homeland's indigenous music. Formed in the early 1990s, they quickly came to exemplify the increasingly eclectic, fusion-oriented roots melting pot that was developing in their home town of Edinburgh.

Their most influential achievement has been in breaking away from the increasingly stagnant confines of folk-rock, with its lumpishly plodding foursquare beats, towards a rhythmic approach much more akin to electronically based dance music. While most of their tunes are still in regular meters, the players slice'n'dice them with syncopations and cross-rhythms. Melodically, too, this groove-based approach is liberating, creating a sense of space among the shifting rhythmic layers that allows the tunes to be fully expressed and embellished, rather than regimented by pounding, 1970s-style guitars and drums. This cross-fertilization of wicked danceability with intoxicating melodic sweetness has elevated Shooglenifty into one of Scotland's most successful roots acts.

Their debut release, **Venus in Tweeds**, announced the arrival of an exciting new act on the Scottish scene and initiated a renaissance of Scottish folk music during the 1990s. With eleven of the album's sixteen individual tunes being Shooglenifty compositions, it's nothing if not an original calling card. It kicks off with *The Pipe Tunes* – an immediate nod to Scotland's traditional heritage, even in the absence of actual bagpipes – which opens with an urgent bass and percussion pulse, swiftly joined by a silvery but similarly edgy acoustic guitar line. The fiddle comes in gradually, starting off high, wild and distant, spiralling into the foreground then ducking cleanly into the first of the set's two reels, where it's shadowed note for note by Iain MacLeod's phenomenally nimble mandolin playing. This high-jinks, knees-up mood is sharpened by the band's split-second agility, plus an assortment of strange clangs, echoes, scratches and other distorted atmospherics sprinkled throughout, which are conjured mainly, though not exclusively, from Garry Finlayson's "banjax" – his own, uniquely customized version of an electric banjo. The next track, *Horace*, does a similarly frolicsome but fiercely honed job with three jigs, before things slow down to a mellower pace in *The Point Road*, a sweetly sauntering mandolin melody. The title track splices insistently choppy beats and a tense, almost menacing initial feel with sudden splashes of East European-tinged extravagance; here as elsewhere, there's a distinct streak of minimalism about Shooglenifty's approach, in their use of repeating figures and incremental progressions.

There's no "almost" about the sense of menace in *Waiting for Conrad*, with its loping dubby beat and late-night, mean-streets ambience, whereas *Two Fifty to Vigo*, with its fluid, lyrical ebb and swell, is a wordless eulogy of ardent, bittersweet beauty. *Paranoia* starts off as a coltish romp through another high-spirited reel, before plunging off the rails into a gleefully cacophonous welter of discord and distortion, while *The Tammienorrie* remains one of Shooglenifty's all-time barnstorming greats, building up a formidable head of steam without forfeiting an iota of effervescence.

> **Further listening:** Martyn Bennett's **Bothy Culture** (Rykodisc) is a more explicit fusion of folk music with clubland styles. Capercaillie's **Beautiful Wasteland** (Survival) occupies more Celtic/pop territory, fronted by the gorgeous Gaelic singing of Karen Matheson.

Paul Simon

Graceland

Warner Brothers, 1986

Paul Simon (vocal, guitar), plus other musicians including Joseph Shabalala and Ladysmith Black Mambazo, General M.D. Shirinda and the Gaza Sisters, Linda Ronstadt, Los Lobos, Rockin' Dopsie and others.

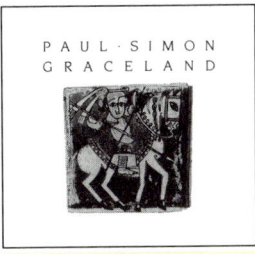

The accordion wheezes its parallel chords for a few bars before the drums and rhythmic bass kick in and drive the song into action: "These are the days of miracle and wonder. This is the long distance call." There was no logical reason for Paul Simon to record The Boy in the Bubble, a meditation on technological progress, in South Africa, but several long-distance calls assembled a variety of local musicians, including a group from Lesotho with Forere Motloheloa on accordion for this opening track. The results were spectacular and not only produced a classic album that sold over ten million copies, but brought the world's attention to a handful of magnificent musicians, some of whom, like Ladysmith Black Mambazo (see p.99), have become stars in their own right.

Simon had been playing a tape called *Gumboots: Accordion Jive Hits Vol. 2* in his car and it was this Soweto "township jive" that first turned him on to South African music. In February 1985 he headed out to Ovation Studios Johannesburg to record with a selection of bands. Five of the eleven tracks came from these sessions, including the fabulous Gumboots, recorded with The Boyoyo Boys who'd performed it on the original cassette. The title track, one of the least African on the album, is a journey across the American South in which the rhythmic, choppy guitar of Chikapa "Ray" Phiri is used to evoke the Mississippi Delta.

According to Simon, the starting point of the song I Know What I Know was hearing a phonetic Anglicization of the title sung stratospherically high by the Gaza Sisters. When Simon arrived in Johannesburg he had no material prepared and the songs were largely improvised in the studio. While the music of this track is South African-flavoured, the words are about a cinematographer's party in New York. Simon has been criticized for not dealing with urgent issues like apartheid, but it's endearing the way the songs emerged tangentially from the material he found in South Africa.

The group really catapulted to success by this album was Ladysmith Black Mambazo, with their a cappella vocals. Simon co-wrote their two tracks with lead singer Joseph Shabalala and recorded them in New York and London. Diamonds on the Soles of Her Shoes and Homeless are both key tracks that somehow define the album. The former includes Youssou N'Dour (see p.129), not that you'd notice, although you do hear his talking-drummer Assane Thiam. The latter is pure a cappella, slipping between English and Zulu and dotted throughout by the little grunts and shrieks typical of Ladysmith. African music and the accordion also led Simon to Louisiana, and Zydeco accordionist Rockin' Dopsie is guest artist on That Was Your Mother, while Tex-Mex band Los Lobos, also accordion-heavy, are the added flavour for All Around the World.

Simon, of course, was attacked for exploiting African musicians and working in South Africa. In fact, the UN anti-apartheid committee declared that he hadn't broken the cultural boycott, which didn't extend to recording, and history has shown that the musicians who took part have benefited from the album. While Under African Skies (about Joseph Shabalala) is the only song that takes Africa as its subject; the musical flavour predominates with its vocal harmony, jangling guitars and township jive rhythms. For many people outside of Africa this album put the continent's music on the map.

Further listening: Peter Gabriel's album **Us** (Virgin) includes Youssou N'Dour as guest vocalist.

Songhai

Songhai

Hannibal, 1988

Toumani Diabate (kora, vocals), Juan Carmona (guitar), José Soto (guitar, vocals), Antonio Carmona (percussion, guitar, vocals), José Miguel Carmona (percussion, guitar, vocals), Danny Thompson (bass), plus guests.

Cross-cultural fusions are a cliché of the World Music boom, as labels have found themselves with a diverse roster of artists and all too often throw them together in a studio to thrash out some East-meets-West, rich-meets-poor, x-meets-y sort of formula. However, certain collaborations stand out way above the rest and Songhai is one of those. A meeting of flamenco and kora music, the disc creates something new by exploring the differences and similarities between the two traditions. It is Hannibal's top-selling title and with good reason.

Toumani Diabate (see p.51) is the leading Malian virtuoso of the kora (the sophisticated West African harp/lute) and Ketama is one of Spain's best "new flamenco" outfits. Both have their own album's on Joe Boyd's Hannibal label and happened to meet each other at a party in London and tried playing together. This record soon followed. The combination of string textures is one of the things that makes it special. The predominantly strummed guitars of Ketama (although there's some mean picking, too) contrast with the intricate plucked sound of the kora, which suddenly sounds like a distant cousin. But more than that, there's a sense of real musicians meeting and communicating together. The tempos shift organically as the soloists are evidently listening closely to each other, their playing sensitively underpinned by Danny Thompson's bass.

Listen to the way Ketama prepare a rhythmic flamenco background for Toumani's first entry on the opening track, Jarabi (a Malian standard). They start with a flamboyant guitar introduction and then settle into a gentle accompanying pattern. The kora enters with the melody and starts to drive things along. The guitars fizz into counter-melodies with the kora, and the music is further charged by hand claps and percussion. The three sections of the piece, concluded by dramatic phrases on kora and guitars, get progressively more animated to create a gloriously rippling texture of swiftly struck strings.

Each of the tracks comes either from the Malian or flamenco tradition. The second track, Mani Mani Kuru, like the first, is distinctly Malian with its languorous melody and female backing vocals (from Mory Kante's group) and virtuoso work on the kora and guitar. Caramelo is more laid-back and distinctly Spanish in character, although after a sustained guitar build-up, the kora gives the melodic lead and, as the melody takes off, there's one of those great moments of organic give and take between the musicians as the tempo races and then holds, before settling down into the groove. It's busy but also cool and sophisticated. A Toumani is another flamenco number, with lead vocals from José Soto dedicated to the kora maestro, who is given moments to shine between the vocals. Vente Pa Madrid is perhaps the most overtly flamenco number on the disc into which the kora fits rather unobtrusively, to be followed by Africa, a gentle Toumani composition (with bowed double bass and vocals in Mande and Spanish) in which the two styles meet. A Mi Tia Marina is gentle and laid-back, but perhaps the padding on the disc, while Ne Ne Koitaa is a relaxing Malian tune carried by a solo from Toumani.

The ingredients of this album are essentially simple, but it's the way that the ingredients combine with such naturalness and joy that make it a real landmark.

> **Further listening**: The equally good sequel, **Songhai 2** (Hannibal), has a slightly stronger Malian ingredient thanks to the participation of Keletigui Diabate on Balafon (xylophone) and Base Kouyate on ngoni (lute)

Mercedes Sosa

30 Años

Polygram Latino, 1994

Mercedes Sosa (voice), numerous musicians from her various groups, and guests including León Gieco, Antonio Tarragó Ros, Horacio Guarany, Charly García and Milton Nascimento.

This is a glorious celebration both of thirty years of the singing of Mercedes Sosa, "the voice of Latin America", and of "new song", one of the most exciting and radical musical traditions of the twentieth century. "New song" supported the struggle for democratic change in Chile, Nicaragua, El Salvador and challenged the iniquitous South American dictatorships. It did so with great energy, through vibrant songs, thoughtful lyrics, infectious rhythms and beautiful melodies. Many artists were imprisoned and exiled for their singing, including Mercedes herself between 1979 and 1982.

"Magnificent Mercedes" is a striking figure, charismatic in performance, her rich voice capable of expressing every nuance of feeling. Such is her passion and conviction, that she has won a strong following, not just in Latin America, but among non-Spanish speakers who feel that they understand her words. "I put all of myself, all of my life into every song I sing," she has said. An interpreter only, Mercedes carefully chooses her material from the output of practically every major Latin American singer-songwriter.

Sosa was a key part of the folk revival in her country and several songs pay tribute to the pioneers who collected material from countryside singers, like the moving *Gracias a la Vida* from Chile discovered by Violeta Parra. With *Luna Tucumana,* by the Argentine Atauhualpa Yupanqui, Mercedes returns home to Tucumán, in northern Argentina, where she was born in 1935. Other early songs include **Al Jardín de la República**, a Tucumán zamba, played with Paraguayan harp and bombo drum, the lyrical **Alfonsina y el Mar**, on which she is supported by a simple piano part, and the jaunty **La Arenosa.**

Mercedes sings **La Maza**, a key song about belief by Cuban troubadour Silvio Rodríguez, is a compassionate serenade. On most of these songs the guitar is her main accompaniment, balanced by percussion. An exception is Rodríguez' **Unicornio,** a song dealing with loss and the importance of dreams, which is here supported by an atmospheric synthesized piano. There's a gentle "live" version of **Años** by Cuban Pablo Milanes, a wistful melody about the passing of love and time. Julio Numhauser's serenade to his native Chile **Todo Cambia**, is sung like a lullaby, a bamboo flute decorating a melody which is underpinned by the rhythms of Chile's "cueca" dance.

The voice of León Gieco and his harmonica can be heard on **Solo le Pido a Dios**, one of the many rock songs which gave strength to young people in Argentina during the "dirty" war, when many of them were "disappeared" by the military. This is one of the great "live" moments of the disc; another is rock singer Charly García's exquisite **Inconsciente Colectivo,** on which he is joined by the achingly tender tones of Brazil's Milton Nascimento.

The philosophical **Si se Calla en Cantor** – "If the singer dies, life does, for life itself is a song" – is sung with its composer Horacio Guarany. And there's **Canción con Todos**, often chosen as the final song at gatherings of these musicians for its poetic lyrics about the unity of the Americas. Mercedes celebrates women's lives in the upbeat **Maria, Maria** and in **Maria Va**, a wonderful duet with Antonio Tarragó Ros and his evocative accordion. Finally, the exuberant **Dale Alegria a Mi Corazon** (Give Happiness to My Heart) completes a terrific album. For many South Americans these songs will capture moments in their lives, while others, less familiar with the world they describe, will be touched and transformed by their emotional power.

> **Further listening:** Víctor Jara, the Chilean singer-songwriter murdered by the Pinochet regime, can be heard on his **Obras Completas** (Pläne). **Dias y Flores** (Hannibal/Ryko) presents the early work of Silvio Rodríguez.

Rachid Taha

Diwân

Barclay, 1998

Rachid Taha (vocals), Nabil Khalidi (oud, banjo, backing vocals), Hossam Ramsy (percussion), Amina Alaoui (vocals), Steve Hillage (guitars, programming), Aziz Ben Salem (flute), Geoffrey Richardson (strings), Bob Loveday (strings), Pete MacGowan (strings), Kaseeme Jalanne (oud).

North African music has been going through a healthy series of mutations and adaptations over the past twenty years but with the release of **Diwân**, Rachid Taha has unveiled a veritable blueprint for modernisation. The album's genesis was a long-held desire on the part of Algerian-born Taha to pay tribute to the many heroes of North African song who have offered inspiration and consolation to generations of fellow beurs (North Africans in France) buffeted by war, emigration and exile. A profusion of different styles – 1960s rai, Moroccan '70s new wave, chaabi from Algiers, classic Egyptian pop, Saharan sahraoui and Berber Kabyle – provide the raw material for Taha's heartfelt exploration of his own musical culture. As his producer/collaborator, Taha chose to team up with Steve Hillage, founding member of hippy icons Gong, prime mover behind electronic trance outfit System 7 and, despite this unlikely pedigree, a musician with a deep and instinctive understanding of modern Arabic music.

Since his days fronting the seminal punk-beur band Carte de Sejour, who managed to "never mind the bollocks" of French racism with considerable panache in the 1980s, Taha has grown into one of the most incisive and radical commentators on North African culture and its place in modern France. When Carte de Sejour split and Taha went solo in the early '90s he embarked on a long process of musical experimentation with the intention of modernising North African music without losing the distinctive flavours of its traditional roots. *Diwan* marks the moment of arrival, of total fusion, where the sounds and shapes of North African music coexist in perfect balance with the world of sequencers, samplers and MIDI.

The album opens with Ya Rayah, a blistering update of an old tune by the Algerian chaabi star Dahmane El Harrachi, who did more than any other song-writer to document the homesickness and sense of loss of North African emigrants in the '40s an '50s. Taha's version was a hit both in his adoptive France and further-flung Arabic countries like Lebanon. Although Taha's gruff guttural vocals don't have the soaring impact of rai superstars like Khaled or Cheb Mami, the deep loping backbeat, insistent melody and swooping violin licks, all perfectly balanced by Hillage's deft production hand, have guaranteed the song's status as a modern North African classic. The album then cruises effortlessly on its reverential journey, paying tribute to the '60s pop rai sound of trumpeter Bellemou Messaoud in Ida, doffing a cap to the Egyptian pop hero Farid El Atrache in Habina, reinventing the raw pounding rhythms of Saharan sahraoui music in Bent Sahra, saluting the maestro of Algerian chaabi Mohammed Hadj el Anka in El H'mame and the hugely influential '70s Moroccan supergroup Nass El Ghiwane in Bani al Insane. What is so remarkable about *Diwân*, is that the voices of all these heroes are incorporated into one coherent sound, song follows song without any sense of chaos, and the whole ends up sounding like a homogenous collection of classic tunes, expertly performed and intelligently produced. With its broad canvas of sources, its uncompromisingly modern production values and its uncluttered yet virtuoso performances, you couldn't hope to find a better introduction to the musical goldmines of North Africa.

> **Further listening:** To explore further new developments in North African music, check out the album **Poulina** (Virgin) by Orchestre National de Barbes or **Halalium** (Apartment 22), the debut from London based Moroccan producer U-cef.

Taraf de Haidouks

Honourable Brigands, Magic Horses and Evil Eye

Cram World, 1994

Musicians include Nicolae Neacşu (voice, fiddle), Caliu (fiddle), Costică (fiddle, voice), Ion Manole (voice, fiddle), Ionică (large and small cimbalom), Ioniţă (accordion), Mitică Cacurică (voice), Fălcaru (flute), Viorel (bass).

In 1990, immediately after the Romanian revolution, Belgian producers Michel Winter and Stéphane Karo went to the village of Clejani near Bucharest to hunt out a Gypsy band. They'd heard them on a CD produced by the French label Ocora in 1988. The rest, as they say, is history. The band was renamed the Taraf de Haidouks – "taraf" is the Romanian term for a village band and Haidouks are the "honourable brigands" of Romanian history. The Taraf have recorded and toured extensively and have now become synonymous with Romanian Gypsy music: a world of swirling violins, punchy accordions, rippling cimbaloms and an athletic plucked bass.

What makes the Taraf exceptional is the way they've transformed themselves into a successful World Music outfit but kept the essential colour and grittiness of their music. They are essentially a functioning wedding band for the Romanian and Gypsy communities of their region and this gives their music its spontaneous, lived-in style. Coming from a dynasty of Gypsy musicians, these aren't scratchy old fiddlers, but masters of their art. In its entirety the band comprises twelve or more musicians, but breaks down into smaller groups, creating a variety of sounds and performing styles.

The first few tracks feature the traditional repertoire of the band's veteran players, who've literally received a new lease of life from their success. Ion Manole and Nicolae Neacşu (both around

80) play with a fantastic old-style fiddle technique, full of character and subtle ornamentation – listen to the high, edgy bowing style on Hora Din Caval, or the gossamer-like accompaniment to Cînd Eram la '48, a song about the peasant uprising in 1848.

Balada lui Corbea, sung by Neacşu, harks back to a semi-mythical world and celebrates the exploits of one of the most renowned Haidouks of the fifteenth century. With the help of his magic horse, the brigand escapes a gory death, and eventually wreaks his vengeance on the emperor, Stephen the Great. It's not surprising that songs like this – the little man getting the better of a cruel ruler – survived so strongly through the fear and corruption of the Ceauşescu regime. Similarly, the lament, Jalea Tiganilor, has a theme which is universal among Gypsy communities and is known throughout the Balkans. Here it's declaimed by Mitică Cacurică in a passionate, emotional voice, accompanied by some formidable accordion playing.

Caliu and Costică are two fast and flashy violinists of the younger generation, who dive into furious dance tunes, like the Geamparale and Turcească, with breathtaking abandon. Gypsy musicians are no slaves to tradition and both these tracks are thrilling examples of the way players are renewing the tradition with infectious, irregular rhythms from Bulgarian and Serbian music. Aside from the breakneck pace, there's the influence of jazz-style solos, with spectacular solo spots for ţimbal (the cimbalom or hammer dulcimer typical of Romanian Gypsy music) and aggressively syncopated walking bass-lines up and down the fingerboard. There are further electrifying instrumental displays in dance numbers like the Brîu, with solo flute, and the Sîrba, an inventive duo for violin and accordion.

For a number of reasons, Romania probably has the richest living folk tradition in Europe, but it's inevitably going to disappear as the country catches up with the twenty-first century. This disc is at least a permanent legacy of the country's music at its very best.

> **Further listening**: The recording that started it all off: **Roumanie: Les Lăutari de Clejani** (Ocora) is a great disc of the old guard, including Neacşu, Manole, Cacurică and others.

Tarika

Son Egal

Xenophile, 1997

Hanitra (vocals, percussion), Noro (vocals, percussion), Donné (vocals, valiha, marovany, accordion, jejy voatavo), Ny Ony (vocals, guitar, bass, kabosy), Solo (vocals, kabosy, drums), plus guests.

Madagascar is the fourth largest island in the world, with a unique and diverse flora, fauna and, of course, music. The original Malagasy settlers were Malayo/Polynesians from Southeast Asia and, since then, African, Arabic and European colonial blood and influence has swept in. This mixture means that the island's music is very distinctive and there's a whole range of fascinating indigenous instruments. Malagasy music hasn't achieved the profile of other African styles, although it deserves to, particularly with groups like Tarika to spread the word. Their music is catchy, exuberant, danceable and full of gorgeous instrumental textures. **Son Egal** is an exceptional album, which addresses important historical and political issues.

The first track, Tsy Kivy (Don't Be Discouraged), is a cracker. Strong syncopated rhythms, a catchy tune and a rippling guitar texture support the virtuoso sound of the valiha – Madagascar's most famous instrument – a bamboo tube with around twenty strings running along its length. Male and female vocals alternate and the Senegalese tama (talking drum) punctuates the vibrant textures of this "be happy" opener. The vocal harmonies of Malagasy music are distinctive and delightful. Avelo (Ghost) is one of the album's most powerful statements. Noro takes the whispering lead vocals, which condemn the current political figures for desecrating Malagasy history and the bones of the ancestors – a hugely important element of

Malagasy culture. Listen for the marovany (box zither) in the accompaniment. The reggae-like rhythm subconsciously connects it to an anthemic stand-up-for-your-rights tradition.

The title track **Sonegaly** (Senegalese) is one of the most politically contentious. Lead vocalist Hanitra tells how as a child the phrase "the Senegalese will come and eat you" was used as a threat to scare children. It goes back to 1947, when there was an uprising against the French colonizers, which was brutally put down by African troops trained in Senegal. Since then, black people have simply been referred to as Senegalese when in fact the story is far more complex. This reflective song tries to lay those ghosts to rest and brings in guesting Senegalese musicians Massamba Diop and Kauwding Cissokho from Baaba Maal's band (see p.109) on tama and kora which, of course, sounds remarkably similar to the valiha. Other songs with a strong political message are **Diso Be** (Very Wrong), about the hypocrisy of a government that mourns the martyrs of 1947 but celebrates the centenary of the French takeover and exile of the last Malagasy queen in 1997, and **Aza Misy Miteniteny** (Don't Say Anything), an allegorical song about misrule that was banned in the 1970s. This last track is purely vocal, with vigorous clapping, whistles and shrieks in jijy style – a sort of Malagasy rap, but much older.

Among the several other tracks which highlight disappearing customs and musical traditions are **Vavaka** (Prayer), **Ady** (Fight) and **Raha Tiany** (Things We Like). The latter celebrates some of the island's unique musical instruments – the valiha, marovany, kabosy (guitar), lokanga (fiddle), jejy voatavo (gourd zither) and others – most of which can be heard on the album. This underlines one of Tarika's other great achievements, which has been to revivify the local roots music scene in Madagascar by demonstrating how successful it can be with audiences worldwide.

> **Further Listening:** For the full range of Malagasy music, try **Big Red: A Musical Journey Through Madagascar** (Nascente) and **The Sunshine Within** (Bush Telegraph), an exuberant recording by valiha virtuoso Justin Vali.

3 Mustaphas 3

Shopping

GlobeStyle, 1987

Uncle Patrel (saz), Hijaz Mustapha (fiddle, bouzouk, guitar), Expensive Mustapha (trumpet, tenor horn), Kemo Mustapha (accordion), Niaveti Mustapha 3rd (flutes, bagpipe), Sabah Habas Mustapha (vocals, bass guitar), Isfa'ani Mustapha (percussion), Houzam Mustapha (drum kit), Lavra Tima Daviz Mustapha (vocals), and guests.

Today there are dozens of bands dabbling in assorted hybrids of other people's music from African to Zydeco. With a scoop of klezmer clarinet, a dash of Gypsy fiddle, tossed timbales on a bed of bongos, you've got a heady Balkan bake or a spicy salsa soup. But in the days before the growth of World Music and ethnic cuisine – the two are definitely linked – this was radical stuff and when the 3 Mustaphas 3 started improvising their own recipe books in the early 1980s they never suspected they'd go down in the history books as "Godfathers of World Beat".

Nothing is certain about the Mustaphas, but legend tells how they hailed from the Balkan town of Szegerely, where they were stalwarts in the Crazy Loquat Club until they followed Uncle Patrel to make their fortune in London. Founder members included Uncle Patrel on saz and Hijaz on fiddle, bouzouk and guitars, while other seminal figures like Kemo Mustapha (accordion/keyboards) and Sabah Habas Mustapha (vocals and electric bass) joined later. It seems the only obligation was to be called Mustapha and to wear a fez. In these early days they were lucky enough to catch the attention of two of Britain's most interesting DJs – Charlie Gillett and John Peel – and they recorded their first vinyl mini-LP in 1985. "A collective revelation of Mustapha decided that people always sound at best when singing in the bath," says the authorized history, so they set out to find the best bathroom, and history was made: "What you hear is five boys and their uncle singing, dancing and running around in giant empty swimming pools. Never before had this phenomenon been better captured."

Shopping was the Mustaphas' first real album. The cover depicts bustling downtown Szegerely. Ringed by an almost impenetrable range of mountains, the city has always been a melting pot of cultures as betrayed by the remarkable range of architectural styles – a Wild West saloon, Cairo minaret, Gothic castle and Classical porticos. Overlooking the marketplace is Fezco, the state recording label, which never released any Mustapha recordings although they're still said to languish in the vaults. Next to a fez supplier, occupying an upper floor on the right is the Crazy Loquat Club itself, with its smoke-filled bar and peeling dancehall. From here music fans would stagger down the stairs to Uncle Patrel's "Slo-Food" stall. On the square itself members of the Mustapha clan are visible doing their shopping in the black market to which the authorities turned a blind eye.

The opening track, Ljubav Kraj Izvora/Skupovo Kolo, is the sort of Yugoslav wedding dance that always went down well at the Club, with wild fiddle and whistles. It's followed by the Oriental-inflected Xamenh Evtexia/Fiz'n, which serves to introduce the band – "the sound of Young Szegerely" – and their sense of humour. Shika Shika is a haunting Swahili language song with the beguiling, breathy vocals of Lavra Tima Daviz Mustapha. Other tracks on the worldwide shopping trip include A Night off Beirut (Arabic), ¿Voulez Vous Danser? (Cuban with a spectacular bouzouki solo), Darling, Don't Say No (a sort of soukous shopping song in English), Shouffī Rhirou (rai), Valle e Pogradecit (funky Bulgarian) and the percussion and bagpipes of Szegerely Farewell. Nothing would be the same again.

Further listening: Bam! Big Mustaphas Play Sterolocalmusic and **3 Mustaphas 3 Meet L'Orchestre "Bam" de Grand Mustapha International & Party**, their first mini-LPs, now appear on a single GlobeStyle CD. In a new incarnation Sabah Habas Mustapha has recorded **Denpasar Moon** (Piranha) – top-quality fake Indonesian that the locals love.

Totó la Momposina

Pacantó

Nuevos Medios, 1999

Totó la Momposina (vocals), and half of Colombia as guest musicians.

Totó la Momposina has long been the queen of roots cumbia, but as Colombia's national dance in its traditional form is essentially just a raw vocals and percussion experience with a few reedy pipes if you're lucky, she's never made an unmissable recording until this one. She ascribes its success to the fact that she has laboured long and hard, working at the coalface of Colombian music and absorbing its power. The world's liveliest musical cultures have grown out of a fusion of different styles. Colombian music, like that of many places in Latin America, is a fruitful mixture of indigenous, African and colonial Spanish traditions. This album is an explosive and energetic seventy-minute, fifteen-track tour of those sounds from breathy flutes, to thunderous drums and strumming guitars and banda brass. Virtually every track should have you moving your butt.

Totó was born into a musical family on the island of Mompos (hence her name) in the Magdalena River. In this region there's a strong percussion-led mix of native and African traditions. Her father was a drummer, her mother a singer and dancer, and Totó started learning from an early age. Possessing a powerful and impressive voice, she formed her own group in 1968 and began to tour and record widely.

One of the things that gives this album its special character is the fizzing brass, which harks back to the street bands and big bands of the 1950s and 1960s. In fact there's only a handful of players involved, although it sounds like half of Cartagena are on trumpets and trombones. Pacantó, the first track, begins with the gentle sound of the marimbula, the African thumb piano transported to the New World and nurtured in a Caribbean grow bag so it's large enough to sit on. Totó is big on the African ingredients in Colombia. A twangy guitar heralds her vocal and the song is transformed into a punchy brass-led invitation to party. It's a glorious start, with Totó firing off the tight salsa-style horn section, the jangling sound of the guitars and smaller tiples and a continually fascinating bed of percussion, plus some spectacular trumpet solos from Freddy Soto. The next track, Goza Plinco Sierra, pushes even harder. This is wild street-band music with a big banda underpinned by an insistent snare drum. Mile is a song from Totó's home village of Talaigua with added soukous guitar courtesy of Papa "Nono" Noel. Several tracks involve link back to Africa, notably the closing Mami Wata which has an easy-going West African feel and was played by Guinean band Bembeya Jazz in the 1970s. It's about a mermaid legend told both in West Africa and Colombia.

There are also some strange and arresting indigenous sounds on this album, notably the breathy gaita flutes on La Ripia, Asi Lo Grita Totó, Porro Magangueleno and the extraordinary funeral piece Bozza y Media with its maracas and drum accompaniments. The counterpoint and clashing harmonies of the flutes interleaving with each other is wonderful. Pozo Brillante clearly demonstrates the tradition into which Totó was born. Her mother takes the lead vocals and her sister and niece provide the chorus. Accompanied by a drum and hand claps, it's the traditional music of her home village. There are no weak tracks here, but possibly the most significant is La Cumbia Esta Herida. Cumbia is injured, it says; the music has become purely commercial and lost its roots and dignity, but nobody protests. A message not only for Colombia, but for countries the world over.

> **Further listening: Cumbia Cumbia** (World Circuit) and **The Rough Guide to Columbia** (World Music Network) are both outstanding introductions to the music.

Ali Farka Toure with Ry Cooder
Talking Timbuktu

World Circuit, 1994

Ali Farka Toure (vocals, acoustic and electric guitar, njarka, etc), Ry Cooder (various guitars), Hamma Sankare (calabash, vocals), Oumar Toure (bongos, congas), and guests including Clarence "Gatemouth" Brown.

Laid-back, mellow and packed with fine musicianship. **Talking Timbuktu** is a great first taste for anyone coming new to World Music. Cooder and Toure had long been aware of each other's music but they first met in 1993 while Toure was on tour in the US. Cooder then guested on some of the dates before the two of them got together in Los Angeles and recorded this album in the space of three days. Cooder has made a speciality of such international collaborations. He has an ear for exceptional music and musicians and seems to approach these projects as a facilitator as much as a participant. He keeps himself in the background and, as the cover states, this is essentially an Ali Farka Toure album – with Ry Cooder. The disc won a Grammy, became a worldwide favourite and also put World Circuit on the map as one of the most interesting labels in the business.

Ali Farka Toure – "the bluesman of Africa" – was born in 1939 and lives in Niafunke, a town on the Niger, not far from Timbuktu in northern Mali. He's not from a griot (musician) family, so music for him is a passion rather than a profession – he claims it was "the spirits" that initially encouraged him to play and his family strongly disapproved. He learned the guitar during the 1950s, performed on Mali Radio and in 1968 was introduced to the recordings of James Brown, Otis Redding and, most importantly, blues guitarist John Lee Hooker. He claims he was not influenced by Hooker, but heard his own traditions in the music and took it as confirmation of the value of the Songhai and Tamasheck music around him. Toure's electric-guitar style is strong and rugged, with lots of bent notes and a generous touch of reverb creating a strangely melancholy and spooky sound.

Every track has its felicitous qualities and attractions. Most of them get into a groove kept alive by details on the guitars and the gentle, crisp percussion tapped on calabash (gourd) and bongos. Particularly attractive is **Soukora** – a Bambara love song – with its simple, repetitive chord progression and lyrical melody. The guitars interweave with each other in the instrumental breaks in a beautiful tapestry of sound. **Gomni** has a darker hue, a repetitive rhythm and splashes of electric guitar from Cooder before the vocals enter. **Sega** and **Banga** are intimate instrumental trios with Toure on njarka (one-string fiddle) accompanied by calabash and congas. Associated with the spirit world, the njarka has a rough-edged sound and it was the first instrument that Toure learned.

Amandrai, with its bluesy feel, is one of Toure's most distinctive songs. It's driven by a repetitive three-note bass pattern, heavier drums (from Jim Keltner), over which Toure picks on electric guitar and sings his mournful vocals while Cooder adds slide guitar. **Bonde** and **Lasidan** are the uptempo numbers, the latter having a particularly airborne feel. **Ai Du** is a bigger production number with guest musicians including Clarence "Gatemouth" Brown on a viola (which sounds for all the world like a bass njarka) and Cooder on mandolin and his distinctive slide guitar. **Diaraby**, a "popular standard", rounds the album off with its relaxed pace, delicate guitar flourishes and mellow feel. An out-and-out triumph.

> **Further listening: Meeting by the River** (Waterlily Acoustics) is another of Cooder's Grammy-winning collaborations, this time with Indian guitarist V.M. Bhatt. On **Kulanjan** (Hannibal), Malian kora player Toumani Diabate teams up with American Blues guitarist Taj Mahal to great effect.

Transglobal Underground

Dream of 100 Nations

Nation, 1993

Hamid Mantu (drums, guitars), Count Dubulah (bass), Alex Kasiek (keyboards), with Goldfinger Man-tharoo (tablas), Natacha Atlas (vocals), T.U.U.P. (vocals), Neil Sparkes (vocals), Sherrif (rapper).

UK dance music in the 1990s was often condemned as "faceless". However, the three Nepalese Temple Guardian masks that hid the faces of the trio behind Transglobal Underground indicate the humour and personality of this seminal world-dance fusion act. Their live shows, augmented by the swaying belly-dance of Natacha Atlas and the formidable presence of gigantic T.U.U.P. brought an irreverent mash of ethnic samples and mixed-up beats into the glossy world of "clubbing".

Their genesis came about through the now legendary recording of the Temple Head single, which kicks off **Dream of 100 Nations**. At the end of the 1980s, the cheap sampler revolutionized Western Dance music and what had once been the preserve of "disco" producers became something that anybody with an imagination and an interesting record collection could collage into powerful and forceful music. Using a sampler, a Simon Harris breakbeat album and a cassette of vocal chants brought back from somebody's Tahitian holiday, the three core members of what was to become TGU recorded a single unlike anything that had gone before it. Drenched in echo, the deep dark voice of rapper Sherrif intones, "Now coming from a different hemisphere we bring you global music . . . " before a loop of Polynesian chants is progressively submerged by a 95bpm breakbeat, some squally rock guitar, a hypnotic "Italian House" piano, looped tablas, a simplistic rap, various non-specific ethnic sounds, and sundry scraps of paranoiac Cold War dialogue from 1950s sci-fi movies.

The track was an instant sensation, but despite several re-releases and the killer hook of "Learn to say peace and na-na-na" it failed to become a hit. However, over the next couple of years TGU were to change from a loose association of friends and family into a genuine "band". Financed by Deconstruction Records, who eventually declined to release it, *Dream of 100 Nations* saw the original participants drawing on their collective past of DJ culture, community politics, Indian classical music, reggae, bhangra, hiphop, and '80s pop, to expand the blueprint of the single into a full-blown album. The twelve tracks explore all the permutations that "Temple Head" opened up – the mix of real and machine percussion, the melding of tribal beats with elastic breaks, and an eclectic library of samples. The album stands the test of time as one of the most comfortable blendings of the "Dance" scene with ethnic sources. **Sirius B** celebrates the Dogon people and their ancient knowledge of Sirius B, a star that is invisible to the eye. Loops of chanting are cut in with North African strings and a four-to-the-floor electro-beat. In the album's closing track, **Hymn to Us**, a splice from a recording of a Nigerian choir (so rough you can hear the edit) soars above a metallic bass-line and a mechanical drum-machine beat. Finally there's a delicate coda after the fade which juggles the machine percussion with the luminous sound of a kora.

The most sensational discovery was the hypnotic pure wail of Natacha Atlas, previously a collaborator with Jah Wobble and now a successful solo artist. It's her presence that unites the sound of this album, drawing together the disparate threads. The handful of tracks she appears on are some of the strongest – from the arid, dignified sway of **I, Voyager** and the impassioned **El Hedudd** to monstrous and orgasmic **Zombie'ites**.

> **Further listening: Backpacking on the Graves of Our Ancestors** (Nation) is their double "Best of" album, augmenting choice cuts from the first album with highlights of their later career. Of Natacha Atlas's solo albums, **Diaspora** (Nation) resembles TGU most closely.

Rokia Traoré

Mouneïssa

Indigo, 1998

Rokia Traoré (vocal, guitar), Andra Kouyaté (ngoni), Baba Sissoko (ngoni, percussion), Oumar Diallo (bass guitar), Abdoul Wahab Berthé (bass guitar), Samba Diarra (baleba), Dimba Camara (percussion), Souleymane Ann (percussion).

Mali may be one of Africa's poorest countries, but in music it's fantastically rich. This vast territory of sub-Saharan West Africa was the heartland of the Manding Empire from the thirteenth to fifteenth centuries, and the musical legacy of that empire is still audible in the repertoire of the hereditary griot musicians and praise singers, and in instruments like the ngoni (lute), balafon (xylophone) and kora (harp/lute). Above all, it's the female vocalists who call the tunes and Rokia Traoré is a stunning recent arrival on the scene. She was selected for the influential Musiques Métisses festival in Angoulême, France and the same year won the Radio France Internationale prize as "African Discovery of 1997".

Rokia doesn't come from one of the griot (musician) families, but in recent years musicians from outside the tradition – like Salif Keita (see p.85) and Ali Farka Toure (see p.181) – have become more common. Rokia's magic comes from her fresh, youthful approach (she was 24 when she recorded this album) combined with a faith in and commitment to the traditional sounds of Malian music. The acoustic instrumental ensemble she uses supports her voice with the light, transparent textures of guitar, ngoni (four-string lute), balafon, bass guitar and the percussive sounds of a scraper and guita – an upturned calabash which is tapped. Rokia's voice is clear and melodic and lacks the hectoring stridency that can be a feature of many of Mali's female singers.

The opening track, **Laïdu**, is a love song that beautifully sets Rokia's voice over the delicate texture of plucked strings and backing vocals. Intricate solos from the two ngoni players, Andra Kouyaté and Baba Sissoko – one on a high instrument, the other on a low one – interleave beautifully with the longer-arched phrases of Rokia's vocals. But the album's hit song must surely be the title track, **Mouneïssa**. It's a soft, gentle lullaby sung to the daughter of separated parents about the pain and sadness of divorce. The vocal line is strong and supportive, but the melodic hook is the repeated name of the girl, Mouneïssa, which sounds strangely vulnerable, partly because of Rokia's lisp – something which might be considered a handicap in a singer but, as here, is actually rather affecting. The pace ups for **Finini**, with attractive harmonized vocals and gently rippling ngoni and guitar. This song was Rokia's first success on Malian radio and TV, although she's still not a well-known name at home. Her international profile, though, is growing and this CD sold over 40,000 copies in Europe – mostly in France.

Djanguina introduces the heavier, slightly buzzing sound of the balaba, the large balafon of the southern region of Mali from where Rokia comes. Apparently the combining of balaba and ngoni is unprencendented and heard here for the first time. It certainly creates a wonderful web of dry textures and combines both solid and delicate sounds. It's a combination explored in different ways in **Tchiwara** and **Sakanto**, the first lithe and springy, the second repetitive and trance-like. The closing track, **Sé**, sets Rokia's voice neatly between the repetitive plucking of treble ngoni and agile bass guitar.

This is a very impressive debut album, which is gentle and seductive but also surprisingly assertive. It was followed by *Wanita*, an excellent successor in 2000, making Rokia one of the rising stars of Malian music.

Further listening: The album just pipped by Rokia in this selection was **Worotan** (World Circuit) by one of Mali's other young singers, Oumou Sangare. **Kita Kan** (Sterns) is a magnificent album by one of the country's greatest praise singers, Kandia Kouyate.

Värttinä

Vihma

Wicklow, 1998

Susan Aho (vocals, 5-row accordion), Mari Kaasinen (vocals), Kirsi Kähkönen (vocals), Janne Lappalainen (bouzouki, kaval, torupill, saxophones), Pekka Lehti (double bass), Kari Reiman (fiddle, 10-string kantele, berimbau), Sirpa Reiman (vocals), Marko Timonen (drums, percussion), Antto Varilo (guitars, banjo, cümbüs, tambur, kantele), with Janne Haavisto (additional percussion).

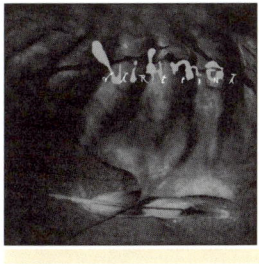

Värttinä burst onto the international scene at the beginning of the 1990s. An exuberant group of feisty women singing modern outspoken versions of ancient songs, they are supported by a brilliant set of male musicians, all of them multi-instrumentalists. Their original high-energy re-interpretations of boastful rants – often delivered with mischievous gestures – offer a raunchy view of men's and young people's behaviour which provokes mirth and joy among audiences, while their versions of slow laments are no less effective.

Founded in 1983 by composer and singer Sari Kaasinen (who left in 1997) and her sister Mari in their home village of Rääkkylä, Värttinä took their inspiration from the rich culture of the surrounding region of Karelia. *Värttinä* means "spindle", a name chosen because the group wished to "prick people awake" and sing from a position of power. By 1987 the original 21 members – who began as teenagers in national dress delivering uptempo songs to accordion-led accompaniment – had been wittled down into a ten-piece ensemble. Along with other figures in the present-day folk revival, they have rejuvenated the lyrical runolaulu (runo-song) of the Finno-Ugric areas, as well as the music of the Setu people of Estonia and the Rönttyskä dance-songs of Ingria. When creating a song, Värttinä often take fragments of an old melody and text and add new sections, mixing past and present, old and new, questioning national stereotypes with irony and humour. Lyrics are often full of mystical feelings, with huge histories distilled into them.

Vihma (The Cold Wind) is the second of three albums that derive from the Karelian runo legend telling the story of the birth of the cosmos. The title track opens with sparkling percussion, while a solo voice begins a characteristic tongue-twisting chant about four girls imploring shelter from the rain. In the undulating movement of the voices, individual personalities emerge from the chorus, vibrantly partnered by rich strings and accordion. A thick swathe of a cappella voices opens Tielle Heitetty, with fiddles, flutes and accordion conjuring an atmosphere of central Europe.

Both Kylän Kävijä and Mieleni Alenevi describe, with almost frenzied agitation, a time when marriage for a woman meant forsaking her family – often for a life of extreme hard work and loneliness. Until the 1960s Finland was largely underpopulated, with many people enduring the long dark winters in isolated homesteads. As a result, lyrics often express feelings bordering on despair: the lone girl in Emoton, backed by a chorus of sisters, sings out her sorrow, her voice framed by fiddle and kantele (a form of zither). Värttinä's tendency to switch voices in solos and in choruses, exchanging and echoing experience as if in conversation, means that an almost pent-up energy bursts through. Uskottu ei Uupuvani expresses similar feelings, but the presence of Tuvan throat singers and members of Finland's premier fiddle group JPP, adds considerable spaciousness and depth to the sound.

The jaunty Neitonen, in contrast, is full of joy at the perfect partner found and everything coming right. Aamu depicts a long-awaited dawn in the Finnish countryside with an almost fanciful wistfulness, and this magical air stays for Kauan Kulkenut, while the Tuvan singers return for a remix of the opening track, Vihmax.

Further listening: The kings of Finnish fiddle playing, JPP, have produced an excellent album in **String Tease** (Rockadillo). **Iho** (Hannibal/Rykodisc) by Finland's premier accordion composer, Maria Kalaniemi, is no less impressive.

Caetano Veloso

Circuladô Vivo

Polygram, 1993

Caetano Veloso (vocals, guitar), Luiz Brasil (guitars), Jaques Morelenbaum (cello, vocals), Marcos Amma (berimbau, percussion), Welington Soares (percussion), Dadi (electric bass), Marcelo Costa (drums).

Brazil is one of the most musical countries on the planet and Caetano Veloso is probably its greatest and most versatile musician. He's Paul McCartney, David Bowie and Bob Dylan rolled into one, with a political edge that is often part of the Latin American songwriter's make-up. He rose to fame in the early days of modern Brazilian popular music (Música Popular Brasileira, or MPB) as one of the leaders of tropicalismo, a progressive mixing of rock guitars and American influence into a cocktail of Brazilian regional styles. Unlike most of the comparable stars in the West, Caetano has remained consistently at the forefront of Brazilian music. He achieved his first million-selling album, *Prenda Minha*, in 1998 when a track was used as the theme tune for a leading TV soap – in Brazil, soaps are BIG.

Caetano was born in 1942 in the northeastern state Bahia. It's where the African influences are strongest, where the carnival is loudest and where, in the state capital of Salvador, the country's most cosmopolitan sounds come from. A large proportion of Brazil's MPB stars hail from Bahia, including Gilberto Gil, Gal Costa, Maria Bethânia (Caetano's sister), Carlinhos Brown, Vinícius de Morães and Virginia Rodrigues – all of whom he's worked with. He started as a philosophy student and film critic in Salvador and his approach to music has always been an intellectual one: alongside fellow musician Chico Buarque (with whom he hosted a TV show in the 1980s), he is widely respected as a poet and lyricist. But it was hearing the bossa nova of João Gilberto and Tom Jobim that inspired him to become a musician and that's audible in the gentle, easy lyricism that characterizes Caetano's best music. The provocative years of tropicalismo earned him and Gilberto Gil prison sentences from the military in 1968, followed by exile in London for two years. Caetano has always experimented across a wide range of styles, but from the early 1990s his work with cellist Jacques Morelenbaum (who produces his albums), has resulted in high production values and brought out the soft, lyrical side of Caetano's music while at the same time maintaining its sophistication.

After a career of thirty years and thirty albums, it's impossible to choose one that really encapsulates the musician, but **Circuladô Vivo** gets pretty close. The album comes from a live show Caetano was touring in 1993, and includes a mixture of old and new songs as well as a variety of styles. There's **Chega de Saudade**, classic bossa nova in a homage to Tom Jobim; a formidable Carlos Gardel tango, **Mano a mano** (sung in Spanish) for just voice and cello; and two English covers: a gentle version of Michael Jackson's **Black or White** – violently juxtaposed with a strident Portuguese rap number **Americanos** – and Dylan's **Jokerman** in a striking arrangement with a strong percussive element.

Distinctive Brazilian instruments pop up from time to time, like the strange, rattling string sound of the berimbau – the Brazilian musical bow that came originally from Africa and opens the album on **A Tua Presença Morena**. **Chuva, Suor e Cerveja**, with its screaming electric guitar solo, reminds you of Caetano's rebellious streak, while several of Caetano's classic ballads are featured, notably **O Leãozinho**, **Quixa** and the exquisite **Você é Linda** – one of his most beautiful songs.

> **Further listening: Fina Estampa** (Polygram/Verve), a collection of classic Spanish rather than Brazilian songs, is one of Caetano's most exquisite albums. **Without Handkerchief Without Document – The Best of Caetano Veloso** (Polygram/Verve) is the best compilation to feature his early hits.

Waterson:Carthy

Waterson:Carthy

Topic, 1994

Norma Waterson (vocals), Martin Carthy (vocals, guitar, mandolin), Eliza Carthy (vocals, fiddle).

With all respect to the worthy Coppers of Sussex, the Watersons from north Yorkshire have been the foremost family of English folk music for more than thirty years. During that time guitarist Martin Carthy has joined the family fold by marrying Norma Waterson, and recently their daughter Eliza Carthy has developed into the most talented performer of her generation working in the English roots field. Together the trio has superseded the original and much-missed Watersons, which included Norma's late sister Lal, brother Mike and cousin John Harrison. All three members of Waterson:Carthy busily pursue parallel and successful solo careers (both Norma and Eliza have been separately short-listed for the prestigious Mercury Music Prize in recent years). They also perform and record in various other groupings and permutations, together and apart. But there is something special about the blending of the voices and personalities of the three of them and the interplay between the two generations which comes from the unique understanding generated by such close family ties.

Their debut album as a threesome was recorded when Eliza was just 19, although both her singing and violin playing already display an astonishing maturity. Perhaps it is less surprising when you hear her describe her earliest preschool memories of curling up to sleep under the stage at folk festivals where mum and dad were playing. By the age of 6, she was wandering onto the stage and pulling her father's trouser leg to demand to be held up to the microphone to join in. She already knew all the songs. All three are avid researchers and students of the folk tradition, seeking and collecting old songs and ballads wherever they can find them. Yet there is nothing remotely dry or academic about their approach, which is characterized by a gusto and vitality based on a profoundly held belief that tradition only counts if it lives and breathes, rather than merely being preserved in the dusty basement of Cecil Sharp House.

As usual with Waterson family recordings, an informative sleeve note by Martin Carthy explains the derivation of all of the dozen songs here. Highlights include Norma's rumbustious rendering of **Bold Doherty** ("young lady be quicker and bring us more liquor and fill us a pitcher") and Martin's plaintive vocal on **Ye Mariners All**. Norma is commanding on **With Kitty I'll Go**, while Martin's exquisite guitar picking on the pastoral **When First I Came to Caledonia** supports Norma in keeningly mournful mood. But we had known for years that Norma was a peerless singer and that Martin's acoustic guitar style had influenced, among others, Bob Dylan and Paul Simon. The real revelation here is Eliza Carthy. Her voice is a sheer delight, particularly on the unaccompanied **The Grey Cock**, and she is almost as impressive on **The Light Dragoon**. When their three voices come together for the a cappella harmonies of **Sleep on Beloved** (with the same tune as the Joseph Spence spiritual "I Bid You Good Night") the result is spine-tingling, with Eliza's high counterpoint particularly outstanding.

As Norma and Martin approach veteran status, Eliza Carthy's presence on this album as the "folk babe" *par excellence* transports the Waterson legend into a new era, and it is clear that the tradition of English roots music is safe in the energetic hands of a new generation.

> **Further listening:** Eliza Carthy's double album **Red Rice** (Topic) maintains the purity of the folk-song tradition while flirting energetically with elements of drum'n'bass and contemporary dance culture. Kate Rusby's **Sleepless** (Pure) represents a more unadulterated approach.

Papa Wemba

Le Voyageur

Real World, 1992

Papa Wemba (vocals), Maika Munan (guitar), Christian Polloni (guitar), Reddy Amisi (vocals), Styno Mubi Matadi (vocals), Shakara Mutela (bass, percussion, programming), John Giblin (bass), Steve Alexander (drums).

Congolese music, known first as rumba and then soukous, has been at the heart of African dance music since the 1950s, influencing almost every other notable African style. Papa Wemba stands pre-eminent among the current exponents, both as a powerful singer with a high-pitched and melancholic voice, and as leader of the sartorial movement known as Les Sapeurs, which has become almost as important among his followers as his music. Since moving to Paris and recording his debut solo album in 1988, he has pursued an increasingly cosmopolitan style, combining modern studio technology with the tough dance rhythms of soukous and working with European-based producers such as Stephen Hague (Pet Shop Boys) and John Leckie (The Fall, Radiohead). **Le Voyageur** was his major breakthrough and is as fine a representation of his international style as anything he has recorded.

Born in 1952, Wemba learned to sing in church (his mother was employed professionally to sing at Catholic funerals). He became one of the leaders of the frenetic new wave of Congolese artists who emerged in Kinshasa in the early 1970s and was a founding member of Zaiko Langa Langa, who combined Western rock stylings with traditional rhythms. He went on to form Viva La Musica, further developing the streetwise sound known as "beau désordre" with a mix of Cuban, rock, funk and authentic

African influences. He also became the figurehead of the fashion-conscious subculture known as "La Société des Ambienceurs et des Personnes d'Élégance" (The Society of Cool and Elegant People) aka Les Sapeurs. Their love of designer labels is not only obsessive, but has even reached the status of a religion. In concert it involves some rather tiresome posturing, and Wemba has been known to turn his clothes inside out to better display the labels.

Like so many Congolese musicians in the 1980s, Wemba moved to Paris, arguably the biggest centre of African music in the world. Although he continued to sing in his native Lingala tongue and use the characteristic spiralling Congolese guitar sound, he began working with European musicians in a style which he refuses to call soukous. "That's just one of the dance styles. We play real World Music," he says. However, he continues to maintain two bands, one playing in a more international style and the other maintaining a rootsier approach.

Le Voyageur opens in high-octane fashion with **Maria Valencia**, Wemba's voice full of a yearning urgency, offset by a soaring trumpet over a vaguely Cuban rhythm and Afro-pop synths. The classic ringing soukous guitar sound with its circular patterns kicks in on **Lingo Lingo**, played not by Rigo Star, the great soukous guitarist who was with Wemba in Viva La Musica, but by Maika Munan, who co-wrote many of the tracks. **Le Voyageur** itself combines traditional percussion with acoustic guitars and finds Wemba in more pastoral mood. The mix of Congolese rhythms and European influences continues on the stunning **Ombela**, while **Jamais Kolong** is more traditional with a hymn-like structure.

It's a rich and smooth set which is typical of the Parisian Afro-modernist school and some will prefer the rawer street sounds of his earlier career. But it showcases Wemba's remarkably soulful voice, like an African version of Otis Redding, his greatest musical hero.

> **Further listening:** Mose Fan Fan has been one of the leading soukous guitarists for thirty years: on the very wonderful **Congo Acoustic** (Triple Earth) he swaps his high-voltage style for a more mellow approach.

Zap Mama

Zap Mama

Cram World, 1991

Marie Daulne, Cecilia Kankonda, Celine 't Hooft, Sabine Kabongo, Sylvie Nawasadio (vocals), and guests.

"Yihoo, yihoo". Pause. "Oo-he. Yihoo, yihoo". Pause. "Oo-ha. Brrrlak-katz katz katz ki-dong. Brrrlak-katz katz katz ki-dong". And a velvety vocal melody slides in over an oral bass. This transliteration completely fails to convey the rhythmic and breathy counterpoint, but when this album hit CD players in 1991 it was a sensation. It's a joyous and exuberant disc. The music draws on a wide range of traditions – mostly Central African – juxtaposes a variety of languages and inhabits a world where ethnic music, vocal sampling, minimalism and pop sensibility meet. The important thing, though, is that there's no sampling or electronics here. Everything is done by the vocal acrobatics of five female singers, plus occasional percussion from David Weemaels and the human rhythm-box (boite à rythme humaine), Jean-Louis Daulne.

Zap Mama was created by Marie Daulne in 1990. She was born in Congo (now the Democratic Republic of Congo) in 1964, but three weeks after her birth her Belgian father was killed in a rebellion and her mother took her children into the forest for eight months, where they were protected by Pygmies. The Belgian Army airlifted the family to Belgium and Daulne grew up in Brussels. There she teamed up with other Belgian Africans and (on this album) one white singer. Drawing on their personal histories they combined Pygmy polyphony, yodelling, all sorts of vocal percussion as well as panting, laughter, sneezes and shrieks into an incredible vocal tapestry. Although they've used electronics and instrumental accompaniments since, this first album was a statement about using limited resources, musical techniques underrated in the modern world, and a lot of imagination and ingenuity.

The opening track, **Mupepe**, is soft and lyrical with a velvety vocal solo over choral harmonies. The song is based on a Central African Pygmy chant and occasionally the lead vocal breaks into little shrieks and bird-like yodels. A whispered French text says, "don't run too fast, but listen what the earth has to tell you". Warm choral harmony also pervades **Guzophela**, an anti-apartheid song sung in Zulu and reminiscent of the popular iscathamiya style made famous by Ladysmith Black Mambazo (see p.000). **Bottom**, sung in English, has overtones of gospel music. Many of the tracks have thrilling vocal effects: for instance, **Ndja Mukanie**, with cries like forest animals; **Abadou**, with its layers of different vocal sounds plus gossiping in the harem, ululations, clapping, neighing and what sounds like somebody disappearing on a horse; and the amazing **Son Cubano**, in which a whole Afro-Cuban-style percussion section of claves, congas, timbales, etc is recreated vocally. In **Etupe** there are complicated interlocking repetitive rhythmic patterns, trance-like in their effect, which are so delicate and precise the whole song seems to take flight. Standing out above even these there are two real showpieces. **Plekete**, subtitled "Motor-Car Polyrhythmy" seems to depict a crazy taxi journey in Brussels. We hear somebody on the taxi radio while voices create mistuned static effects. The streets are busy, there's laughter, sudden hoots of horns, cars whizzing past and it all ends with a crash and sirens. A brilliantly depicted tale of urban life. Closing the album is **Brrrlak!**, quoted at the top, in which rich vocal harmonies alternate with frenetic rhythmic polyphony. This is highly skilled and sassy music, performed with confidence and a great sense of fun.

Further listening: Try Vocal Sampling's **Una Forma Mas** (Wea/Elektra) – six guys romp through a selection of Cuban classics with, it's hard to believe, no help from instruments.

Various Artists

The Indestructible Beat of Soweto: Vol.1

Earthworks/Virgin, 1985

Udokotela Shange Namajaha, Nelcy Sedibe, Umahlathini Nabo, Amaswazi Emvelo, Mahlathini and the Mkgona Tsohle Band, Moses Mchunu, Nganeziyamfisa No Khambalomvaleliso, Johnson Mkhalali, Ladysmith Black Mambazo.

Township music combines a celebratory joy in the resilience of the human spirit with a profound sense of the tragedy of South Africa's recent history. **The Indestructible Beat of Soweto: Vol.1** was recorded during some of the grimmest days in apartheid's blood-stained history, between 1981 and 1984, and remains the defining set in this indispensable series. Everything about this album is perfectly conceived as a chronicle of life in the townships during a turbulent period in the struggle for freedom and justice, from the defiant image of the street dancers on the cover to the informed sleeve notes by the London-based South African exiles Trevor Herman and Jumbo Vanrenen who also compiled the collection.

Billed as Mbaqanga ("homemade"), the dozen tracks showcase a wide range of styles drawing upon a panoply of township sounds, including traditional Zulu and Sotho rhythms, African-American influences, sax jive, swinging jazz, the pennywhistle music of kwela and the boisterous rhythms of marabi.

Udokotela Shange Namajaha opens the album in dramatic fashion with **Awungilobolele** (Can You Pay Lobola for Me), like a township John Lee Hooker with an atmospheric half-sung, half-spoken delivery over a heavy and insistent guitar riff. Zulu stomper Moses Mchunu is heard to great effect on **Qhwayilahle** (Leave Him Alone), which includes a Cajun-style violin. **Sini**

Lindili (We Are Waiting for You), by the magnificently named Nganeziyamfisa No Khambalomvaleliso, is in similar Zulu beat style and features a great accordion part and an early example of township rap. Among the best-known artists represented are Mahlathini and the Mahotella Queens, backed by the Makgona Tsohle Band. They offer **Emthonjeni Womculo** (The Stream of Music) and **Ngicabange Ngaqeda** (I Have Made up My Mind), classic examples of vocal mbaqanga, with the groaning bass voice of Simon "Mahlathini" Nkabinde (who died in 1999) balanced by the exquisite female harmonies of the backing singers.

Mahlathini is also heard on **Qhude Manikiniki** (Fair Fight) by Umahlathini Nabo, a kind of township supergroup which includes his older brother Zeph, originally a member of the 1960s band Alexandra Black Mambazo, from which the successful Ladysmith troupe later took its name. Johnson Mkhalali is a jive accordionist who played on Paul Simon's *Graceland* (see p.000) and here contributes a joyously uplifting instrumental. Nelcy Sedibe, who sings the moving **Holotelani** (Daughter-in-Law), is a female singer in the great Miriam Makeba/Dorothy Masuka tradition, while the top male vocal group Amaswazi Emvelo offers the infectious **Indoda Yejazi Elimnyama** (The Man in the Black Coat), backed by a driving guitar band.

Congratulations if you've got this far through some of the most impossible spellings and pronunciations to be found anywhere in World Music. Now go and buy the album. You will soon discover that unfamiliar languages won't stop dancing feet. But remember too, the tragic circumstances in which this joyous music was made. While none of the songs is overtly political, they do have an inner strength and pride in black culture. "We are the source of music," sings Mahlathini. "We are calling the young and old not to forget/That music never ends/Everybody knows that 'where the water has been, it will be again'."

Further listening: For the post-apartheid township sounds, listen to **South African Rhythm Riot**, Vol.6 in the Indestructible Beat of Soweto series. Bhusi Mhlongo's magnificent **Urban Zulu** (M.E.L.T.) is one of the best recent albums from South Africa.

Various Artists

Road of the Gypsies

Network, 1996

Camarón, Goran Bregovic, Ando Drom, Esma Redzepova, Taraf de Haidouks, Romica Puceanu, Mustafa Kandirali, Romano Dives, Kocani Orkestar, Taraf Mociu, Abdullah and Gholam Sakhi, Bratsch, Angelo Debarre, Serge Camps, Frank Anastasio, Titi Winterstein Quintet, Jelem, Loyko, Yiorgos Mangas, Blehorkestar Bakija Bakic, Gabi Lunca, Kályi Jag, Valerie Buchacová, Pedro Bacan, Lida Goulesco, Matelo Ferret, Istanbul Oriental Ensemble, Musicians of the Nile, Suva Devi Kálbelya.

Gypsies are among the most flamboyant and idiosyncratic of musicians, and the leading exponents of a range of popular styles from belly dance to flamenco. This double album samples that range, with music from Rajasthan to Andalucia, from Russia to Egypt, with a major focus on the Balkans where the majority of European Gypsies live. In most of these areas the Gypsies, or Roma as they're more correctly known, have become the leading folk musicians, practising music as a trade and bringing to it a highly distinctive showmanship.

Arab and Persian historians describe how Shah Bahram Gur, who ruled Persia from 420 to 438 AD, invited musicians and dancers from northwest India to entertain his people. In return they were given corn, oxen and donkeys so they could become farmers, but they ate the oxen and corn and returned after a year, starving. The shah told them to fit their instruments with strings of silk, put their possessions on their donkeys and wander the world. Whether the story is true or not, it's a potent tale of how the Gypsies are perceived – as nomadic musicians surviving on the fringes of civilization, unsuited to settled life.

The opening track on this compilation, Camarón's **Nana del Caballo Grande** makes an impressive and appropriate connection between the beginning and the end of the Gypsy road stretching from northern India to southern Spain. Here we have Spain's greatest Gypsy flamenco singer accompanied not by a guitar but by a sitar. It's a self-conscious, but dignified, statement about ties of Gypsy culture, and the raw passion in his voice sounds across the centuries to the music's roots. The common characteristics that run through the music are a raw and declamatory singing style, a tendency to make exaggerated slides between notes and expressive vocal gestures wringing out the emotion. But what this collection actually demonstrates is the variety and diversity of Gypsy music although it usually makes its impact through a typical raw energy or emotional punch.

When singer and dancer Suva Devi Kálbelya performs **Kaman Song**, from Rajasthan, to the accompaniment of a snake charmer's pipe and drum, it's easy to hear the connection between her childlike but knowing singing style and that of the famous song **Ederlezi**, from the film *The Time of the Gypsies*. The singer Mitsou, performing **Lindráji Szi** with Hungarian Gypsy group Andro Drom, has a similar quality. One of the greatest Gypsy vocalists of the Balkans is Esma Redzepova and she performs her signature song **Szelem Szelem**, a Macedonian number which was adopted as the Romani anthem in 1979. She plays on the musical tensions of dissonant suspensions; the melody notes clash with the underlying harmony, she draws out these passages, pointing up the pain and longing and then finally resolves them with an inevitable resignation and relief. It's a well-practised art, and a successful one. The compilation includes several famous names, like Esma, the Taraf de Haidouks and Turkish clarinettist Mustafa Kandirali, but also some wonderful unknowns, like the Slovak singer Valerie Buchacová and Russian diva Lida Goulesco.

> **Further listening: Gitans** (Auvidis/Silex) is a landmark album by Thierry Robin, a Gypsy from the south of France, with excellent collaborations between Spanish and Rajasthani Gypsies.